An Introduction to
Qualitative Research

An Introduction to
Qualitative Research

Uwe Flick

SAGE Publications
London • Thousand Oaks • New Delhi

SAGE Publications Ltd
6 Bonhill Street
London EC2A 4PU

SAGE Publications Inc.
2455 Teller Road
Thousand Oaks, California 91320

SAGE Publications India Pvt Ltd
32, M-Block Market
Greater Kailash – I
New Delhi 110 048

Originally published as *Qualitative Forschung* in the 'rowohlts enzyklopädie' series. Copyright © 1995 by Rowohlt Taschenbuch Verlag GmbH, Reinbek bei Hamburg.

British Library Cataloguing in Publication data

A catalogue record for this book is available from the British Library

ISBN 0 7619 5587 9
ISBN 0 7619 5588 7 (pbk)

Library of Congress catalog card number 98–060079

Typeset by Mayhew Typesetting, Rhayader, Powys
Printed in Great Britain by Butler & Tanner Ltd, Frome and London

CONTENTS

BOXES

FIGURES

TABLES

PREFACE AND ACKNOWLEDGEMENTS

This book is the revised and extended edition of an introduction to qualitative research written and published in German in 1995 with the title *Qualitative Forschung: Theorie, Methoden, Anwendung in Psychologie und Sozialwissenschafen* (*Qualitative Research: Theory, Methods, Applications in Psychology and Social Sciences*). Thus a little more space is given to some methods and discussions which are mainly found in German-speaking areas, which hopefully have some fruitful impact on qualitative research in other areas. These methods and discussions may complement the discussions and methods in Anglo-Saxon contexts, which are also central issues in this book.

The elaboration of this English edition is based on teaching experiences with the material presented here and discussions at the Technical University of Berlin and the Free University of Berlin, at the Hannover Medical School, at the Methodology Institute at the London School of Economics, and at the Faculty of Political and Social Sciences at the University of Cambridge. Barry Sherlock has contributed a lot to improving the English.

The book has benefited from the discussions in the cross-sectional projects 'Qualitative Methods in Public Health' (as part of the Berlin Research Association Public Health) and 'Qualitative Methods Consulting' (as part of the North German Research Association Public Health) (both supported by the German Ministry of Research and Technology), and last but not least from the questions and suggestions by Ines Steinke.

┌─────┐
│ 1 │
└─────┘

QUALITATIVE RESEARCH: RELEVANCE, HISTORY, FEATURES

Qualitative research is establishing itself in the social sciences and in psychology. There is now available a great variety of specific methods each of which starts from different premises and pursues different aims. Each method is based on a specific understanding of its object. However, qualitative methods cannot be regarded independently of the research process and the issue under study. They are specifically embedded in the research process and are best understood and described using a processual perspective. Therefore a presentation of the different steps in the process of qualitative research will be the central concern of this book. The most important procedures for collecting and interpreting data and for assessing and presenting results will be located in this processual framework. This will provide readers with an overview of the field of qualitative research, of concrete methodological alternatives and of their claims, applications and limits. This should enable readers to choose the most appropriate methodological strategy with respect to their research question and issues.

THE RELEVANCE OF QUALITATIVE RESEARCH

Qualitative research is of specific relevance to the study of social relations, owing to the fact of the pluralization of life worlds. Key expressions for this pluralization are the 'new obscurity' (Habermas 1985), the growing 'individualization of ways of living and biographical patterns' (Beck 1986) and the dissolution of 'old' social inequalities into the new diversity of milieus, subcultures, lifestyles and ways of living (Hradil 1992). This pluralization requires a new sensitivity to the empirical study of issues. Advocates of postmodernism have argued that the era of big narratives and theories is over: locally, temporally and situationally limited narratives are now required. With regard to the pluralization of lifestyles and patterns of interpretation in modern and postmodern society, Herbert Blumer's statement becomes relevant once again and has new implications: 'The initial position of the social scientist and the psychologist is practically always one of lack of familiarity with what is actually taking place in the sphere of life chosen for study' (1969, p. 33).

Rapid social change and the resulting diversification of life worlds are increasingly confronting social researchers with new social contexts and perspectives. These are so new for them that their traditional deductive methodologies – deriving research questions and hypotheses from theoretical models and testing them against empirical evidence – are failing in the differentiation of objects. Thus, research is increasingly forced to make use of inductive strategies: instead of starting from theories and testing them, 'sensitizing concepts' are required for approaching social contexts to be studied. However, contrary to widespread misunderstanding, these concepts are themselves influenced by previous theoretical knowledge. But here, theories are developed from empirical studies. Knowledge and practice are studied as *local* knowledge and practice (Geertz 1983).

Concerning research in psychology in particular, it is argued that it lacks relevance for everyday life because it is not sufficiently dedicated to exactly describing the facts of a case (Dörner 1983). The study of subjective meanings and everyday experience and practice is as essential as the contemplation of narratives (Bruner 1991; Sarbin 1986) and discourses (Harré 1998).

LIMITS OF QUANTITATIVE RESEARCH AS A STARTING POINT

Traditionally, psychology and social sciences have taken the natural sciences and their exactness as a model, paying particular attention to developing quantitative and standardized methods. Guiding principles of research and of planning research have been used for the following purposes: to clearly isolate causes and effects, to properly operationalize theoretical relations, to measure and to quantify phenomena, to create research designs allowing the generalization of findings and to formulate general laws. For example, random samples of populations are selected in order to ensure representativeness. General statements are made as independently as possible of the concrete cases that have been studied. Observed phenomena are classified on their frequency and distribution. In order to classify causal relations and their validity as clearly as possible, the conditions under which the phenomena and relations under study occur are controlled as far as possible. Studies are designed in such a way that the researcher's (interviewer's, observer's etc.) influence can be excluded as far as possible. This should guarantee the objectivity of the study, whereby the subjective views of the researcher as well as those of the individuals under study are largely eliminated. General obligatory standards for carrying out and evaluating empirical social research have been formulated. Procedures such as how to construct a questionnaire, how to design an experiment and how to statistically analyse data have become increasingly refined.

For a long time, psychological research has almost exclusively used experimental designs. Through these, vast quantities of data and results have been produced, which demonstrate and test psychological relations among variables and the conditions under which they are valid. For the reasons mentioned above, for a long period empirical social research was mainly based on standardized surveys. The aim was to document and analyse the frequency and distribution of social phenomena in the population – for example certain attitudes. To a lesser and lesser extent, standards and procedures of quantitative research have been fundamentally examined and analysed in order to clarify to which research objects and questions they are appropriate and to which they are not.

When research carried out with the above targets is balanced overall, the results prove rather negative. The ideals of objectivity are largely shattered: some time ago Max Weber (1919) proclaimed the 'shattering of the world' as the task of science. More recently, Bonß and Hartmann (1985) have proposed the increasing shattering of the sciences, their methods and their findings. In the case of the social sciences, the low degree of applicability and connectability of results is taken as an indicator of this. Less widely than expected – and above all in a very different way – have the findings of social research found their way into political and everyday contexts. 'Utilization research' (Beck and Bonß 1989) has demonstrated that scientific findings are not carried over into political and institutional practices as much as expected. When they are taken up, they are obviously reinterpreted and picked to pieces: 'Science no longer produces "absolute truths", which can uncritically be adopted. It furnishes limited offers for interpretation, which reach further than everyday theories but can be used in practice comparatively flexibly' (1989, p. 31).

It has also become clear that social science results are rarely perceived and used in everyday life because – in order to fulfil methodological standards – their investigations and findings often remain too far removed from everyday questions and problems. On the other hand, analyses of research practice have demonstrated that a large part of the ideals of objectivity formulated in advance cannot be fulfilled. Despite all the methodological controls, the research and its findings are unavoidably influenced by the interests and the social and cultural backgrounds of those involved. These factors influence the formulation of research questions and hypotheses as well as the interpretation of data and relations.

Finally, the shattering that Bonß and Hartmann state has consequences for the form of knowledge that psychology and the social sciences can strive for and above all are able to produce: 'Under the condition of the shattering of objectivist ideals, we can no longer unreflectively start from the notion of objectively true sentences. What remains is the possibility of statements which are related to subjects and situations, and which a sociologically articulated concept of knowledge would have to establish' (1985, p. 21). The empirically well-founded formulation of such subject- and situation-related statements is a goal which can be attained with qualitative research.

ESSENTIAL FEATURES OF QUALITATIVE RESEARCH

The central ideas guiding qualitative research are different from those in quantitative research. The essential features of qualitative research (Box 1.1) are the correct choice of appropriate methods and theories; the recognition and analysis of different perspectives; the researchers' reflections on their research as part of the process of knowledge production; and the variety of approaches and methods.

Appropriateness of methods and theories

In his influential textbook on empirical research, Bortz (1984) for example suggests that one should check the 'suitability of ideas for investigations' and should choose only those research ideas that can be studied empirically. For him, the following ideas explicitly do not fit into this range:

> ideas for investigations of . . . philosophical content (e.g. . . . the meaning of life) and investigations dealing with imprecise concepts . . . the study of exceptional persons (e.g. the psychological problems of dwarfs) or situations . . . Finally, studies on the causal relevance of isolated features, which in reality are only effective in combination with other influential factors.

There is no doubt that it makes sense to reflect on whether a research question can be studied empirically or not (see Chapter 5). But for Bortz, the

---

Box 1.1   Features of qualitative research: preliminary list

- Appropriateness of methods and theories
- Perspectives of the participants and their diversity
- Reflexivity of the researcher and the research
- Variety of approaches and methods in qualitative research

---

criterion for assessing the object of research is whether the methods available (and, even more, accepted) can be used to study it or not. Exceptional persons or situations can be found, but not necessarily in sufficient numbers to justify a sample for a quantifying study and generalizable findings. That most phenomena in reality indeed cannot be explained in isolation is a result of the complexity of reality and phenomena. If all empirical studies were exclusively designed according to the model of clear cause–effect relations, all complex objects would have to be excluded. This is the first solution to the problem of analysing causes comprising different features mentioned by Bortz. A second solution is to take contextual conditions into account in complex quantitative research designs (e.g. multi-level analyses: Saldern 1986) and to understand complex models empirically and statistically. The necessary methodological abstraction makes it more difficult to reintroduce findings in the everyday situation under study. The basic problem – that the study can only show what the underlying model of reality already comprises – is not solved in this way.

The third way to solve the problem is pursued in qualitative research: to design methods so open that they do justice to the complexity of the object under study. Here, the object under study is the determining factor for choosing a method and not the other way round. Objects are not reduced to single variables but are studied in their complexity and entirety in their everyday context. Therefore, the fields of study are not artificial situations in the laboratory but the practices and interactions of the subjects in everyday life. Here, in particular, exceptional situations and persons are frequently studied (see Chapter 7). In order to do justice to the diversity of everyday life, methods are characterized by an openness towards their objects, which is guaranteed in different ways (see Chapters 8 to 17). The goal of research is less to test the already well known (for example theories already formulated in advance) than to discover the new and to develop empirically grounded theories. Also, the validity of the study is assessed with reference to the object under study and does not exclusively follow abstract academic criteria of science as in quantitative research. Rather, central criteria in qualitative research are whether findings are grounded in empirical material and whether the methods have been appropriately selected and applied to the object under study. The relevance of findings and the reflexivity of proceedings are further criteria (see Chapter 18).

Perspectives of the participants and their diversity

The example of mental disorders allows us to explain another feature of qualitative research. Epidemiological studies show the frequency of schizophrenia in the population and furthermore how its distribution varies: in lower social classes, serious mental disorders like schizophrenia occur much more frequently than in higher classes. These correlations were found by Hollingshead and Redlich (1958) in the 1950s and have been confirmed repeatedly since then. However, the direction of the correlation could not be clarified: do the conditions of living in a lower social class promote the occurrence and outbreak of mental disorders, or do people with mental problems slip down into the lower classes (see Keupp 1982)? Moreover, these findings do not tell us anything about what it means to live with mental illness. Neither is the subjective meaning of this illness (or of health) for those directly concerned made clear, nor is the diversity of perspectives on the illness in their context grasped. What is the subjective meaning of schizophrenia for the patient and what is it for his or her relatives? How do the various people involved deal with the disease in their actual lives? What has led to the outbreak of the disease in the course of the patient's life and what has made it a chronic disease? What were the influences of the various institutions that have treated the patient in his or her life on this trajectory? Which ideas, goals and routines guide their concrete handling of this case?

Qualitative research into a topic like mental illness concentrates on questions like these (for an overview see Flick 1995b). It demonstrates the variety of perspectives (those of the patient, of his or her relatives, of professionals) on the object and starts from the subjective and social meanings related to it. Qualitative research studies participants' knowledge and practices. It analyses interactions about and ways of dealing with mental illness in a particular field. Interrelations are described in the concrete context of the case and explained in relation to it. Qualitative research takes into account that viewpoints and practices in the field are different because of the different subjective perspectives and social backgrounds related to them.

Reflexivity of the researcher and the research

Unlike quantitative research, qualitative methods take the researcher's communication with the field and its members as an explicit part of knowledge production instead of excluding it as far as possible as an intervening variable. The subjectivities of the researcher *and* of those being studied are part of the research process. Researchers' reflections on their actions and observations in the field, their impressions, irritations, feelings and so on, become data in their own right, forming part of the interpretation, and are documented in research diaries or context protocols (see Chapter 14).

Variety of approaches and methods in qualitative research

Qualitative research is not based on a unified theoretical and methodological concept. Various theoretical approaches and their methods characterize the discussions and the research practice. Subjective viewpoints are a first starting point. A second string of research studies the making and course of interactions, while a third seeks to reconstruct the structures of the social field and the latent meaning of practices (see the next chapter for more details). This variety of different approaches results from different developmental lines in the history of qualitative research, which evolved partly in parallel and partly in sequence.

HISTORY OF QUALITATIVE RESEARCH

Here, only a brief and rather cursory overview of the history of qualitative research can be given. The use of qualitative methods has long traditions in psychology as well as in social sciences. In psychology, Wilhelm Wundt (1900–20) used methods of description and *verstehen* in his folk psychology alongside the experimental methods of his general psychology. Roughly at the same time, an argument between a more monographic conception of science, which was oriented towards induction and case studies, and an empirical and statistical approach began in German sociology (Bonß 1982, p. 106). In American sociology, biographical methods, case studies, and descriptive methods were central for a long time (until the 1940s). This can be demonstrated by the importance of Thomas and Znaniecki's study *The Polish Peasant in Europe and America* (1918–20) and more generally with the influence of the Chicago School of sociology.

During the further establishment of both sciences, however, increasingly 'hard', experimental, standardizing and quantifying approaches have asserted themselves against 'soft', understanding, open and qualitative-descriptive strategies. It was not until the 1960s that in American sociology the critique of standardized, quantifying social research became relevant again (Cicourel 1964; Glaser and Strauss 1967). This critique was taken up in the 1970s in German discussions. Finally, this led to a renaissance of qualitative research in the social sciences and also (with some delay) in psychology (Jüttemann 1985). The developments and discussions in the USA and in Germany not only took place at different times but also are marked by differing phases.

Developments in German-speaking areas

In Germany, Jürgen Habermas (1967) first recognized that a 'different' tradition and discussion of research was developing in American sociology, related to names like Goffman, Garfinkel and Cicourel. Since the translation of Cicourel's (1964) methodological critique, various collections (e.g. Arbeitsgruppe Bielefelder Soziologen 1973; Bühl 1972; Gerdes 1979; Hopf and Weingarten 1979; Steinert 1973; Weingarten et al. 1976) imported contributions from the American discussions. This has made basic texts on ethnomethodology or symbolic interactionism available for German discussions. From the same period, the model of the research process created by Glaser and Strauss (1967) has attracted a lot of attention (e.g. in Hoffmann-Riem 1980; Hopf and Weingarten 1979; Kleining 1982). Discussions are motivated by the aim to do more justice to the objects of research than is possible in quantitative research, as Hoffmann-Riem's claim for the 'principle of openness' demonstrates. Kleining (1982, p. 233) has argued that it is necessary to regard the understanding of the object of research as preliminary until the end of the research, because the object 'will present itself in its true colours only at the end'. Also the discussions about a 'naturalistic sociology' (Schatzman and Strauss 1973) and about appropriate methods are determined by a similar, initially implicit and later also explicit assumption: that to realize the principle of openness and the rules that Kleining suggests (e.g. to postpone a theoretical formulation of the research object) enables the researcher to avoid constituting the object by the very methods used for studying it. Rather it becomes possible 'to take everyday life first and always again in the way it presents itself in each case' (Grathoff 1978; quoted in Hoffmann-Riem 1980, p. 362, who ends her article with this quotation).

At the end of the 1970s, a broader and more original discussion began in Germany which no longer relied exclusively on the translation of American literature. This discussion deals with interviews, their application (e.g. Hopf 1978; Kohli 1978), their interpretation (Mühlefeld et al. 1981) and methodological questions (Kleining 1982) and has stimulated extensive research (see Flick et al. 1991 for an overview). The characteristic question for this period is formulated by Küchler (1980): whether this should be seen as 'a fashionable trend or a new beginning'.

Crucial for this developmental push at the beginning of the 1980s was that two original methods appeared and were widely discussed: the *narrative interview* by Schütze (1977; see also Riemann and Schütze 1987) and *objective hermeneutics* by Oevermann et al. (1979). Both methods were no longer just an import of American developments as was the case in applying participant observation or interviews with an interview guide oriented towards the focused interview (see Hopf 1978). Both methods have stimulated an extensive research praxis (mainly in biographical research: for overviews see Bertaux 1981; Kohli and Robert 1984; Krüger and Marotzki 1994). But the influence of these methodologies on the general discussion of qualitative methods is at least as crucial as the results obtained from them.

In the middle of the 1980s, problems of validity and the generalizability of findings obtained with qualitative methods attracted broader attention (see for example Flick 1987; Gerhardt 1985; Legewie 1987). Related questions of presentation and the transparency of results have been discussed.

The quantity and above all the unstructured nature of the data require the use of computers in qualitative research too (Böhm et al. 1994; Fielding and Lee 1991; Flick 1991a; Huber 1991; Richards and Richards 1994; Weitzman and Miles 1995). Finally, the first textbooks or introductions have been published on the background of the discussions in the German-speaking area (e.g. Bohnsack 1991; Lamnek 1988, 1989; Spöhring 1989).

Discussions in the United States

Denzin and Lincoln (1994a, pp. 6–11) refer to phases different from those just described for the German-speaking area. They see 'five moments of qualitative research', as follows.

The *traditional period* ranges from the early twentieth century to World War II. It is related to the research of Malinowski (1916) in ethnography and the Chicago School in sociology. During this period, qualitative research was interested in the other, the foreign or the strange, and in its more or less objective description and interpretation. Foreign cultures were the issue in ethnography, and outsiders within one's own society in sociology.

The *modernist phase* lasts until the 1970s and is marked by attempts to formalize qualitative research. For this purpose, more and more textbooks were published in the USA. The attitude of this kind of research is still alive in the tradition of Glaser and Strauss (1967), Strauss (1987), and Strauss and Corbin (1990) as well as in Miles and Huberman (1994).

Blurred genres (Geertz 1983) characterize the developments up to the mid 1980s. Various theoretical models and understandings of the objects and methods stand side by side, from which researchers can choose and which they can weigh up against each other or combine: symbolic interactionism, ethnomethodology, phenomenology, semiotics or feminism are some of these 'alternative paradigms' (see also Guba 1990; Jacob 1987).

In the mid 1980s, the *crisis of representation* discussed up to then in artificial intelligence (Winograd and Flores 1986) and ethnography (Clifford and Marcus 1986) impacts upon qualitative research as a whole. This makes the process of displaying knowledge and findings a substantial part of the research process. The findings *per se* attract more attention. Qualitative research becomes a continuous process of constructing versions of reality. The version somebody presents in an interview does not necessarily correspond to the version he or she would have formulated at the moment when the reported event happened. It does not necessarily correspond to the version he or she would have given to a different researcher with a different research question. The researcher, who interprets this interview and presents it as part of his or her findings, produces a new version of the whole. Different readers of the book, article or report interpret the researcher's version differently, so that further versions of the event emerge. Specific interests brought to the reading in each case play a central part. In this context, the evaluation of research and findings becomes a central topic

TABLE 1.1 *Phases in the history of qualitative research*

Germany	United States
Early studies (end of nineteenth and early twentieth centuries)	Traditional period (1900 to 1945)
Phase of import (early 1970s)	Modernist phase (1945 to the 1970s)
Beginning of original discussions (late 1970s)	Blurred genres (until the mid 1980s)
Developing original methods (1970s and 1980s)	Crisis of representation (since the mid 1980s)
Consolidation and procedural questions (late 1980s and 1990s)	Fifth moment (the 1990s)

in methodological discussions. This is connected with the question of whether traditional criteria are valid any more and, if not, which other standards should be applied for assessing qualitative research.

The recent situation is characterized by Denzin and Lincoln as the *fifth moment*: narratives have replaced theories, or theories are read as narratives. But here we learn about the end of grand narratives – as in postmodernism in general. The accent is shifted towards theories and narratives that fit specific, delimited, local, historical situations and problems.

Comparing the two lines of development (Table 1.1), in Germany we find increasing methodological consolidation complemented by a concentration on procedural questions in a growing research practice. In the United States, on the other hand, a trend to question further or once again the apparent certainties provided by methods characterizes recent developments: the role of presentation in the research process, the crisis of representation, and the relativity of what is presented have been stressed, and this has made the attempts to formalize and canonize methods rather secondary. The 'correct' application of procedures of interviewing or interpretation counts less than the 'art and politics of interpretation' (Denzin 1994). Qualitative research therefore becomes – or is linked still more strongly with – a specific attitude based on the researcher's openness and reflexivity.

PROCESSUAL PRESENTATION AS ORIENTATION IN THE FIELD OF QUALITATIVE METHODS

Aims of the presentation in this book

Over the historical period outlined, there has emerged a variety of methods which are characterized by different starting points and targets. They differ in their understanding of the object under study, and each contributes in a specific way to the general discussion on qualitative research and its further developments. Instead of discussing qualitative methods in isolation, it seems necessary to discuss them in the framework of the research process, premised on three grounds: experiences from applying them in empirical studies, experiences from teaching them to students, and experiences from training researchers in ongoing projects. This book seeks to give such a processual presentation. On the one hand, an overview is given as a basis for choosing specific methods of collecting and interpreting data. On the other hand, this overview allows us to assess how far a specific method fits the other parts of the research process: how far does the method of interpretation chosen from possible alternatives (Chapter 17) fit the method of collecting the data (Chapters 11 and 13) and the design of the research process (Chapter 4) or the applied sampling strategy (Chapter 7)? For further consideration and for the application of individual methods it will be necessary to consult the original literature. Suggestions for further reading and references to central works are given in each chapter.

The procedure in the presentation

The starting point of the presentation in this book is that qualitative research above all works with texts. Methods for collecting information – like interviews or observations – produce data which are transformed into texts by recording and transcription. Methods of interpretation start from these texts. Different routes lead towards the texts at the centre of the research and away from them. Very briefly, the qualitative research process can be represented as a path from theory to text and another from text back to theory. The intersection of the two paths is the collection of verbal or visual data and their interpretation in a specific research design.

On the path from theory to text, there is a theoretical position implicit in each method later applied. Several theoretical positions, which have traditionally and also recently determined the field of qualitative research, may be distinguished, but they have some features in common (Chapter 2). One of these is that in addition to using texts as empirical material, qualitative research is concerned with constructions of reality – its own constructions and in particular those constructions it meets in the field or in the people it studies. Chapter 3 highlights these relations of construction, text and reality in greater detail.

Before encountering empirical data for the first time, a certain understanding of the research process – as linear or interlinked (Chapter 4) – is transformed into a research design. Also, the research question is formulated (Chapter 5) and an answer to the problem of access to the field and the individuals being studied is sought and found (Chapter 6). A specific strategy is applied for sampling cases or groups (Chapter 7).

Qualitative research mainly works with two sorts of data. *Verbal data* are collected in semi-structured interviews (Chapter 8) or as narratives (Chapter 9), sometimes using groups instead of individuals (group interviews and discussions, focus groups, joint narratives: Chapter 10). In Chapter 11 the methodological alternatives for collecting verbal data are compared. The criteria for choosing a specific method and for assessing this choice are presented. As a second major group, *visual data* result from applying the various observational methods, ranging from participant and non-participant observation to ethnography and analysing photos and films (Chapter 12). They are again compared on the basis of the criteria for choosing a specific method and for assessing this choice (Chapter 13).

In the next step, verbal and visual data are transformed into texts by documenting them and by transcription. Research starts the second part of its journey – *from text to theory*. Documenting data is not simply a neutral recording of but is an essential step in the construction of reality in the qualitative research process (Chapter 14). Interpreting data is oriented either towards coding and categorizing (Chapter 15) or towards analysing sequential structures in the text (Chapter 16). Comparing the main methods for both strategies of interpreting texts gives useful advice on the decision about which specific method to use (Chapter 17). Grounding qualitative research (Chapter 18) engages the researcher in questions such as how to assess the validity and appropriateness of the research process and of the data produced. Alternatives are either to apply traditional criteria (reliability, validity) or to develop new criteria. It is in this context that ways of writing qualitative research – its strategies and results – have attracted greater attention (Chapter 19).

Finally, various perspectives for further developments of qualitative research are summarized: the use of computers, the combination of qualitative and quantitative research, and the taking up of concepts and strategies from the fields of quality management and processual evaluation as new ways of grounding qualitative research (Chapter 20).

QUALITATIVE RESEARCH AT THE END OF MODERNITY

At the beginning of this introduction, some changes to the potential objects were mentioned in order to show the relevance of qualitative research. Additionally, the greater need for the turn to qualitative research can be derived from recent diagnoses of sciences in general. In his discussion of the 'hidden agenda of modernity', Toulmin (1990) explains in great detail why he judges modern sciences to be dysfunctional. As a way forward for philosophy and sciences in general and thus for empirical social research, he sees four tendencies:

- the return to the oral, which is manifested in trends in the formulation of theories and in the carrying out of empirical studies in philosophy, linguistics, literature and social sciences in narratives, language and communication;

- the return to the particular, which is manifested in the formulation of theories and in the carrying out of empirical studies with the aim 'not only to concentrate on abstract and universal questions but to treat again specific, concrete problems which do not arise generally but occur in specific types of situations' (1990, p. 190);

- the return to the local, which finds its expression in studying systems of knowledge, practices and experiences again in the context of those (local) traditions and ways of living in which they are embedded, instead of assuming and attempting to test their universal validity;

- the return to the timely, manifested in the need to put problems to be studied and solutions to be developed in their temporal or historical context and to describe them in this context and explain them from it.

Qualitative research is oriented towards analysing concrete cases in their temporal and local particularity, and starting from people's expressions and activities in their local contexts. Therefore, qualitative research is in a position to design ways for psychology and social sciences to make concrete the tendencies that Toulmin mentions, to transform them into research programmes and to maintain the necessary flexibility towards their objects and tasks:

> Like buildings on a human scale, our intellectual and social procedures will do what we need in the years ahead, only if we take care to avoid irrelevant or excessive stability, and keep them operating in ways that are adaptable to unforeseen – or even unforeseeable – situations and functions. (1990, p. 186)

Concrete suggestions and methods for realizing such programmes of research will be outlined in what follows.

FURTHER READING

The first two references extend the short overview given here of the German and United States discussions, whilst Strauss's book represents the research attitude behind this book and qualitative research in general.

Denzin, N., Lincoln, Y.S. (eds) (1994a), *Handbook of Qualitative Research*. London: Sage.

Flick, U., Kardorff, E.v., Keupp, H., Rosenstiel, L.v., Wolff, S. (eds) (1991), *Handbuch Qualitative Sozialforschung* (2nd edn 1995). Munich: Psychologie Verlags Union.

Strauss, A.L. (1987), *Qualitative Analysis for Social Scientists*. Cambridge: Cambridge University Press.

PART 1
FROM THEORY TO TEXT

2

THEORETICAL POSITIONS

CONTENTS

RESEARCH PERSPECTIVES IN THE FIELD OF QUALITATIVE RESEARCH

Under the umbrella heading of qualitative research, various research approaches are summarized which are different in their theoretical assumptions, in the way they understand their object and in their methodological focus. Generally speaking, these approaches orient towards three basic positions: the tradition of symbolic interactionism, concerned with studying subjective meanings and individual ascriptions of sense; ethnomethodology, interested in routines of everyday life and their production; and structuralist or psychoanalytic positions, starting from processes of psychological or social unconsciousness. It is possible to differentiate those approaches foregrounding the 'subject's viewpoint' (Bergold and Flick 1987) from those seeking descriptions of given (everyday, institutional, or more generally social) milieus (e.g. Hildenbrand 1983). Additionally we find strategies interested in how social order is produced (e.g. ethnomethodological analyses of language) or oriented towards reconstructing 'deep structures that generate action and meaning' from psychoanalysis or 'objective hermeneutics' (Lüders and Reichertz 1986).

Each of these positions conceptualizes how the subjects under study – their experiences, actions and interactions – relate to the context in which they are studied in different ways.

SUBJECTIVE MEANING: SYMBOLIC INTERACTIONISM

In the first perspective, the empirical starting point is the subjective meanings individuals attribute to their activities and their environments. These research approaches refer to the tradition of symbolic interactionism:

> The name of this line of sociological and sociopsychological research was coined in 1938 by Herbert Blumer (1938). Its focus is processes of interaction – social action that is characterized by an immediately reciprocal orientation – and the investigations of these processes are based on a particular concept of interaction which stresses the symbolic character of social actions. (Joas 1987, p. 84)

As Joas shows, this position has been developed from the philosophical tradition of American pragmatism. Generally, it represents the understanding of theory and method in the Chicago School (H.W.I. Thomas, Robert Park, Charles Horton Cooley, George Herbert Mead) in American sociology. The central role this approach plays in qualitative research in general can be demonstrated both recently and historically: sociologists such as Anselm Strauss, Barney Glaser, Norman K. Denzin, Howard Becker and others directly refer to this position; and Blumer's (1969) work on the 'methodological position of symbolic interactionism' had a big influence on the methodological discussions of the 1970s.

Basic assumptions

Blumer summarizes the starting points of symbolic interactionism as 'three simple premises':

> The first premise is that human beings act toward things on the basis of the meanings that the things have for them ... The second premise is that the meaning of such things is derived from, or arises out of, the social interaction that one has with one's fellows. The third premise is that these meanings are handled in, and modified through, an interpretative process used by the person in dealing with the things he encounters. (1969, p. 2)

The consequence is that the different ways in which individuals invest objects, events, experiences etc. with meaning form the central starting point for research. The reconstruction of such subjective viewpoints becomes the instrument for analysing social worlds. Another central

assumption is formulated in the so-called Thomas theorem, further
grounding the methodological principle[1] just mentioned. Thomas's

> claim that when a person defines a situation as real, this situation is real in its
> consequences, leads directly to the fundamental methodological principle of
> symbolic interactionism: the researcher has to see the world from the angle of
> the subjects he or she studies. (Stryker 1976, p. 259)

From this basic assumption, the methodological imperative is drawn to
reconstruct the subject's viewpoint (Bergold and Flick 1987) in different
respects. The first is in the form of subjective theories, used by people to
explain the world – or at least a certain area of objects as part of this world
– for themselves. Thus there is a voluminous research literature on
subjective theories of health and illness (for overviews see e.g. Faltermaier
1994; Flick 1993), on subjective theories in pedagogy (Dann 1990; Groeben
1990) and in counselling actions (e.g. Flick 1992a). The second is in the form
of autobiographical narratives, biographical trajectories that are reconstructed from the perspective of the subjects. But it is important that these
should give access to the temporal and local contexts, reconstructed from
the narrator's point of view (for overviews see Bertaux 1981; Kohli and
Robert 1984).

Recent developments in sociology: Interpretive interactionism

In recent years, Denzin has argued from a position which starts from
symbolic interactionism but integrates several alternative and more recent
streams. Here we find phenomenological considerations (following
Heidegger), structuralist ways of thinking (Foucault), feminist and postmodern critiques of science, the approach of 'thick descriptions' (Geertz
1973) and that of concepts from literature.[2] This approach is specified or
limited by Denzin in two respects. On the one hand it 'should only be used
when the researcher wants to examine the relationship between personal
troubles, for example wife-battering or alcoholism, and the public policies
and public institutions that have been created to address those personal
problems' (1989a, p. 10). On the other hand, Denzin restricts the perspective
taken when he repeatedly emphasizes that the processes being studied
should be understood biographically and necessarily interpreted from this
angle (e.g. 1989a, pp. 19–24).

Recent developments in psychology: subjective theories as research programme

The aim of analysing subjective viewpoints is pursued in a most consistent
way in the framework of research on subjective theories (Flick 1993;
Groeben 1990). Here, the starting point is that individuals in everyday life –

like scientists – develop theories on how the world and their own activities function. They apply and test these theories in their activities and revise them if necessary. Assumptions in such theories are organized in an interdependent way and with an argumentative structure corresponding to the structure of statements in scientific theories (in the sense of the statement view of theories: see Stegmüller 1973). This type of research seeks to reconstruct these subjective theories. For this purpose, a specific interview method has been developed (see Chapter 8 for the semi-standardized interview). In order to reconstruct subjective theories as close as possible to the subject's point of view, special methods for a (communicative) validation of the reconstructed theory have been created (see Chapter 18).

The concentration on the subjects' points of view and on the meaning they attribute to experiences and events, as well as the orientation towards the meaning of objects, activities and events, informs a large part of qualitative research. Combining subject-oriented research with symbolic interactionism, as has been done here, certainly cannot take place without reservations. For example, the reference to symbolic interactionism in recent research on subjective theories usually remains rather implicit. Also there are other research perspectives arising out of the traditions of Blumer and Denzin which are more interested in interactions than in subjective viewpoints (e.g. the contributions to Denzin 1993). For such interactionist studies, however, it remains essential to focus the subjective meanings of objects for the participants in interactions. With regard to methods, this approach mainly uses different forms of interviews (see Chapters 8 and 9) and participant observation (see Chapter 12).

These two positions – the study of subjective viewpoints and the theoretical background of symbolic interactionism – mark one pole in the field of qualitative research.

THE MAKING OF SOCIAL REALITIES: ETHNOMETHODOLOGY

The limitations of interactionism's concern with the subjects' viewpoints are exceeded theoretically and methodologically in the framework of ethnomethodology. This school was founded by Harold Garfinkel (1967). It addresses the question of how people produce social reality in and through interactive processes. Its central concern is with the study of the methods used by members to produce reality in everyday life.[3] A definition of the research interests related to ethnomethodology is given by Garfinkel:

> Ethnomethodological studies analyse everyday activities as members'
> methods for making those same activities visibly-rational-and-reportable-for-
> all-practical-purposes, i.e. 'accountable', as organizations of commonplace
> everyday activities. The reflexivity of that phenomenon is a singular feature of

practical actions, of practical circumstances, of common sense knowledge of social structures, and of practical sociological reasoning. (1967, p. vii)

The interest in everyday activities, in their execution and beyond – in the constitution of a locally oriented context of interaction in which activities are carried out – characterizes the ethnomethodological research programme in general. This research programme has been realized mainly in the empirical researches of conversation analysis.

Basic assumptions

The premises of ethnomethodology and conversation analysis are encapsulated in three basic assumptions by Heritage:

(1) Interaction is structurally organized; (2) contributions of interaction are both context shaped and context renewing; and (3) thus two properties inhere in the *details* of interaction so that no order of detail in conversational interaction can be dismissed *a priori* as disorderly, accidental or irrelevant. (1985, p. 1)

Crucial points in these basic assumptions are that interaction is produced in a well-ordered way, and that context is the framework of interaction which is produced in and through the interaction at the same time. Decisions as to what is relevant to members in social interaction can only be made through an analysis of that interaction and not *a priori* taken for granted. The focus is not the subjective meaning for the participants of an interaction and its contents but how this interaction is organized. The research topic becomes the study of the routines of everyday life rather than the outstanding events consciously perceived and invested with meaning.

In order to uncover the methods through which interaction is organized, the researcher seeks to adopt an attitude of 'ethnomethodological indifference' (Garfinkel & Sacks 1970). He or she should abstain from an *a priori* interpretation as well as from adopting the perspectives of the actors or one of the actors. Crucial for understanding the perspective of ethnomethodology is the role of the context in which interactions take place, and how this can be shown to be demonstrably relevant to the participants (see Sacks 1992) through its empirical study. Wolff et al. hold on this:

The fundamental starting point of an ethnomethodological . . . proceeding is to regard any event as constituted through the production efforts of the members on the spot. This is the case not only for the actual facts in the interaction, as for example the unwinding of question–answer sequences, but also for realizing so-called macro-facts, like the institutional context of a conversation. (1988, p. 10)

According to such a notion, a counselling conversation becomes a counselling conversation (different from other types of conversation) through the members' efforts in creating this situation. We are thus concerned not with the researcher's *a priori* definition of the situation but rather with members' conversational contributions, as it is through the turn-by-turn organization of the talk that the conversation is constituted as a consultation. On the other hand, the institutional context is also made relevant in the conversation and constituted in and through the members' contributions. Only the specific practices of the counsellor and the client turn a conversation into a consultation, and turn a consultation into a consultation in a specific context – for example in a 'sociopsychiatric service' (see Flick 1989).

Recent developments of ethnomethodology in the social sciences: Studies of work

Ethnomethodological research has focused and narrowed more and more on the increasingly formal analysis of conversations. But since the 1980s, in the 'studies of work', the analysis of work processes is pursued as its second main focus (see Bergmann 1991a; Garfinkel 1986). Here, processes of work are studied in a broad sense and particularly in the context of scientific work in laboratories or for example how mathematicians construct proofs (Livingston 1986). In these studies, various methods for describing work processes as exactly as possible are used, among which conversation analysis is just one approach. The scope is enlarged from studying interactive practices to a concern with 'embodied knowledge', materializing in such practices as well as in their results (Bergmann 1991a, p. 270). These studies contribute to the wider context of recent research on the sociology of scientific knowledge (see Amann and Knorr-Cetina 1991; Knorr-Cetina and Mulkay 1983). In general the sociology of scientific knowledge has been developed from the tradition of ethnomethodology.

Recent developments in psychology: Discursive psychology

Starting from conversation analysis and laboratory studies, a programme of 'discursive psychology' has been developed in British social psychology (see Edwards and Potter 1992; Harré 1998; Harré and Stearns 1995; Potter and Wetherell 1998). Here, psychological phenomena such as cognition or memory are studied by analysing relevant discourses concerned with certain topics. These discourses range from everyday conversations to texts in media. The stress lies on communicative and constructive processes in interactions. The methodological starting point is to analyse the 'interpretive repertoires' that the participants of certain discourses use to produce a specific version of reality and to assert it: 'Interpretive repertoires are broadly discernible clusters of terms, descriptions, and figures of speech often assembled around metaphors or vivid images. They can be thought of as the building blocks used for manufacturing versions of actions, self, and social structures in talk' (Potter and Wetherell 1998, pp. 146–7). The contents and procedures of cognitive processes are reconstructed from such discourses as well as the ways in which social or collective memories referring to certain events are constructed and mediated (see Middleton and Edwards 1990).

In these approaches, the perspective remains restricted to describing the *how* in the making of social reality. Ethnomethodological analyses often provide impressively exact descriptions of how social interaction is organized and are able to develop typologies of conversational forms in this way. However, the aspect of subjective ascription of meaning remains rather neglected, as does the question of what role pre-existing contexts such as specific cultures play in the construction of social practices.

CULTURAL FRAMING OF SOCIAL AND SUBJECTIVE REALITY: STRUCTURALIST MODELS

Qualitative research is based on a third type of theoretical approach. A common feature of this is – although with various degrees of emphasis – that cultural systems of meaning are assumed to somehow frame the perception and making of subjective and social reality (for overviews see Bude 1991; Streeck 1991).

Basic assumptions

Here, a distinction is made between the surface of experience and activity on the one hand and the deep structures of activities on the other. While the surface is accessible to the participant subject, the deep structures are not accessible to everyday individual reflections. The surface is associated with intentions and the subjective meaning related to actions, whereas deep structures are understood as generating activities. Deep structures like these are contained in cultural models (D'Andrade 1987), in interpretive patterns and latent structures of meaning (Oevermann et al. 1979), and finally in those latent structures that remain unconscious according to psychoanalysis (Devereux 1967; Erdheim 1984). Psychoanalysis attempts to reveal the unconscious both in society and in the research process. Analysing this process and the relation of the researcher to those who are interviewed or observed becomes a resource for discovering how the 'societal production of unconsciousness' (Erdheim 1984) works. For these analyses, the implicit and explicit rules of action are of special importance. For objective hermeneutics, which is taken here as an example of the other approaches mentioned, it is argued:

> On the basis of rules, which may be reconstructed, texts of interaction constitute the *objective meaning structures*. These objective meaning structures

represent the *latent structures* of sense of the interaction itself. These objective meaning structures of texts of interaction, prototypes of objective social structures in general, are reality (and exist) analytically (even if not empirically) independent of the concrete intentional representation of the meanings of the interaction on the part of the subjects participating in the interaction. (Oevermann et al. 1979, p. 379)

In order to reconstruct rules and structures, various methodological procedures for analysing 'objective' (i.e. non-subjective) meanings are applied – such as linguistic analyses to extrapolate cultural models, strictly sequential analyses of expressions and activities to uncover their objective structure of meanings, and the researcher's 'evenly suspended attention' in the psychoanalytical process of interpretation (see Devereux 1967; Erdheim 1984).

In particular objective hermeneutics following Oevermann et al. (1979), has attracted wide attention and stimulated voluminous research in German-speaking areas (see Chapter 16). However, there is an unsolved problem in the theoretical basics of the approach, which is the unclear relation of acting subjects to the structures to be extrapolated. Lüders and Reichertz (1986, p. 95), for example, criticize the 'metaphysics of structures' which are almost studied as 'autonomously acting subjects'. Other problems are the naive equation of text and world ('the world as text': see Garz 1994) and the assumption that, if analyses were pursued far enough, they would lead to the structures which generate the activities of the case under study. This assumption is based on the structuralist background of Oevermann's approach.

Recent developments in social sciences: Poststructuralism

After Derrida (1976), such structuralist assumptions have been questioned in qualitative research as well (see Lincoln and Denzin 1994, p. 578). It is asked, for example, whether the text produced for the purposes of interpretation, as well as the text formulated as a result of the interpretation, corresponds not only to the interests (of research or whatever) of the interpreter, but also to the interests of those being studied and forming a topic in the text (1994, p. 578). According to this view, texts are neither the world *per se* nor an objective representation of parts of this world. Rather they result from the interests of those who produced the text as well as of those who read it. Different readers resolve the vagueness and ambiguity every text contains in different ways – depending on the perspectives they bring to the particular text (Agger 1991, p. 112). On the basis of this background, the reservations formulated about the objective hermeneutics concept of structure – that 'between the surface and deep structures of language use . . . in objective hermeneutics there is a methodological "hiatus", which at best can be closed by teaching and treating the method as art' (Bonß 1991, p. 38) – become yet more relevant (see also Reichertz 1988; 1991).

Recent developments in psychology: Social representations

What remains unclear in structuralist approaches is the relation between implicit social knowledge and individual knowledge and actions. To answer this question, one might take up a research programme in social psychology which was engaged in studying the 'social representation' of objects (e.g. scientific theories on cultural objects and processes of change: for a recent overview see Flick 1998). Such a programme would address the problem of how such socially and culturally shared knowledge influences individual ways of perception, experience and action. A social representation is understood as

> a system of values, ideas and practices with a twofold function: first to establish an order which will enable individuals to orient themselves in their material and social world and to master it; and secondly to enable communication to take place among the members of a community by providing them with a code for social exchange and a code for naming and classifying unambiguously the various aspects of their world and their individual and group history. (Moscovici 1973, p. xvii)

This approach is increasingly used as a theoretical framework for qualitative studies dealing with the social construction of phenomena such as health and illness (Herzlich 1973), madness (Jodelet 1991) and technological change in everyday life (Flick 1995a; 1996). Here again, social rules deriving from social knowledge about each topic are studied without being conceived as a reality *sui generis*. From a methodological point of view, different forms of interviews (see Chapter 8) and participant observation (see Chapter 12) are used (e.g. in Jodelet 1991).

RIVALRY OF PARADIGMS OR TRIANGULATION OF PERSPECTIVES

The different perspectives in qualitative research and their specific starting points may be put in a scheme as in Figure 2.1.

The first perspective starts from the subjects involved in a situation under study and from the meanings that this situation has for them. The situational context, the interactions with other members and – as far as possible – the social and cultural meanings are reconstructed step by step from these subjective meanings. As the example of counselling shows, in this perspective the meaning and the course of the event 'counselling' is reconstructed from the subjective viewpoint (e.g. a subjective theory of counselling). If possible, the cultural meaning of the situation 'counselling' is disclosed on this path. The second perspective starts from the interaction in counselling,

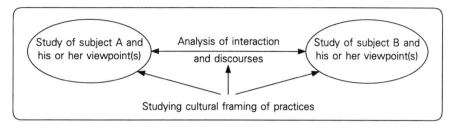

FIGURE 2.1 *Research perspectives in qualitative research*

and the discourse (of helping, on certain problems etc.) is studied. Here, participants' subjective meanings are treated as less interesting than the way in which the conversation is formally organized as a consultation and how participants mutually allocate their roles as members. Cultural and social contexts outside the interaction only become relevant in the context of how they are produced or continued in the conversation. The third perspective asks which implicit or unconscious rules govern the explicit actions in the situation and which latent or unconscious structures generate activities. The corresponding culture and the structures and rules it offers the individuals in and for situations are the main focus. Subjective views and interactive perspectives are especially relevant as means to expose or reconstruct structures.

Beyond such juxtapositions, two ways of responding to different perspectives of research can be found. On the one hand, a single position and its perspective on the phenomenon under study are adopted as the 'one and only' and other perspectives are critically rejected. This kind of demarcation has determined discussion in German-speaking areas for a long time. In the American discussion as well different positions have been formalized into paradigms and then juxtaposed in terms of competing paradigms or even 'paradigm wars' (see Guba and Lincoln 1994, p. 116).

Alternatively, different theoretical perspectives can be understood as different ways of accessing the phenomenon under study. Any perspective may be examined as to which part of the phenomenon it discloses and which part remains excluded. Starting from this understanding, different research perspectives may be combined and supplemented. Such a triangulation of perspectives (Flick 1992a) enlarges the focus on the phenomenon under study, for example by reconstructing the participants' viewpoints and analysing afterwards the unfolding of shared situations in interactions.

COMMON FEATURES OF THE DIFFERENT POSITIONS

Despite differences of perspective, one may summarize the following points as common features across these different theoretical positions:

- *Verstehen as epistemological principle* Qualitative research aims at understanding the phenomenon or event under study from the interior (see Hopf 1985). It is the view of one subject or of different subjects, the course of social situations (conversations, discourse, processes of work), or the cultural or social rules relevant for a situation, which are to be understood. How this understanding is put into methodological terms depends on the theoretical position underpinning the research.

- *Reconstructing cases as starting point* A second feature common to the different positions is that the single case is analysed more or less consistently, before comparative or general statements are made. For instance, first, the single subjective theory, the single conversation and its course or the single case is reconstructed. Later, other case studies and their results are used in comparison (see Hildenbrand 1991) to develop a typology (of the different subjective theories, of the different courses of conversations, of the different case structures). What in each case is understood as 'case' – an individual and his or her viewpoint, a locally and temporally delimited interaction, or a specific social or cultural context in which an event unfolds – depends on the theoretical position used to study the material.

- *Construction of reality as basis* The reconstructed cases or typologies contain various levels of construction of reality: subjects with their views on a certain phenomenon construe a part of their reality; in conversations and discourses, phenomena are interactively produced and thus reality is constructed; latent structures of sense and related rules contribute to the construction of social situations with the activities they generate. Therefore, the reality studied by qualitative research is not a given reality, but is constructed by different 'actors': which actor is regarded as crucial for this construction depends on the theoretical position taken to study this process of construction.

- *Text as empirical material* In the process of reconstructing cases, texts are produced on which the actual empirical analyses are made: the view of the subject is reconstructed as his or her subjective theory or is formulated this way; the course of an interaction is recorded and transcribed; reconstructions of latent structures of meaning can only be formulated from texts given in the necessary detail. In all these cases, texts are the basis of reconstruction and interpretation. What status the text is given depends on the theoretical position of the study.

The theoretical positions and their common features are summarized in Table 2.1.

Thus the list of features of qualitative research discussed in Chapter 1 may now be completed as in Box 2.1.

TABLE 2.1 *Theoretical positions in qualitative research*

	Subjects' points of view	*Making of social realities*	*Cultural framing of social realities*
Traditional theoretical background	Symbolic interactionism	Ethnomethodology	Structuralism, psycholanalysis
Recent developments in social sciences	Interpretive interactionism	Studies of work	Poststructuralism
Recent developments in psychology	Research programme 'subjective theories'	Discursive psychology	Social representations
Common features	• *Verstehen* as epistemological principle • Reconstructing cases as starting point • Construction of reality as basis • Text as empirical material		

Box 2.1   Features of qualitative research: completed list

- Appropriateness of methods and theories
- Perspectives of the participants and their diversity
- Reflexivity of the researcher and the research
- Variety of approaches and methods in qualitative research
- *Verstehen* as epistemological principle
- Reconstructing cases as starting point
- Construction of reality as basis
- Text as empirical material

NOTES

1 One starting point is the symbolic interactionist assumption: 'One has to get inside of the defining process of the actor in order to understand his action' (Blumer 1969, p. 16).

2 'Epiphany' in the sense of James Joyce as 'a moment of problematic experience that illuminates personal characteristics, and often signifies a turning point in a person's life' (Denzin 1989a, p. 141).

3 Bergmann holds for the general approach and the research interests linked to it: 'Ethnomethodology characterizes the methodology used by members of a society for proceeding activities, which simply makes the social reality and order which is taken as given and for granted for the actors. Social reality is understod by Garfinkel as a procedural reality, i.e. a reality which is produced locally (there and then, in the course of the action), endogenously (i.e. from the interior of the

situation), audiovisually (i.e. in hearing and speaking, perceiving and acting) in the interaction by the participants. The aim of ethnomethodology is to grasp the 'how', i.e. the methods of this production of social reality in detail. It asks, for example, how the members of a family interact in such a way that they can be perceived as a family' (1980, p. 39).

FURTHER READING

The first four references give overviews of the more traditional positions discussed here, while the latter two represent more recent developments.

Blumer, H. (1969), *Symbolic Interactionism: Perspective and Method.* Berkeley, CA: University of California.

Devereux, G. (1967), *From Anxiety to Methods in the Behavioral Sciences.* The Hague: Mouton.

Garfinkel, H. (1967), *Studies in Ethnomethodology.* Englewood Cliffs, NJ: Prentice-Hall.

Oevermann, U., Allert, T., Konau, E., Krambeck, J. (1979), Die Methodologie einer 'objektiven Hermeneutik' und ihre allgemeine forschungslogische Bedeutung in den Sozialwissenschaften. In: Soeffner, H.G. (ed.), *Interpretative Verfahren in den Sozial- und Textwissenschaften,* pp. 352–433. Stuttgart: Metzler.

Denzin, N.K. (1989), *Interpretative Interactionism.* London: Sage.

Flick, U. (ed.) (1998), *Psychology of the Social.* Cambridge: Cambridge University Press.

3

CONSTRUCTION AND UNDERSTANDING OF TEXTS

CONTENTS

In the previous chapter, it was argued that the common features of qualitative research across different theoretical positions include *verstehen*, reference to cases, construction of reality, and using texts as empirical material. From these features, various questions emerge. How can one understand the process of constructing social reality in the phenomenon under study but also in the process of studying it? How is reality represented or produced in the case that is (re)constructed for investigative purposes? What is the relation between text and realities?

TEXT AND REALITIES

Texts serve three purposes in the process of qualitative research: they are not only the essential data on which findings are based, but also the basis of interpretations and the central medium for presenting and communicating findings. This is the case not only for objective hermeneutics, which has made the textualization of the world a programme (see Garz 1994), but more generally for the current methods in qualitative research. Either interviews comprise the data, which are transformed into transcripts (i.e.

texts), and interpretations of them are produced afterwards (in observations, field notes are often the textual database); or research starts from recording natural conversations and situations to arrive at transcriptions and interpretations. In each case, we find text as the result of the data collection and as the instrument for interpretation. If qualitative research relies on understanding social realities through the interpretation of texts, two questions become especially relevant: what happens in the translation of reality into text, and what happens in the retranslation of texts into reality or in inferring from texts to realities?

In this process, text is substituted for what is studied. As soon as the researcher has collected the data and made a text out of them, this text is used as a substitute for the reality under study in the further process. Originally biographies were studied but now the narrative produced in the interview is available for interpretation. From this narrative there remains only what the recording has 'caught' and what is documented by the chosen method of transcription. The text produced in this way is the basis of further interpretations and the findings so derived: checking back to the acoustic recordings is as unusual as checking back to the subjects interviewed (or observed). It is difficult to establish control of how much and what this text contains and reproduces of the original issue – for example of a biography. The social sciences, which have necessarily turned into a textual science (Gross 1981) and which rely on texts as ways of fixing and objectifying their findings, should pay more attention to these kinds of questions. The rarely mentioned question of producing *new* realities (e.g. life as narrative) in generating and interpreting data as texts and texts as data has to be further discussed.

TEXT AS WORLD MAKING: FIRST DEGREE AND SECOND DEGREE CONSTRUCTIONS

That the relation of text and reality cannot be reduced to a simple representation of given facts has been discussed for quite a while in different contexts as a 'crisis of representation'. In the discussion around the question of how far the world can be represented in computer systems or cognitive systems, Winograd and Flores (1986) express heavy doubts about this simple idea of representation, while Paul Ricoeur sees such discussions as a general topic of modern philosophy. Starting from debates in ethnography (e.g. Berg and Fuchs 1993; Clifford and Marcus 1986), this crisis is discussed for qualitative research as a double crisis of representation and of legitimation. In terms of the crisis of representation, and as a consequence of the linguistic turn in the social sciences, it is doubted that social researchers can 'directly capture lived experience. Such experience, it is now argued, is created in the social text written by the researcher. This is the crisis of representation . . . It . . . makes the direct link between experience and text problematic' (Denzin and Lincoln 1994b, p. 11). The second crisis is the crisis of legitimation, in which the classic criteria for assessing research are rejected for qualitative research or – following postmodernism – the possibility of legitimizing scientific knowledge is rejected in general (see Chapter 18).

The crucial point in these discussions is how far – especially in social research – we are still able to suppose a reality existing outside subjective or socially shared viewpoints and on which we can validate its 'representation' in texts or other products of research. The several varieties of social constructivism (see Knorr-Cetina 1989 for a short overview) or constructionism (Gergen 1985) reject such suppositions. Rather, they start from the idea that realities are actively produced by the participants through the meanings ascribed to certain events and objects and that social research cannot escape these ascriptions of meanings if it wants to deal with social realities. The questions that are asked and have to be asked in this context are summarized by Matthes as follows: 'What do the social subjects themselves hold for real and *how*? And: under which conditions – in the perspective of the observers turning towards them – does this holding-for-real stand? And: under which conditions do the observers themselves hold the things they observe this way for real?' (1985, p. 59). Thus, the points of departure for research are the ideas of social events, of things or facts which we meet in a social field under study and the way in which these ideas communicate with one another – i.e. compete, conflict, succeed, are shared and taken for real.

Social constructions as starting points

That facts only become relevant through their selection and interpretation has already been stated by Alfred Schütz:

> Strictly speaking there are no such things as facts, pure and simple. All facts are from the outset facts selected from a universal context by the activities of our mind. They are, therefore, always interpreted facts, either facts looked at as detached from their context by an artificial abstraction or facts considered in their particular setting. In either case, they carry their interpretational inner and outer horizons. (1962, p. 5)

Here we can draw parallels with Goodman (1978). For Goodman, the world is socially constructed through different forms of knowledge – from everyday knowledge to science and art as different 'ways of world making'. According to Goodman – and Schütz – social research is an analysis of such ways of world making and the constructive efforts of the participants in their everyday lives. A central idea in this context is the distinction Schütz makes between first degree and second degree constructions. According to Schütz 'the constructs of the social sciences are, so to speak,

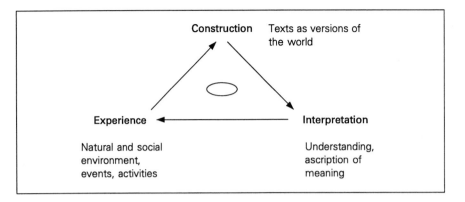

FIGURE 3.1 *Understanding between construction and interpretation*

constructs of the second degree, that is, constructs of the constructs made by the actors on the social scene.' In this sense, Schütz holds that 'the exploration of the general principles according to which man in daily life organizes his experiences, and especially those of the social world, is the first task of the methodology of the social sciences' (1962, p. 59).

According to this, everyday perception and knowledge are the basis for social scientists to develop a more formalized and generalized 'version of the world' (Goodman 1978). Correspondingly Schütz (1962, pp. 208ff.) assumes 'multiple realities', of which the world of science is only one, and which is organized partly according to the same principles by which the world of everyday life is organized and partly according to other principles.

In particular, social science research is confronted with the problem that it encounters the world it wants to study always and only in those versions of this world existing in the field or constructed by interacting subjects commonly or concurrently. Scientific knowledge and displays of inter-relations include different processes of constructing reality: everyday, subjective constructions on the part of those who are studied, and scientific (i.e. more or less codified) constructions on the part of the researchers in collecting, treating and interpreting data and in the presentation of findings (Figure 3.1).

In these constructions, taken-for-granted relations are translated: everyday experience into knowledge by those who are studied, reports of those experiences or events and activities into texts by the researchers. How can these processes of translation be made more concrete?

WORLD MAKING IN THE TEXT: MIMESIS

To answer this question, the concept of mimesis will be taken from aesthetics and literary sciences (see Iser 1991; *Kunstforum* 1991) which can offer insights for a social science based on texts. Mimesis refers to the transformation of (originally, e.g. in Aristotle, natural) worlds into symbolic worlds. It was first understood as 'imitation of nature'; however, this concept has been discussed more extensively (Gebauer and Wulf 1995). A succinct example of mimesis, and one repeatedly used, would be the presentation of natural or social relations in literary or dramatic texts or on the stage: 'In this interpretation, mimesis characterizes the act of producing a symbolic world, which encompasses both practical and theoretical elements' (1995, p. 3). However, the interest in this concept now goes beyond presentations in literary texts or in the theatre. Recent discussions treat mimesis as a general principle with which to map out one's under-standing of the world and of texts:

> The individual 'assimilates' himself or herself to the world via mimetic pro-cesses. Mimesis makes it possible for individuals to step out of themselves, to draw the outer world into their inner world, and to lend expression to their interiority. It produces an otherwise unattainable proximity to objects and is thus a necessary condition of understanding. (1995, pp. 2–3)

In applying these considerations to qualitative research and to the texts used within such research, mimetic elements can be identified in the following respects:

- in the transformation of experience into narratives, reports etc. on the part of the persons being studied;

- in the construction of texts on this basis and in the interpretation of such constructions on the part of the researchers;

- finally, when such interpretations are fed back into everyday contexts, for example in reading the presentations of these findings.

To analyse the mimetic processes in the construction and interpretation of social science texts, the considerations of Ricoeur (1981; 1984) offer a fruitful starting point. For literary texts, Ricoeur has separated the mimetic process 'playfully yet seriously' into the three steps of mimesis$_1$, mimesis$_2$ and mimesis$_3$:

> Hermeneutics, however, is concerned with reconstructing the entire arc of operations by which practical experience provides itself with works, authors, and readers . . . It will appear as a corollary, at the end of this analysis, that the reader is that operator *par excellence* who takes up through doing something – the act of reading – the unity of the traversal from mimesis$_1$ to mimesis$_3$ by way of mimesis$_2$. (1984, p. 53)

Reading and understanding texts becomes an active process of producing reality, which involves not only the author of – in our case social science – texts, but also the person for whom they are written and who reads them. Transferred to qualitative research, this means that in the production of texts (on a certain subject, an interaction or an event) the person who reads and interprets the written text is as involved in the construction of reality as the person who writes the text. According to Ricoeur's understanding of mimesis, three forms of mimesis may be distinguished in a social science based on texts:

- Everyday and scientific interpretations are always based on a pre-conception of human activity and of social or natural events, *mimesis$_1$*: 'Whatever may be the status of these stories which somehow are prior to the narration we may give them, our mere use of the word 'story' (taken in this pre-narrative sense) testifies to our pre-understanding that action is human to the extent it characterizes a life story that deserves to be told. Mimesis$_1$ is that pre-understanding of what human action is, of its semantics, its symbolism, its temporality. From this pre-under-standing, which is common to poets and their readers, arises fiction, and with fiction comes the second form of mimesis which is textual and literary' (Ricoeur 1981, p. 20).

- The mimetic transformation in 'processing' experiences of social or natural environments into texts – whether in everyday narratives recounted for other people, in certain documents or in producing texts for research purposes – should be understood as a process of construction, *mimesis$_2$*: 'Such is the realm of mimesis$_2$ between the antecedence and the descendance of the text. At this level mimesis may be defined as the configuration of action' (1981, p. 25).

- The mimetic transformation of texts in understanding occurs through processes of interpretation, *mimesis$_3$* – in the everyday understanding of narratives, documents, books, newspapers etc. just as in the scientific interpretations of such narratives, research documents (protocols, transcripts etc.) or scientific texts: 'mimesis$_3$ marks the intersection of the world of text and the world of the hearer or reader' (1981, p. 26).

According to this view, which has been formulated by Ricoeur in dealing with literary texts, mimetic processes can be located in social science understanding as the interplay of construction and interpretation of experiences (Figure 3.2). Mimesis includes the passage from pre-understanding across the text to interpretation. The process is executed in the act of construction and interpretation as well as in the act of understanding.

Understanding as an active process of construction involves the one who understands. According to this conception of mimesis, this process is not limited to access to literary texts but extends to understanding as a whole

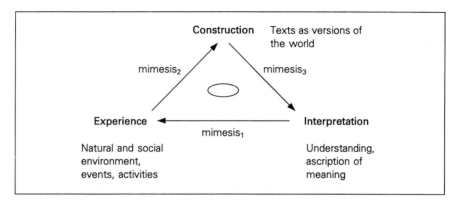

FIGURE 3.2 *Process of mimesis*

and thus also to understanding as a concept of knowledge in the framework of social science research. This is clarified by Gebauer and Wulf (1995) in their generalizing discussion of mimesis. They refer to Goodman's (1978) theory of the different ways of world making and the resulting versions of the world as outcome of knowledge:

> Knowing in terms of this model is a matter of invention: modes of organization 'are not found in the world but *built into a world*'. Understanding is creative. With the aid of Goodman's theory of worldmaking, mimesis can be rehabilitated in opposition to a tradition that rigidly deprived it of the creative element – and that itself rests on false presuppositions: the isolated object of knowledge, the assumption of a world existing outside codification systems, the idea that truth is the correspondence between statements and an extralinguistic world, the postulate that thought can be traced back to an origin. Nothing of this theory remains intact after Goodman's critique: worlds are made '*from other worlds*'. (1995, p. 17)

Thus, mimesis is discussed by Gebauer and Wulf in terms of the construction of knowledge in general, and by Ricoeur for processes of understanding literature in a particular way, without invoking the narrow and strict idea of representation of given worlds in texts and without the narrow concept of reality and truth.[1]

MIMESIS IN THE RELATION OF BIOGRAPHY AND NARRATIVE

For further clarification, this idea of the mimetic process will be applied to a common procedure in qualitative research. A big part of research practice concentrates on reconstructing life stories or biographies in interviews. The starting point is to assume that a narrative is the appropriate form of presenting biographical experience (for more details see Chapters 9, 10 and 16). In this context, Ricoeur maintains 'the thesis of a narrative or pre-narrative quality of experience as such' (1981, p. 20). For the mimetic relation between life stories and narratives, Bruner highlights

> that the mimesis between life so-called and narrative is a two-way affair . . . Narrative imitates life, life imitates narrative. 'Life' in this sense is the same kind of construction of the human imagination as 'a narrative' is. It is constructed by human beings through active ratiocination, by the same kind of ratiocination through which we construct narratives. When someone tells you his life . . . it is always a cognitive achievement rather than a through the clear-crystal recital of something univocally given. In the end, it is a narrative achievement. There is no such thing psychologically as 'life itself'. At very least, it is a selective achievement of memory recall; beyond that, recounting one's life is an interpretive feat. (1987, pp. 12–13)

This means that a biographical narrative of one's own life is not a representation of factual processes. It becomes a mimetic presentation of experiences, which are constructed in the form of a narrative for this purpose – in the interview. On the other hand, the narrative in general provides a frame in which experiences may be located, presented and evaluated – in short, in which they are lived. The issue studied by qualitative research (here) is already constructed and interpreted in everyday life in the form in which it wants to study it, i.e. as a narrative. In the situation of the interview, this everyday way of interpreting and constructing is used to transform these experiences into a symbolic world – social science and its texts. The experiences are then reinterpreted from this world: 'In mimetic reference, an interpretation is made from the perspective of a symbolically produced world of a prior (but not necessarily existing) world, which itself has already been subject to interpretation. Mimesis construes anew already construed worlds' (Gebauer and Wulf 1995, p. 317).

In the reconstruction of a life from a specific research question, a version of the experiences is constructed and interpreted. To what extent life and experiences really have taken place in the reported form cannot be verified in this way. But it is possible to ascertain which constructions the narrating subject presents of both and which versions evolve in the research situation. No later than in the presentation of the findings of this reconstruction, these experiences and the world in which they have been made will be presented and seen in a specific way – for example in (new) theory with claims to validity: 'Mimetic action involves the intention of displaying a symbolically produced world in such a way that it will be perceived as a specific world' (1995, p. 317). Mimesis comes to fruition at the intersections of the world symbolically generated in research and the world of everyday life or the contexts that research is empirically investigating: 'Mimesis is by nature intermediary, stretched between a symbolically produced world and another one' (1995, p. 317).

Following the views of several of the authors mentioned here, mimesis avoids those problems which led to the concept of representation ending up in a crisis and becoming an illusion.[2] Mimesis can be released from the context of literary presentation and understanding and used as a concept in the social sciences which takes into account that the things to be understood are always presented on different levels: mimetic processes can be identified in the processing of experiences in everyday practices, in interviews, and through these in the construction of versions of the world that are textualized and textualizable, i.e. accessible for social science, as well as in the production of texts for research purposes. In mimetic processes, versions of the world are produced which may be understood and interpreted in social research (for an application see Flick 1996). Ricoeur's differentiation of various forms of mimesis and Schütz's distinction between everyday and scientific constructions may further contribute to the framework claimed by Goodman with the assumption of different versions of the world constructed in everyday, artistic and scientific ways. This allows the researcher to avoid the illusions and crises which are characteristic of the idea of representation, whilst not disregarding the constructive elements in the process of representation (or better presentation) as well as in the process of understanding.

Qualitative research, which takes as its epistemological principle the understanding realized in different methodological procedures, is already confronted with the construction of reality on the part of its 'object'. Experiences are not simply mirrored in narratives or in the social science texts produced about them. The idea of mirroring reality in presentation, research and text has ended in crisis. It may be replaced by the multistage circle of mimesis according to Ricoeur in a way that takes into account the constructions of those who take part in the scientific understanding – i.e. the individual being studied, the author of the texts on him or her, and their reader. The difference between everyday and scientific understanding in qualitative research lies in its methodological organization in the research process, which the following chapters will deal with in greater detail.

NOTES

1 'Mimesis in this sense is ahead of our concepts of reference, the real and truth. It engenders a need as yet unfilled to think more' (Ricoeur 1981, p. 31).
2 'Mimesis, which seems to me less shut in, less locked up, and richer in polysemy, hence more mobile and more mobilizing for a sortie out of the representative illusion' (Ricoeur 1981, p. 15).

FURTHER READING

The epistemological position which is briefly outlined here is based on the first four references and is detailed further and put into empirical terms in the fifth.

Gebauer, G., Wulf, C. (1995), *Mimesis: Culture, Art, Society*. Berkeley, CA: University of California Press.

Goodman, N. (1978), *Ways of Worldmaking*. Indianapolis: Hackett.

Ricoeur, P. (1984), *Time and Narrative*, Vol. 1. Chicago: University of Chicago Press.

Schütz, A. (1962), *Collected Papers*, Vol. 1. Den Haag: Nijhoff.

Flick, U. (1996), *Psychologie des technisierten Alltags*. Opladen: Westdeutscher Verlag.

PART 2
RESEARCH DESIGN

4

PROCESS AND THEORIES

Qualitative research cannot be characterized by its choice of certain methods over and above others. Qualitative and quantitative research are not incompatible opposites which should not be combined (see Chapter 20); nor will old and unfruitful methodological debates on fundamental questions be reopened here. However, qualitative research does presuppose a different understanding of research in general, which goes beyond the decision to use a narrative interview or a questionnaire, for example. Qualitative research comprises a specific understanding of the relation between issue and method (see Becker 1996). Furthermore, only in a very restricted way is it compatible with the logic of research familiar from experimental or quantitative research. In this type of research, the process of research can be neatly arranged in a linear sequence of conceptual, methodological and empirical steps. Each step can be taken and treated one after the other and separately. In qualitative research, on the other hand, there is a mutual interdependence of the single parts of the research process and this has to be taken into account much more. This idea has been developed most clearly in the approach of grounded theory research by Glaser and Strauss (1967), Corbin and Strauss (1990) and Strauss (1987).

RESEARCH AS LINEAR PROCESS

The traditional version of quantitative social sciences starts from building a model: before entering the field to be studied, and while still sitting at his or her desk, the researcher constructs a model of the assumed conditions and relations. The researcher's starting point is the theoretical knowledge taken from the literature or earlier empirical findings. From this, hypotheses are derived which are operationalized and tested against empirical conditions. The concrete or empirical 'objects' of research, like a certain field or real persons, have the status of the exemplary, against which assumed general relations (in the form of hypotheses) are tested. The aim is that the representativeness of the data and findings can be guaranteed, for example across random samples of the persons that are studied. A further aim is the breaking down of complex relations into distinct variables, which allows the researcher to isolate and test their effects. Theories and methods are prior to the object of research. Theories are tested and perhaps falsified on the way. If they are enlarged it is through additional hypotheses, which are again tested empirically, and so on.

THE CONCEPT OF PROCESS IN GROUNDED THEORY RESEARCH

In contrast to this, the grounded theory approach gives preference to the data and the field under study as against theoretical assumptions. These should not be applied to the subject being studied but are 'discovered' and formulated in dealing with the field and the empirical data to be found in it. It is their relevance to the research topic rather than their representativeness which determines the way in which the people to be studied are selected. The aim is not to reduce complexity by breaking it down into variables but rather to increase complexity by including context. Methods too have to be appropriate to the issue under study and have to be chosen accordingly. The relation of theory to empirical work in this type of research is outlined as follows: 'The principle of openness implies that the theoretical structuring of the issue under study is postponed until the structuring of the issue under study by the persons being studied has emerged' (Hoffmann-Riem 1980, p. 343). Here, it is postulated that the researcher should at least suspend the *a priori* theoretical knowledge that he or she brings into the field. However, in contrast to a widespread misunderstanding, this is postulated above all for the way to treat hypotheses and less for the decision about the research question (see the following chapter): 'The delay in structuring implies the abandonment of the *ex ante* formulation of hypotheses. In fact, the research question is outlined under theoretical aspects . . . But the elaboration does not culminate in . . . the set of hypotheses' (1980, p. 345).

This understanding of qualitative research suggests that the researcher should adopt an attitude of what, in a different context, has been termed 'evenly suspended attention'. According to Freud, this allows one to avoid the ensuing problems:

> For as soon as anyone deliberately concentrates his attention to a certain degree, he begins to select from the material before him; one point will be fixed in his mind with particular clearness and some other will be correspondingly disregarded, and in making this selection he will be following his expectations or inclinations. This, however, is precisely what must not be done. In making this selection, if he follows his expectations he is in danger of never finding anything but what he already knows; and if he follows his inclinations, he will certainly falsify what he may perceive. (1958, p. 112)

Applied to qualitative research, this means that researchers – partly because of their own theoretical assumptions and structures, which direct their attention to concrete aspects, but also because of their own fears – remain blind to the structures in the field or person under study. This makes them and their research lose the discovery of the actual 'new'.

The model of the process in grounded theory research mainly includes the following aspects: theoretical sampling (see Chapter 7), theoretical coding (see Chapter 15) and writing the theory (see Chapter 19). This approach strongly focuses on the interpretation of data no matter how they were collected. Here, the question of which method to use for collecting data becomes minor. Decisions on data to be integrated and methods to be used for this are based on the state of the developing theory after analysing the data already at hand at that moment.

Various aspects of Glaser and Strauss's model have become relevant in their own right in methodological discussions and qualitative research practice. Theoretical sampling in particular, as a strategy of defining a sample step by step, is also applied in research in which methods of interpretation are used that are completely different from those Glaser and Strauss suggest or in which the claim for developing a theory is not made. Theoretical coding as a method of interpreting texts has also gained its own relevance. The idea of developing theories by analysing empirical material has become essential in its own right to the discussions of qualitative research, quite independently from using the methods of the approach at the same time. But often the consistency with which the approach of Strauss interrelates its individual components is ignored. Theoretical sampling, for example, actually is only feasible as a strategy if the consequence is appreciated that not all interviews are completed in the first stage and the interpretation of the data starts only after interviewing is finished. It is rather the immediate interpretation of collected data which is the basis for sampling decisions. These decisions are not limited to selecting cases, but also comprise the decisions about the type of data to integrate next and – in extreme cases – about changing the method.

LINEARITY AND CIRCULARITY OF THE PROCESS

This circularity of the processual parts in the model of grounded theory research is a central feature of the approach. It was the force behind a multitude of approaches starting from case analyses (e.g. Hildenbrand 1991; Ragin and Becker 1992). However, this circularity causes problems where the general linear model of research (theory, hypotheses, operationalization, sampling, collecting data, interpreting data, validation) is used to evaluate research. In general, this is the case in two respects: in proposing a research project or in applying for a grant, and in the evaluation of this research and its results by the use of traditional quality indicators (see Chapter 18).

However, notwithstanding that problem, this circularity is one of the strengths of the approach, because it forces the researcher to permanently reflect on the whole research process and on particular steps in the light of the other steps – at least when it is applied consistently. The close (also temporal) link between collecting and interpreting data on the one hand and the selection of empirical material on the other, unlike in the traditional linear method of proceeding, allows the researcher not only to ask the following question repeatedly but also to answer it: how far do the methods, categories and theories that are used do justice to the subject and the data?

THEORIES IN THE RESEARCH PROCESS AS VERSIONS OF THE WORLD

Now, what is the function of theories[1] in a research process in the style of Glaser and Strauss? There are two starting points for answering this question. The first is Goodman's (1978) concept that theories – similar to other forms of presenting empirical relations – are versions of the world. These versions undergo a continuous revision, evaluation, construction and reconstruction. According to this, theories are not (right or wrong) representations of given facts, but versions or perspectives through which the world is seen. By the formulation of a version and by the perspective on the world hidden in it, the perception of the world is determined in a way which feeds back into the social construction of this perspective and thus the world around us (see Chapter 3). Theories as versions of the world thus become preliminary and relative. Further developing the version – for example by additional interpretations of new materials – leads to an increased empirical grounding in the object that is studied. But here the research process, too, does not start as a *tabula rasa*. The starting point is rather a pre-understanding of the subject or field under study.

Accordingly, the second point of reference for defining the role of theories in the model of grounded theory research is the first rule that Kleining formulates for qualitative research: 'The pre-understanding of the facts under study should be regarded as preliminary and should be exceeded with new, non-congruent information' (1982, p. 231).

Theoretical assumptions become relevant as preliminary versions of the understanding of and the perspective on the object being studied, which are reformulated and above all are further elaborated in the course of the research process. These revisions of versions on the basis of the empirical material drive forward the construction of the subject under study. The researcher's methodological decisions, as designed in the model of Glaser and Strauss, contribute to this construction.

Qualitative research fits the traditional, linear logic of research only in a limited way. Rather, the circular interlinking of empirical steps, as the model of Glaser and Strauss suggests (see Figure 4.1), does justice to the character of discovery in qualitative research. The context of this processual model should be referred to when single parts – like theoretical sampling – are taken from it and used in isolation. This processual understanding allows one to realize the epistemological principle of *verstehen* with a greater degree of sensitivity than in linear designs. The relative relevance of theories as versions of the object to be reformulated takes the construction of reality in the research process into account more seriously. The central part reserved for the interpretation of data (compared with their collection or the *a priori* construction of elaborated designs) takes into account the fact that text is the actual empirical material and the ultimate basis for developing the theory.

NOTE

1   Here, 'theories' means assumptions about the subject under study, whereas the notion 'theoretical positions' in Chapter 2 refers to differing assumptions about the methods and goals of research.

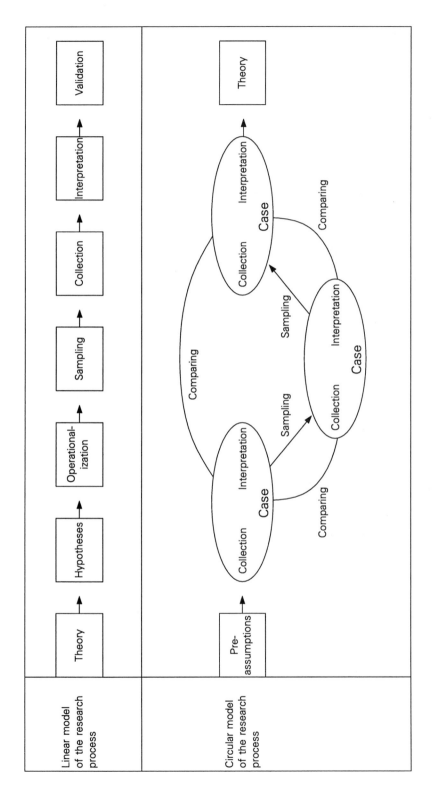

FIGURE 4.1 *Models of process and theory*

FURTHER READING

The epistemological positions of qualitative research are outlined in the first text, whereas the others give both classical and more recent versions of the process model of grounded theory research.

Becker, H.S. (1996), The Epistemology of Qualitative Research. In: Jessor, R., Colby, A., Shweder, R.A. (eds), *Ethnography and Human Development*, pp. 53–72. Chicago: University of Chicago Press.

Glaser, B.G., Strauss, A.L. (1967), *The Discovery of Grounded Theory: Strategies for Qualitative Research*. New York: Aldine.

Strauss, A.L. (1987), *Qualitative Analysis for Social Scientists*. Cambridge: Cambridge University Press.

RESEARCH QUESTIONS

CONTENTS

A central step, and one which essentially determines success in qualitative research, but tends to be ignored in most presentations of methods,[1] is how to formulate the research question(s). The researcher is confronted with this problem not only at the beginning, when the study or the project is conceptualized, but in several phases of the process: in conceptualizing the research design, in entering the field, in selecting the cases and in collecting data. Particularly in the decision about the method(s) of collecting data, in conceptualizing interview schedules, but also in conceptualizing the interpretation, i.e. the method used and the material selected, reflection on and reformulation of the research question are central points of reference for assessing the appropriateness of the decisions taken. The formulation of research questions in concrete terms is guided by the aim of clarifying what the field contacts will reveal. The less clearly a research question is formulated, the greater is the danger that researchers will ultimately find themselves in front of mountains of data helplessly trying to interpret them (see Südmersen 1983). Although the quoted 'principle of openness' questions the *a priori* formulation of hypotheses (Hoffmann-Riem 1980) it by no means implies that researchers should abandon attempts to define and formulate research questions. It is important, that the researcher develops a clear idea of his or her research question, but remains open to new and perhaps surprising results. Clear ideas about the nature of the research questions that are pursued are also necessary for checking the appropriateness of methodological decisions in the following respects: which

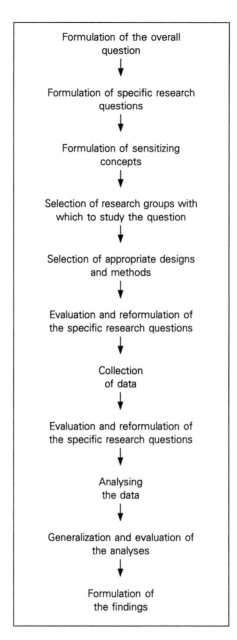

FIGURE 5.1 *Research questions in the research process*

methods are necessary to answer the questions? Is it possible to study the research question with the chosen methods at all? Is qualitative research the appropriate strategy to answer these questions?[2] More generally, the elaboration of the research question in the research process may be characterized in Figure 5.1.

CUTTING QUESTIONS TO SIZE

Research questions do not come from nowhere. In many cases, their origin lies in the researcher's personal biography and his or her social context. The decision about a specific question mostly depends on the researcher's practical interests and his or her involvement in certain social and historical contexts. Everyday and scientific contexts both play a part here. Recent research studying scientific processes has demonstrated repeatedly how much traditions and styles of thinking (Fleck 1935) influence the formulation of research questions in scientific laboratories and in work groups in social sciences (for overviews see Amann and Knorr-Cetina 1991; Knorr-Cetina and Mulkay 1983).

Deciding upon a concrete research question is always linked to reducing variety and thus to structuring the field under study: certain aspects are brought to the fore, others are regarded as less important and (at least for the time being) left in the background or excluded. For instance in collecting data, such a decision is particularly crucial when single interviews (see Chapters 8 to 10) are used. However, if the data are collected in a processual manner, as for example in participant observation (see Chapter 12) or with repeated interviews, the consequences of such a decision can be changed more easily.

SPECIFYING AN AREA OF INTEREST AND DELIMITING THE ISSUE

The result of formulating research questions is that a specific area of a more or less complex field is circumscribed which is regarded as essential, although the field would allow various research definitions of this kind. For studying the situation 'counselling', for example, one could specify any of the following as areas of interest:

- interactive processes between counsellor and client;

- organization of the administration of clients as 'cases';

- organization and maintenance of a specific professional identity (for example to be a helper under unfavourable circumstances);

- subjective or objective manifestations of the patient's 'career'.

All these areas are relevant aspects of the complexity of everyday life in an institution (counselling service, sociopsychiatric service). Each of these areas could be focused on in a study and embodied in a research question. For example, the researcher could approach a complex (e.g. institutional) field with the aim of focusing on gaining an understanding of the viewpoint of one person or of several persons acting in this field (Bergold and Flick 1987). He or she could focus on describing a life world (see Legewie 1987). Similarly, he or she could be dedicated to reconstructing subjective (Holzkamp 1986) or objective (Oevermann 1983) reasons for activities and thus to explaining human behaviour. Alternatively, he or she could concentrate on the relation between subjective interpretations and the structural features of activity environments that can be described objectively. Only in very rare cases in qualitative research does it make sense and is it realistic to include this multitude of aspects. Rather it is crucial that the field and the research question are defined in such a way that the latter can be answered with the available resources and a sound research design can be derived. This also calls for the formulation of a research question in such a way that it does not implicitly raise a lot other questions at the same time, which would result in too indistinct an orientation to the empirical activities.

KEY CONCEPTS AND THE TRIANGULATION OF PERSPECTIVES

The researcher faces the problem of which aspects to include (the essential, the manageable, the relevant perspective etc.) and which to exclude (the secondary, the less relevant etc.). How should this decision be shaped in order to ensure the least 'frictional loss' possible, i.e. ensure that the loss of authenticity remains limited and justifiable through an acceptable (degree of) neglect of certain aspects?

On the one hand, key concepts that give access to as wide as possible a spectrum of processes relevant in a field may be the starting point of the research. Glaser and Strauss call these 'analytical and sensitizing concepts' (1967, p. 38). For instance, in studying the institutional everyday life of counselling, a concept like 'trust' has proved to be useful. This concept may be applied, for example, to aspects of interactions between counsellor and client as well as of the task, to the client's impression of the institution and his or her perception of the counsellor's competence, to the problematic of how to make a conversation a consultation, and so on (Flick 1989).

On the other hand, the frictional loss in decisions between research perspectives can be reduced by the approach of systematic triangulation of perspectives (Flick 1992a). This refers to the combination of appropriate research perspectives and methods that are suitable for taking into account as many different aspects of a problem as possible. An example of this would be the combination of attempts at understanding a person's point of view with attempts at describing the life world in which he or she acts. According to Fielding and Fielding (1986, p. 34) structural aspects of a problem should be linked with reconstructing its meaning for the people involved (see Chapter 18 for triangulation). In the previous example, one could realize this by linking the reconstruction of counsellors' subjective theories on trust with a description of the process of producing trust in a conversation in the special world of 'counselling'.

The use of key concepts to gain access to the relevant processes, and the use of the triangulation of perspectives to disclose as many different aspects as possible, increase the degree of proximity to the object in the way cases and fields are explored. This process may also enable the opening up of new fields of knowledge.

Generally speaking, the precise formulation of the research question is a central step in conceptualizing the research design. Research questions should be examined critically as to their origins (what has led to the actual research question?). They are a point of reference for checking the soundness of the research design and the appropriateness of methods used for collecting and interpreting data. This is relevant for evaluating any generalizations: the level of generalization that is appropriate and obtainable depends on the research questions pursued.

TYPES OF RESEARCH QUESTIONS

There are different types of research questions, which may be located in a schema comprising (according to Lofland and Lofland 1984, p. 94) the components displayed in Table 5.1. There are also links to the 'coding paradigm' that Strauss (1987, p. 27) suggests for formulating questions on text to be interpreted (for more details see Chapter 15).

Generally speaking, we can differentiate between research questions oriented towards describing states and those describing processes (Bude 1995). In the first case, it should be described how a certain given state (which type, how often) has come about (causes, strategies) and how this state is maintained (structure). In the second case, the aim is to describe how something develops or changes (causes, processes, consequences, strategies).

The description of states and the description of processes as the two main types of research question may be classified in terms of the increasingly complex 'units' (Lofland and Lofland 1984) in the left-hand column of Table 5.1. This schema can be used for locating research questions in this space of possibilities and also for checking the selected research question for additional questions raised.

Finally, research questions may be assessed or classified as to how far they are suitable for confirming existing assumptions (like hypotheses) or how far they aim at discovering new ones, or at least allow this. Strauss calls the latter 'generative questions' and defines them as follows: 'Questions that stimulate the line of investigation in profitable directions; they lead to hypotheses, useful comparisons, the collection of certain classes of

TABLE 5.1 *Types of research questions*

Units	What type is it?	What is its structure?	How frequent is it?	What are the causes?	What are its process?	What are its consequences?	What are people's strategies?
				Questions			
Meanings							
Practices							
Episodes							
Encounters							
Roles							
Relationships							
Groups							
Organizations							
Settlements							
Worlds							
Lifestyles							

Source: Lofland and Lofland © 1984, p. 94. (Reprinted with kind permission of Wadsworth, Inc. Belmont, CA)

data, even to general lines of attack on potentially important problems' (1987, p. 22).

Research questions are like a door to the research field under study. Whether empirical activities investigated produce answers or not depends on the formulation of such questions. Also dependent on this is the decision as to which methods are appropriate and who (i.e. which persons, groups or institutions) or what (i.e. what processes, activities, lifestyles) should be included in the study. The essential criteria for evaluating research questions include their soundness and clarity, but also whether they can be answered in the framework of given and limited resources (time, money etc.).

NOTES

1   Almost no textbook dedicates a separate chapter to this topic. In most subject indexes, one looks for it in vain. Exceptions can be found in Silverman (1985, Chapter 1; 1993), Strauss (1987, p. 17) and Strauss and Corbin (1990, pp. 37–40).
2   If the research question in a study implicitly or explicitly leads to the determination of the frequencies of a phenomenon, quantitative methods are not only more appropriate but generally also simpler to apply.

FURTHER READING

The first two texts deal with linking perspectives in research questions in some detail, whereas the other two give classical and more elaborate information about how to deal with research questions in qualitative research.

Fielding, N.G., Fielding, J.L. (1986), *Linking Data.* Beverley Hills, CA: Sage.

Flick, U. (1992a), Triangulation Revisited: Strategy of or Alternative to Validation of Qualitative Data. *Journal for the Theory of Social Behaviour,* 22, pp. 175–97.

Lofland, J., Lofland, L.H. (1984), *Analyzing Social Settings* (2nd edn). Belmont, CA: Wadsworth.

Strauss, A.L. (1987), *Qualitative Analysis for Social Scientists.* Cambridge: Cambridge University Press.

6

ENTERING THE FIELD

CONTENTS

DEMANDS OF QUALITATIVE RESEARCH AND THE PROBLEM OF ACCESS

The question of how to gain access to the field under study is more crucial in qualitative research than in quantitative research. Here, the contact that researchers look for is either closer or more intense, and this can briefly be demonstrated in terms of the problems faced by some of the current qualitative methods. For example, open interviews require that the interviewed person and the researcher get more closely involved than would be necessary for simply handing over a questionnaire. The recording of everyday conversations is linked to a degree of disclosing by members of their own everyday life which they cannot easily control in advance. Participant observers normally come to the field for longer periods. From a methodological point of view, research does more justice to its object through these procedures. From the perspective of everyday practicability, they lead to much more extensive demands on the persons involved. This is why the question of how to gain access to a field, and to those persons and processes in it which are of particular interest, deserves special attention. The general term 'field' may mean a certain institution, a subculture, a family, a specific group of 'biography carriers' (Schütze 1983), decision-makers in administrations or enterprises, and so on. In each of these cases, one faces the same problems: how does the researcher secure the collaboration of his or her potential participants in the study? How does he or she achieve not only that a willingness is expressed, but that this also leads to concrete interviews or other data?

ROLE DEFINITIONS IN ENTERING AN OPEN FIELD

In qualitative research, the person that is the researcher has a special importance. Researchers and their communicative competencies are the main 'instrument' of collecting data and of cognition. Because of this, they cannot adopt a neutral role in the field and in their contacts with the persons to be interviewed or observed. Rather they have to take or are allocated certain roles and positions – sometimes vicariously and/or unwillingly. Which information a researcher gains access to and which he remains debarred from depends essentially on the successful adoption of an appropriate role or position. Taking or being assigned a role should be seen as a process of negotiation between researcher and participants, which runs through several stages. 'Participants' here refers to those persons to be interviewed or observed. For research in institutions, it also refers to those who have to authorize or facilitate access. The growing insight into the importance of the interactive process of negotiating and allocating roles to the researchers in the field finds its expression in the metaphors used to describe it.

Using the example of participant observation in ethnographic field research (see Chapter 12), Adler and Adler (1987) have presented a system of membership roles in the field (see Figure 6.1). They show how this problem has been treated differently in the history of qualitative research. At one pole, they position the studies of the Chicago School (see Chapter 1) and their use of pure observation of the members in a field, of open and well-directed interaction with them and of active participation in their everyday life. The dilemma of participation and observation becomes relevant in questions of necessary distancing (how much participation is needed for a good observation, how much participation is permissible in the context of scientific distancing?). For Douglas's (1976) 'existential sociology', in an intermediate position, Adler and Adler see the problem solved in participation aiming at revealing the secrets of the field. At the other pole, the concern of recent ethnomethodology (see Chapter 2) is with describing members' methods rather than their perspectives in order to describe the process under study from the inside. Here the problem of access is managed by immersion in the work process observed and by membership in the researched field.

For Adler and Adler, the Chicago School's handling of this problem is too committed to scientific distancing from the 'object' of research. On the other

```
┌─────────────────────────────────────────────────────────────────────────┐
│  Observe members          ⎫                                              │
│  Interact with members    ⎬ ──────── Chicago School                      │
│  Participate with members ⎭                                              │
│                                                                          │
│  Investigative participation       ──────── Existential sociology        │
│                                                                          │
│  Membership roles:                                                       │
│      peripheral member                                                   │
│      active member                                                       │
│      complete member                                                     │
│                                                                          │
│  Good faith membership             ──────── Ethnomethodology             │
└─────────────────────────────────────────────────────────────────────────┘
```

FIGURE 6.1 *Membership roles in the field (Adler and Adler 1987, p. 33)*

hand, they are rather critical of the types of access obtained by ethnomethodology as well as by existential sociology (although positioned at
different poles in their systematic): In both cases, access is obtained by
completely fusing with the research object. Their concept of membership
roles seems to them to be a more realistic solution located between these
two poles. They work out the types of 'membership roles: the peripheral,
the active and the complete member'. For studying delicate fields (in their
case, drug dealers) they suggest a combination of 'overt and covert roles'
(1987, p. 21). This means that they do not disclose their actual role (as
researchers) to all the members in a field, in order to gain insights that are
as open as possible.

ACCESS TO INSTITUTIONS

When researching institutions (e.g. counselling services), this problem
becomes more complicated. In general, different levels are involved in the
regulation of access. First, there is the level of the persons responsible for
authorizing the research: in case of difficulties, they are held responsible
for this authorization by external authorities. Second, we find the level of
those to be interviewed or observed, who will be investing their time and
willingness.

For research in administrations, Lau and Wolff (1983, p. 419) have outlined the process as follows. In an institution like social administration,
researchers with their research interest are defined as clients. Like a client,
the researcher has to make his request in formal terms. This request, its
implications (research question, methods, time needed), and the person of
the researcher have to undergo an 'official examination'. The treatment of a
researcher's request is 'pre-structured' by the fact that the researcher has
been sent by other authorities. On the one hand, this means that the

authorization or support for the request by a higher authority in the first instance may produce distrust in the people to be interviewed (why is this higher authority in favour of this research?). On the other hand, being endorsed by other people (e.g. colleagues from another institution) facilitates access. In the end, the researcher's request can be fitted into administrative routines and treated using institutionally familiar procedures. This process, termed 'work of agreement', is a 'joint product, in some cases an explicit working problem for both sides'. For instance, the main task is the negotiation of common linguistic rules between researchers and practitioners. The analysis of this entry as a constructive process, and more importantly the analysis of failures in this process (see Kroner and Wolff 1986), allow the researcher to reveal central processes of negotiation and routinization in the field in an exemplary manner (for example with 'real' clients).

Wolff (1993) summarizes the problems of entering institutions as a research field as follows:

1 Research is always an intervention into a social system.
2 Research is a disruptive factor for the system to be studied, to which it reacts defensively.
3 A mutual opacity exists between the research project and the social system to be researched.
4 Exchanging a whole mass of information on entering the research field does not reduce the opacity. Rather, it leads to increasing complexity in the process of agreement and may lead to increased 'immune reactions'. On both sides, myths are produced which are fed by increased exchange of information.
5 Instead of mutual understanding at the moment of entry, one should strive for an agreement as a process.
6 Protection against infringement of rights through storage of data is necessary, but may contribute to increased complexity in the process of agreement.
7 The field reveals itself when the research project enters the scene, e.g. the limits of a social system are perceived.
8 The research project cannot offer anything to the social system. At most, it can be functional. The researcher should take care not to make promises about the usefulness of the research for the social system.
9 The social system has no real reasons for rejecting the research.

These nine points already contain within themselves various reasons for a possible failure in the agreement about the purpose and necessity of the research. A research project is an intrusion into the life of the institution to be studied. Research is a disturbance, and it disrupts routines, with no perceptible immediate or long-term pay off for the institution and its members. Research unsettles the institution with three implications: that the limitations of its own activities are to be disclosed; that the ulterior motives of the 'research' are and remain unclear for the institution; and finally, that there are no sound reasons for refusing research requests. Thus, reasons have to be invented and sustained if research is to be prevented. Here the part played by irrationality in the ongoing process of agreement is situated. Finally, providing more information on the background, intentions, procedure and results of the planned research does not necessarily lead to more clarity, but rather may lead to more confusion and produce the opposite of understanding. That is, negotiating entry to an institution is less a problem of providing information than one of establishing a relationship. In this relationship, enough trust must be developed in the researchers as persons, and in their request, that the institution – despite all reservations – gets involved in the research. However, it remains necessary to underline that the discrepancies of interests and perspectives between researchers and the institutions under study cannot in principle be removed. However, they can be minimized by developing trust far enough to forge a working alliance in which research becomes possible.

ACCESS TO INDIVIDUALS

Once the researcher has gained access to the field or the institution in general, he or she faces the problem of how to reach those persons within it, who are the most interesting (see Chapter 7). For example, how can one recruit experienced and practising counsellors for participation in the study and not simply trainees without practical experience who are not yet allowed to work with the relevant cases, but have – for that reason – more time for participating in the research? How can one access the central figures in a setting and not merely the marginals? Here again, processes of negotiation, strategies of reference in the sense of snowballing and above all competencies in establishing relationships play a major part. Often, the reservations in the field caused by certain methods are different in each case. This may be demonstrated by examining various methods used to study the question of trust in counselling. Here, interviews and conversation analyses were used. The individual counsellor was approached with two requests: for permission to be interviewed for one to two hours and for permission to record one or more consultations with clients (who had also agreed beforehand). After they had agreed in general to participate in the study, some of the counsellors had reservations about being interviewed (time, fear of 'indiscreet' questions), whereas they saw the recording of a counselling session as routine. Other counsellors had no problem with being interviewed, but big reservations about allowing someone to delve into their concrete work with clients. Precautions guaranteeing anonymity may dispel such reservations only up to a point. This example shows that various methods may produce different problems, suspicions and fears in different persons.

With regard to access to persons in institutions and specific stituations, the researcher above all faces the problem of willingness. However, with regard to access to individuals, the problem of how to find them proves just as difficult. In the framework of studying individuals who cannot be approached as employees or clients in an institution or as being present in a particular setting, the main problem is how to find them. We can take the biographical study of the course and subjective evaluation of professional careers as an example. In such a study, for example, it would be necessary to interview men living alone after retirement. The question then is how and where to find this kind of person. Strategies could be to use the media (advertisements in papers, announcements in radio programmes) or notices in institutions (education centres, meeting points) which these persons might frequent. Another route to interviewees for the researcher is to snowball from one case to the next. In using this strategy, often friends of friends are chosen and thus persons from one's own broader environment. Hildenbrand warns of the problems linked to this strategy:

> While it is often assumed that access to the field would be facilitated by studying persons well known to the researcher and accordingly finding cases from one's own circle of acquaintances, exactly the opposite is true: the stranger the field, the more easily may researchers appear as strangers, whom the people in the study have something to tell which is new for the researcher. (1991, p. 258)

STRANGENESS AND FAMILIARITY

The question of gaining access (to persons, institutions or fields) raises a problem which can be expressed by the metaphor of the researcher as professional stranger (Agar 1980) (Box 6.1). On the one hand, the need to orient oneself in the field and to find one's way around it gives the researcher a glimpse into routines and self-evidence. These have been familiar to the members for a long time and are routinized by them as 'unquestioned and taken for granted' (Schütz 1962). The individuals no longer reflect on such routines, because they are often no longer accessible for them. A potential way of gaining further knowledge is to take and (at least temporarily) maintain the perspective of an outsider – the 'attitude of principled doubting of social self-evidence' (Hitzler 1988, p. 19). This status of a stranger can be differentiated – depending on the strategy of the research – into the roles of the 'visitor' and the 'initiate'. The 'visitor' appears in the field – in the extreme case – only once for a single interview, but is able to receive knowledge through questioning the routines mentioned above. In the case of the initiate, it is precisely the process of giving up the outsider's perspective step by step in the course of the participant observation which is fruitful. Above all, the detailed description of this process from the subjective perspective of the researcher can become a

---

Box 6.1 Roles in the field

- Stranger
- Visitor
- Initiate
- Insider

---

fruitful source of knowledge. Lau and Wolff (1983) describe entering the field as a sociological process of learning.

On the other hand, certain activities in the field remain hidden from the view of the researcher as stranger. In the context of social groups, Adler and Adler mention 'two sets of realities about their activities: one presented to outsiders and the other reserved for insiders' (1987, p. 21). Qualitative research is normally not simply interested in the exterior presentation of social groups. Rather, 'one wants to get involved in a different world or subculture and first to understand it as far as possible from its own action directing ideas' (Wahl et al. 1982, p. 77). A source of knowledge in this context is to gradually take an insider's perspective – to understand the individual's viewpoint or the organizational principles of social groups from a member's perspective. The limits of this strategy become relevant in Adler and Adler's (1987) example mentioned above – dealing drugs. Here aspects of reality remain hidden and are not disclosed to researchers – even if they are integrated in the field and the group as persons. These areas will only be accessible if researchers conceal from certain members in the field their role as researchers. Fears of passing on information and of negative sanctions by third parties for the people researched, as well as ethical problems in the contact with the people under study are here trenchantly revealed. But they play a part in all research. Issues are raised here of how to protect the trust and interests of the people researched, of how to protect them against infringements of their rights by the research, and of how the researchers deal with their own aims.

In summary, the researcher faces the problem of negotiating proximity and distance in relation to the person(s) studied. The problems of disclosure, transparency and negotiation of mutual expectations, aims and interest are also relevant. Finally, the decision has to be made between adopting the perspective of either an insider or an outsider with regard to the object of the research. Being an insider and/or an outsider with regard to the field of research may be analysed in terms of the strangeness and familiarity of the researcher. Where researchers locate themselves in this area of conflict between strangeness and familiarity will determine in the continuation of the research which concrete methods are chosen and also which part of the field under study will be accessible and which inaccessible to the researcher. A specific role again is played by the partly unconscious fears (according to Devereux 1967) which prevent the researcher from meddling in a certain field. For the researcher, it depends on the form of access permitted by the field, and on his or her personality, how instructive descriptions of the cases will be and how far the knowledge obtained remains limited to confirming what was known in advance.

FURTHER READING

The first two texts deal with concrete problems and examples of entering a field and taking a role and position in it. Schütz's paper is a good sociological description of the qualities of being a stranger which allows insights into what is familiar to members of a field.

Adler, P.A., Adler, P. (1987), *Membership Roles in Field Research.* Beverley Hills, CA: Sage.

Lau, T., Wolff, S. (1983), Der Einstieg in das Untersuchungsfeld als soziologischer Lernprozeß. *Kölner Zeitschrift für Soziologie und Sozialpsychologie*, 35, pp. 417–37.

Schütz, A. (1962), The Stranger. In: Schütz, A. (1962) *Collected Papers*, Vol. II. Den Haag: Nijhoff.

7

SAMPLING STRATEGIES

SAMPLING DECISIONS IN THE RESEARCH PROCESS

The issue of sampling emerges at different points in the research process (Table 7.1). In an interview study, it is connected to the decision about which persons to interview (case sampling) and from which groups these should come (sampling groups of cases). Furthermore, it emerges with the decision about which of the interviews should be further treated, i.e. transcribed and interpreted (material sampling). During interpretation of the data, the question again arises with the decision about which parts of a text should be selected for interpretation in general or for particular detailed interpretations (sampling within the material). Finally, it arises when presenting the findings: which cases or parts of text are best used to demonstrate the findings (presentational sampling)?

In the literature, various suggestions have been made for the problem of sampling. But quite unambiguously they are located at two poles: on more or less abstract criteria or on more or less concrete criteria.

TABLE 7.1 *Sampling decisions in the research process*

Stage in research	Sampling methods
While collecting data	Case sampling Sampling groups of cases
While interpreting data	Material sampling Sampling within the material
While presenting the findings	Presentational sampling

A PRIORI DETERMINATION OF THE SAMPLE STRUCTURE

At one pole, criteria are abstract in so far as they start from an idea of the researched object's typicality and distribution. This should be represented in the sample of the material which is studied (i.e. collected and analysed) in a way which allows the inference of the relations in the object. This is the logic of statistical sampling, in which material is put together according to certain (e.g. demographic) criteria, for example a sample which is homogeneous in age or social situation (women with a certain profession at a specific biographical stage) or a sample representing a certain distribution of such criteria in the population. These criteria are abstract, because they have been developed independently of the concrete material analysed and before its collection and analysis, as the following examples show.

Example: Sampling with social groups defined in advance
In a study on the social representation of technological change in everyday life (Flick 1996), the starting point was that perceptions and evaluations of technological change in everyday life are dependent upon the profession of the interviewee as well as on his or her gender, and finally that they are influenced by the cultural and political context. In order to take these factors into account, several dimensions of the sample were defined: the professions of information engineers (as developers of technology), social scientists (as professional users of technology) and teachers in human disciplines (as everyday users of technology) should be represented in the sample by cases with a certain minimum of professional experience. Male and female persons should be integrated. The different cultural backgrounds were to be taken by selecting cases from the contexts of West Germany, East Germany and France. This led to a sample structure of nine fields (Table 7.2) which were filled as evenly as possible with cases representing each group. The number of cases per field depended on the resources (how many interviews could be conducted, transcribed and interpreted in the time available?) and on the goals of the study (what do the individual cases or the totality of the cases stand for?).

Sampling cases for data collection is oriented towards filling the cells of the sample structure as evenly as possible or towards filling all cells

TABLE 7.2 *Example of a sampling structure with dimensions given in advance*

	CONTEXT AND GENDER						
	West Germany		East Germany		France		Total
Profession	Female	Male	Female	Male	Female	Male	
Information engineers							
Social scientists							
Teachers							
Total							

Source: Flick 1996

sufficiently. Inside the groups or fields, theoretical sampling (see below) may be used in the decision as to which case to integrate next.

Complete collection in qualitative research

An alternative method of sampling is the strategy of complete collection, which Gerhardt (1986a, p. 67) has applied: 'To learn more about events and courses of patients' careers in chronic renal failure, we decided to do a complete collection of all patients (male, married, 30 to 50 years at the beginning of the treatment) of the five major hospitals (renal units) serving the south-east of Britain.' The sampling is limited in advance by certain criteria: a specific disease, a specific age, a specific region, a limited period, and a particular marital status characterize the relevant cases. These criteria delimit the totality of possible cases in such a way that all the cases may be integrated in the study. But here, as well, sampling is carried out because virtual cases which do not meet one or more of these criteria are excluded in advance. It is possible to use such methods of sampling mainly in regional studies.

In research designs using *a priori* definitions of the sample structure, sampling decisions are taken with a view to selecting cases or groups of cases. In complete collection, the exclusion of interviews already done will be less likely in that data collection and analysis is aimed at the keeping and the integration of all cases available in the sample. Thus whilst the sampling *of* materials is less relevant, questions about sampling *in* the material (which parts of the interview are interpreted more intensely, which cases are contrasted?) and about sampling *in* presentation are as relevant as in the method of gradual definition of the sampling structure.

Limitations of the method

In this strategy, the structure of the groups taken into account is defined in advance of data collection. This restricts the variational range of possible comparison. At least on this level, there will be no real new findings. If the development of theory is the aim of the study, this form of sampling restricts the developmental space of the theory in an essential dimension. Thus, this procedure is suitable for further analysing, differentiating and perhaps testing assumptions about common features and differences between specific groups.

GRADUAL DEFINITION OF THE SAMPLE STRUCTURE IN THE RESEARCH PROCESS: THEORETICAL SAMPLING

Gradual strategies of sampling are mostly based on 'theoretical sampling' developed by Glaser and Strauss (1967). Decisions about choosing and putting together empirical material (cases, groups, institutions etc.) are made in the process of collecting and interpreting data. This strategy is described by Glaser and Strauss as follows:

> Theoretical sampling is the process of data collection for generating theory whereby the analyst jointly collects, codes and analyzes his data and decides what data to collect next and where to find them, in order to develop his theory as it emerges. This process of data collection is controlled by the emerging theory. (1967, p. 45)

Sampling decisions in theoretical sampling may start from either of two levels: They may be made on the level of the groups to be compared; or they may directly focus on specific persons. In both cases, the sampling of concrete individuals, groups or fields is not based on the usual criteria and techniques of statistical sampling. The representativeness of a sample is guaranteed neither by random sampling nor by stratification. Rather, individuals, groups etc. are selected according to their (expected) level of new insights for the developing theory, in relation to the state of theory elaboration so far. Sampling decisions aim at that material which promises the greatest insights, viewed in the light of the material already used and the knowledge drawn from it. The main question for selecting data is: 'What groups or subgroups does one turn to *next* in data collection? And for *what* theoretical purpose? ... The possibilities of multiple comparisons are infinite, and so groups must be chosen according to theoretical criteria' (1967, p. 47).

Given the theoretically unlimited possibilities of integrating further persons, groups, cases etc., it is necessary to define criteria for a well-founded

---

Box 7.1   Example of theoretical sampling

Visits to the various medical services were scheduled as follows. I wished first to look at services that minimized patient awareness (and so first looked at a premature baby service and then at a neurosurgical service where patients were frequently comatose). Next I wished to look at the dying in a situation where expectancy of staff and often of patients was great and dying was quick, so I observed on an Intensive Care Unit. Then I wished to observe on a service where staff expectations of terminality were great but where the patient's might or might not be, and where dying tended to be slow. So I looked next at a cancer service. I wished then to look at conditions where death was unexpected and rapid, and so looked at an emergency service. While we were looking at some different types of services, we also observed the above types of services at other types of hospitals. So our scheduling of types of service was directed by a general conceptual scheme – which included hypotheses about awareness, expectedness and rate of dying – as well as by a developing conceptual structure including matters not at first envisioned. Sometimes we returned to services after the initial two or three or four weeks of continuous observation, in order to check upon items which needed checking or had been missed in the initial period.

Source: Glaser and Strauss 1967, p. 59

---

limitation of the sampling. These criteria are defined here in relation to the theory. The theory developing from the empirical material is the point of reference. Examples of such criteria are how promising the next case is and how relevant it might be for developing the theory.

An example of applying this form of sampling is found in Glaser and Strauss's (1967) study on awareness of dying in hospitals. In this study, the authors did participant observation in different hospitals and institutions in order to develop a theory about how dying in hospital is organized as a social process (see also Chapter 15 for more details). The memo in Box 7.1 describes the decision and sampling process.

A second question, as crucial as the first, is how to decide when to stop integrating further cases. Glaser and Strauss suggest the criterion of 'theoretical saturation' (of a category etc.): 'The criterion for judging when to stop sampling the different groups pertinent to a category is the category's theoretical saturation. Saturation means that no additional data are being found whereby the sociologist can develop properties of the category' (1967, p. 61). Sampling and integrating further material is finished when the 'theoretical saturation' of a category or group of cases has been reached, i.e. nothing new emerges any more.

TABLE 7.3　*Theoretical versus statistical sampling*

Theoretical sampling	Statistical sampling
Extension of the basic population is not known in advance	Extension of the basic population is known in advance
Features of the basic population are not known in advance	Distribution of features in the basic population can be estimated
Repeated drawing of sampling elements with criteria to be defined again in each step	One-shot drawing of a sample following a plan defined in advance
Sample size is not defined in advance	Sample size is defined in advance
Sampling is finished when theoretical saturation has been reached	Sampling is finished when the whole sample has been studied

Source: Wiedemann 1991, p. 441

The main features of theoretical sampling are highlighted in the comparison with statistical sampling shown in Table 7.3.

Example: Gradual Integration of Groups and Cases

A study of the role of trust in therapy and counselling (Flick 1989) comprised cases taken from specific professional groups, institutions, and fields of work. They were selected step by step in order to fill the blanks in the database that became clear according to the successive interpretation of the data incorporated at each stage. First, cases from two different fields of work were collected and compared (prison versus therapy in private practice). After that, a third field of work (sociopsychiatric services) was integrated to increase the meaningfulness of the comparisons on this level. During the interpretation of the collected material, sampling on a further dimension promised additional insights: the range of professions in the study up to that point (psychologists and social workers) was extended by a third one (physicians) to further elaborate the differences of viewpoints in one field of work (sociopsychiatric services). Finally it became clear that the epistemological potential of this field was so big that it seemed less instructive to contrast this field with other fields than to systematically compare different institutions within this field. Therefore, further cases from other sociopsychiatric services were integrated (see Table 7.4, in which the sequence and order of the decisions in the selection are indicated by the letters A to C).

TABLE 7.4　*Example of a sample structure resulting from the process*

	Prison	Private practice	Sociopsychiatric services
Psychologists	A	A	B
Social workers	A	A	B
Physicians			C

Source: Flick 1989

In the end, it can be seen that a structured sample results from the use of this method as well as from the use of the method of statistical sampling. However, the structure of the sample here is not defined before collecting and interpreting data. It is developed step by step during the collection of data and their interpretation and is completed by new dimensions or limited to certain dimensions and fields.

GRADUAL SELECTION AS A GENERAL PRINCIPLE IN QUALITATIVE RESEARCH

Comparing different conceptions of qualitative research in this respect shows that this principle of selecting cases and material has also been applied beyond Glaser and Strauss. The basic principle of theoretical sampling is to select cases or case groups according to concrete criteria concerning their content instead of using abstract methodological criteria. Sampling proceeds according to the relevance of cases instead of their representativeness. This principle is also characteristic of related strategies of collecting data in qualitative research.

On the one hand, parallels can be drawn with the concept of 'data triangulation' in Denzin (1989b) which refers to the integration of various data sources, differentiated by time, place and person (see Chapter 18). Denzin suggests studying 'the same phenomenon' at different times and places and with different persons. Denzin also claims to have applied the strategy of theoretical sampling in his own way as a purposive and systematic selection and integration of persons and groups of persons, and temporal and local settings. The extension of the sampling procedure to temporal and local settings is an advantage of the system of access in Denzin's method compared with that of Glaser and Strauss. In the example just mentioned, this idea was taken into account by purposively integrating different institutions (as local settings) and professions and by using different sorts of data.

'Analytic induction', originally put forward by Znaniecki (1934) (see Chapter 18), may also be seen as a way of making concrete and further developing theoretical sampling. But here attention is focused less on the question of which cases to integrate in the study in general. Rather this concept starts from developing a theory (pattern, model etc.) at a given moment and state and then specifically looking for and analysing deviant cases (or even case groups). Whereas theoretical sampling mainly aims to enrich the developing theory, analytic induction is concerned with securing it by analysing or integrating deviant cases. Whereas theoretical sampling wants to control the process of selecting data by the emerging theory, analytic induction uses the deviant case to control the developing theory. The deviant case here is a complement to the criterion of theoretical saturation. This criterion remains rather indeterminate but is used for continuing and assessing the collection of data. In the example mentioned above, cases were minimally and maximally contrasted in a purposive way instead of applying such strategies starting from deviant cases (see Chapter 18).

This brief comparison of different conceptions of qualitative research may demonstrate that the basic principle of theoretical sampling is the genuine and typical form of selecting material in qualitative research. This assumption may be supported by reference to Kleining's (1982) idea of a typology of social science methods. According to this idea, all methods have the same source in everyday techniques; qualitative methods are the first and quantitative methods are the second level of abstraction from these everyday techniques. If this is applied analogously to strategies for selecting empirical material, theoretical sampling (and basically related strategies as mentioned before) is the more concrete strategy and is closer to everyday life. Criteria of sampling like representativeness etc. are the second level of abstraction. This analogy of levels of abstraction may support the thesis that theoretical sampling is the more appropriate sampling strategy in qualitative research, whereas classical sampling procedures remain oriented to the logic of quantitative research. To what extent the latter should be imported into qualitative research has to be checked in every case. Here we can draw parallels with the discussion about the appropriateness of quality indicators (see Flick 1987; and see Chapter 18).

RECENT CONCEPTS OF GRADUAL SELECTION

Gradual selection is not merely the original principle of sampling in various traditional approaches in qualitative research. It is also repeatedly taken up in more recent discussions which concentrate on describing strategies for how to proceed with the steps of selection. In the framework of evaluation research, Patton (1990, pp. 169–81) contrasts random sampling in general with purposive sampling and makes some concrete suggestions:

- One is to integrate purposively *extreme* or deviant cases. In order to study the functioning of a reform programme, particularly successful examples of realizing it are chosen and analysed. Or cases of failure in the programme are selected and analysed for the reasons for this failure. Here, the field under study is disclosed from its extremities to arrive at an understanding of the field as a whole.

- Another suggestion is to select particularly *typical* cases – i.e. those cases in which success and failure are particularly typical for the average or the majority of the cases. Here, the field is disclosed from inside and from its centre.

- A further suggestion aims at the *maximal variation* in the sample – to integrate only a few cases, but those which are as different as possible, to disclose the range of variation and differentiation in the field.

- Additionally, cases may be selected according to the *intensity* with which the interesting features, processes, experiences etc. are given or assumed in them. Either cases with the greatest intensity are chosen or cases with different intensities are systematically integrated and compared.

- The selection of *critical cases* aims at those cases in which the relations to be studied become especially clear – for example in the opinion of experts in the field – or which are particularly important for the functioning of a programme to be evaluated.

- It may be appropriate to select politically important or *sensitive cases* in order to present positive findings in evaluation most effectively – which is an argument for integrating them. However, where these may endanger the programme as a whole owing to their explosive force, they should rather be excluded.

- Finally, Patton mentions the criterion of *convenience*, which refers to the selection of those cases which are the easiest to access under given conditions. This may simply be to reduce the effort. However, from time to time it may be the only way to do an evaluation with limited resources of time and people.

In the end, the generalizability of results depends on these strategies of selection. In random sampling this may be greatest, whereas in the strategy of least effort, mentioned last, it will be most restricted. However, it must be noted that generalizability is not in every case the goal of a qualitative study, whereas the problem of access may be one of the crucial barriers.

Correspondingly, Morse (1994, p. 228) defines several general criteria for a 'good informant'. These may serve more generally as criteria for selecting meaningful cases (especially for interviewees). They should have the necessary knowledge and experience of the issue or object at their disposal for answering the questions in the interview or – in observational studies – for performing the actions of interest. They should also have the capability to reflect and articulate, should have time to be asked (or observed), and should be ready to participate in the study. If all these conditions are fulfilled, this case is most likely to be integrated into the study. Integrating such cases is characterized by Morse as *primary selection* which she contrasts with *secondary selection*. The latter refers to those cases that do not fulfil all the criteria previously mentioned (particularly of knowledge and experience), but are willing to give their time for an interview. Morse suggests not investing too many resources in these cases (e.g. for transcription or interpretation). Rather one should only work with them further if it is clear that there really are not enough cases of the primary selection to be found.

Box 7.2 summarizes the sampling strategies discussed.

> **Box 7.2   Sampling strategies in qualitative research**
>
> - *A priori* determination
> - Complete collection
> - Theoretical sampling
> - Extreme case sampling
> - Typical case sampling
> - Maximal variation sampling
> - Intensity sampling
> - Critical case sampling
> - Sensitive case sampling
> - Convenience sampling
> - Primary selection
> - Secondary selection

WIDTH OR DEPTH AS AIMS OF SAMPLING

What is decisive for choosing one of the sampling strategies just outlined, and for success in putting together the sample as a whole, is whether it is rich in relevant information. Sampling decisions always fluctuate between the aims of covering as wide a field as possible and of doing analyses which are as deep as possible. The former strategy seeks to represent the field in its diversity by using as many different cases as possible in order to be able to present evidence on the distribution of ways of seeing or experiencing certain things. The latter strategy, on the other hand, seeks to further permeate the field and its structure by concentrating on single examples or certain sectors of the field. Considering limited resources (manpower, money, time etc.) these aims should be seen as alternatives rather than projects to combine. In the example mentioned above, the decision to deal more intensively with one type of institution (sociopsychiatric services) and, owing to limited resources, not to collect or analyse any further data in the other institutions, was the result of weighing width (to study trust in counselling in as many different forms of institutions) against depth (to proceed with the analyses in one type of institution as far as possible).

CASE CONSTITUTION IN THE SAMPLE

In this context, the question arises of what is the case that is considered in a sample and – more concretely – what this case represents each time. In the example of the studies of trust in counselling and technological change which have already been mentioned several times, the *case was treated as a case*: sampling as well as collecting and interpreting data proceeded as a sequence of case studies. For the constitution of the sample in the end, each case was representative in five respects:

- The case represents itself. According to Hildenbrand, the 'single case ... dialectically can be understood as an individualized universal' (1987, p. 161). Thus, the single case is initially seen as the result of specific individual socialization against a general background – for example as physician or psychologist with a specific individual biography against the background of the changes in psychiatry and in the understanding of psychiatric disorders in the 1970s and 1980s. This also applies to the socialization of an information engineer against the background of the changes in information science and in the cultural context of each case. This socialization has led to different, subjective opinions, attitudes and viewpoints, which can be found in the actual interview situation.

- In order to find out what the 'individualized universal' here concretely means, it proved to be necessary to also conceptualize the case as follows. The case represents a specific institutional context in which the individual acts, and which he or she also has to represent to others. Thus, the viewpoints in subjective theories on trust in counselling are influenced by the fact that the case (e.g. as doctor or social worker) orients his or her practices and perceptions to the goals of the institution of 'sociopsychiatric services'. Or he or she may even transform these viewpoints into activities with clients or statements in the interview – perhaps in critically dealing with these goals.

- The case represents a specific professionalization (as doctor, psychologist, social worker, information engineer etc.) which he or she has attained and which is represented in his or her concepts and ways of acting. Thus, despite the existence of teamwork and cooperation in the institution, it was possible to identify differences in the ways professionals from the same sociopsychiatric services presented clients, disorders and starting points for treating them.

- The case represents a developed subjectivity as a result of acquiring certain stocks of knowledge and of evolving specific ways of acting and perceiving.

- The case represents an interactively made and makeable context of activity (e.g. counselling, developing technology).

Sampling decisions cannot be made in isolation. There is no decision or strategy which is right *per se*. The appropriateness of the structure and contents of the sample, and thus the appropriateness of the strategy chosen for obtaining both, can only be assessed with respect to the research question of the study: which and how many cases are necessary to answer the questions of the study? On the other hand, the appropriateness of the selected sample can be assessed in terms of the degree of generalizability which is striven for. It may be difficult to make generally valid statements based only on a single case study. However, it is also difficult to give deep descriptions and explanations of a case which was found by applying the principle of random sampling. Sampling strategies describe ways of disclosing a field. This can start from extreme, negative, critical or deviant cases and thus from the extremities of the field. It may be disclosed from the inside, starting from particularly typical or developed cases. It can be tapped by starting from its supposed structure – by integrating cases as different as possible in their variation. The structure of the sample may be defined in advance and filled in through collecting data, or it may be developed and further differentiated step by step during selection, collection, and interpretation of material. Here, in addition, the decision between defining in advance and gradually developing the sample should be determined by the research question and the degree of generalization one is seeking.

The characteristics of qualitative research mentioned in Chapter 2 also apply to sampling strategies. Implicit in the selection made in sampling decisions resides a specific approach to understanding the field and the selected cases. In a different strategy of selection, the understanding would be different in its results. As sampling decisions start from integrating concrete cases, the origin of reconstructing cases is concretely realized. In sampling decisions, the reality under study is constructed in a specific way: certain parts and aspects are highlighted, others are phased out. Sampling decisions determine substantially what becomes empirical material in the form of text and what is taken from available texts concretely and how it is used.

FURTHER READING

The first text is the classical text about theoretical sampling. The other two texts offer recent concepts for refining this strategy.

Glaser, B.G., Strauss, A.L. (1967), *The Discovery of Grounded Theory: Strategies for Qualitative Research*. New York: Aldine.

Morse, J.M. (1994), Design in Funded Qualitative Research. In: Denzin, N., Lincoln, Y.S. (eds.), *Handbook of Qualitative Research*, pp. 220–35. London: Sage.

Patton, M.Q. (1990), *Qualitative Evaluation and Research Methods*. London: Sage.

PART 3
VERBAL DATA

┌─────┐
│ 8 │
└─────┘

SEMI-STRUCTURED INTERVIEWS

In the United States and particularly in earlier periods of qualitative research, methodological discussion has revolved for a long time around observation as the main method for collecting data. Open interviews are more dominant in the German speaking area (e.g. Hoffmann-Riem 1980; Hopf 1978; 1991; Kohli 1978) and now attract more attention in the Anglo-Saxon areas as well (see e.g. Kvale 1996; Smith 1995). Semi-structured interviews, in particular, have attracted interest and are widely used. This interest is linked to the expectation that the interviewed subjects' view-points are more likely to be expressed in a relatively openly designed interview situation than in a standardized interview or a questionnaire (e.g. in Kohli 1978). Several types of semi-structured interviews can be distinguished. Some of them will be discussed here both in terms of their own logic and also in terms of their contribution to further developing the semi-structured interview as a method in general.

THE FOCUSED INTERVIEW

Merton and Kendall (1946) have developed the focused interview for media research. After a uniform stimulus (a film, a radio broadcast etc.) is presented, its impact on the interviewee is studied using an interview guide. The original aim of the interview was to provide a basis for interpreting statistically significant findings (from a parallel or later quantified study) on the impact of media in mass communication. The stimulus presented is content analysed beforehand. This enables a distinction to be made between the 'objective' facts of the situation and the interviewees' subjective definitions of the situation with a view to comparing them.

Four criteria need to be met during the design of the interview guide and the conducting of the interview itself: non-direction, specificity, range, and the depth and personal context shown by the interviewer. The different elements of the method will serve to meet these criteria.

Elements of the focused interview

Non-direction is achieved by several forms of questions.[1] The first is unstructured questions ('What impressed you most in this film?'). In the second, semi-structured questions, either the concrete issue (e.g. a certain scene in a film) is defined and the response is left open ('How did you feel about the part describing Jo's discharge from the army as a psycho-neurotic?'); or the reaction is defined and the concrete issue is left open ('What did you learn from this pamphlet which you hadn't known before?'). In the third form of questioning, structured questions, both are defined ('As you listened to Chamberlain's speech, did you feel it was propagandistic or informative?'). Unstructured questions are asked first, and increased structuring is introduced only later during the interview to prevent the interviewer's frame of reference being imposed on the interviewee's viewpoints (Box 8.1). In this respect, Merton and Kendall call for the flexible use of the interview schedule. The interviewer should restrain himself or herself as far as possible from making early evaluations and should perform a non-directive style of conversation which leans on Rogers (1944). Problems may arise if questions are asked at the wrong moment, and the interviewee is thus prevented from rather than supported in presenting his or her view, or if the wrong type of question is used at the wrong time.

The criterion of *specificity* means that the interview should bring out the specific elements which determine the impact or meaning of an event for the interviewee, in order to prevent the interview from remaining on the level of general statements. For this purpose, the most appropriate forms of questions are those which handicap the interviewee as little as possible. To increase specificity, *retrospective inspection* should be encouraged. Here, the interviewee can be supported in recalling a specific situation by using

---

Box 8.1   Example questions from the focused interview

- What impressed you most in this film?
- How did you feel about the part describing Jo's discharge from the army as a psycho-neurotic?
- What did you learn from this pamphlet which you hadn't known before?
- Judging from the film, do you think that the German fighting equipment was better, as good as, or poorer than the equipment used by the Americans?
- Now that you think back, what were your reactions to that part of the film?
- As you listened to Chamberlain's speech, did you feel it was propagandistic or informative?

Source: Merton and Kendall 1946

---

materials (e.g. an excerpt of a text, a picture) and corresponding questions ('Now that you think back, what were your reactions to that part of the film?'). Alternatively, this criterion may be achieved by 'explicit reference to the stimulus situation' ('Was there anything in the film that gave you that impression?'). As a general rule, Merton and Kendall suggest that 'specifying questions should be explicit enough to aid the subject in relating his responses to determinate aspects of the stimulus situation and yet general enough to avoid having the interviewer structure it' (1946, p. 552).

The criterion of *range* aims at securing that all aspects and topics relevant to the research question are mentioned during the interview. On the one hand the interviewee must be given the chance to introduce new topics of his or her own in the interview. On the other hand, the interviewer's double task is mentioned here: step by step, to cover the topical range (contained in the interview guide) by introducing new topics or initiating changes in the topic. This means as well that he or she should lead back to topics that have already been mentioned but not detailed deeply enough, especially if he or she has the impression that the interviewee led the conversation away from a topic in order to avoid it. Here the interviewer should reintroduce the earlier topic again with 'reversional transitions' (1946, p. 553). However, in realizing this criterion, Merton and Kendall see the danger of 'confusing range with superficiality' (1946, p. 554). To what extent this becomes a problem depends on the way the interviewer introduces the topical range of the interview guide and whether he or she becomes too dependent on the interview guide. Therefore the interviewer should only mention topics if he or she really wants to ensure that they are treated in detail.

Depth and *personal context* on the part of the interviewer mean that he or she should ensure that emotional responses in the interview go beyond simple assessments like 'pleasant' or 'unpleasant'. The goal is rather 'a maximum of self-revelatory comments concerning how the stimulus material was experienced' by the interviewee (1946, pp. 554–5). A concrete task for the interviewer resulting from this goal is to continuously diagnose the current level of depth, in order to 'shift that level toward whichever end of the "depth continuum" he finds appropriate to the given case'. Strategies for raising the degree of depth are for example to 'focus on feelings', 'restatement of implied or expressed feelings' and 'referring to comparative situations'. Here reference to the non-directive style of conducting a conversation of Rogers (1944) can also be seen.

The application of this method in other fields of research is mainly oriented to the general principles of the method. Focusing in the interview is understood as related to the topic of study rather than to the use of stimuli such as films.

Example: Persons' concepts of human nature

Based on Merton and Kendall's method, Oerter (1995; see also Oerter et al. 1996, pp. 43–7) has developed the 'adulthood interview' for studying concepts of human nature and adulthood in different cultures (United States, West Germany, Indonesia, Japan and Korea) (Box 8.2):

> The semi-structured interview is divided into four main parts. In the first part, general questions about adulthood are asked; for example, what should an adult look like, what is appropriate for adulthood. The second part deals with the three main roles of adulthood: the family, occupational, and political. The third part draws attention to the past of the interviewee, asking for developmental changes during the previous 2 or 3 years. The last part of the interview deals with the near future of the interviewee, asking for his or her goals in life and his or her further development. (1995, p. 213)

The interviewee is then confronted with dilemma stories, which are followed again by a focused interview:

> The subject is asked to describe the situation [in the story] and to find a solution. The interviewer is asking questions and tries to reach the highest possible level the subject can achieve. Again, the interviewer must be trained in understanding and assessing the actual level of the individual in order to ask questions at the level proximal to the individual's point of view. (1995, p. 213)

In order to focus the interview more on the subject's point of view, the interview guide includes 'general suggestions' like 'Please encourage the subject as often as necessary: Can you explain this in more detail? What do you mean by . . .?' (Oerter et al. 1996, pp. 43–7).

Problems in conducting the interview

The criteria Merton and Kendall (1946) suggest for conducting the interview incorporate some targets which cannot be matched in every situation (e.g.

Box 8.2   Example questions from the adulthood interview

1   *General questions about childhood*

(a)   How should an adult behave? Which abilities/capabilities should he or she have? What is your idea of an adult?

(b)   How would you define real adults? How do real adults differ from ideal adults? Why are they as they are?

(c)   Can the differences between the ideal and the real adult (between how an adult should behave and how an adult actually does behave) be narrowed down? How? (If the answer is 'no': why not?)

(d)   Many people consider responsibility to be an important criterion of adulthood. What does responsibility mean to you? . . .

(e)   Striving for happiness (being happy) is often viewed as the most important goal for human beings. Do you agree? What is happiness and what is being happy in your opinion?

(f)   What is the meaning of life in your opinion? Why are we alive?

2   *Further explanations about the three leading roles of an adult*

(a)   Conceptions about one's professional role
Questions:
What do you think you need to get a job?
Are work and a job really necessary? Are they part of being an adult or not?

(b)   Conceptions about one's future family
Questions:
Should an adult have a family of his or her own?
How should he or she behave in his or her family? How far should he or she be involved in it?

(c)   Political role
. . .
Questions:
What about an adult's political role? Does he or she have political tasks? Would he or she engage in political activities? Should he or she care about public affairs? Should he or she take on responsibilities for the community?

Source: Oerter et al. 1996, pp. 43–7)

specificity and depth versus range). Fulfilling these criteria cannot be realized in advance – for example in designing the interview guide. How far they are really met in an actual interview, depends to a great extent on the actual interview situation and how it goes off. These criteria highlight the decisions that the interviewer has to make and the necessary priorities he or she has to establish *ad hoc* in the interview situation. They emphasize that there is no unambiguous definition of the 'right' behaviour for the interviewer in the focused (or any other semi-structured) interview. The successful carrying out of such interviews depends essentially on the interviewer's situational competence. This competence may be increased by practical experience of making decisions necessary in interview situations, in rehearsal interviews and in interview training. In such training, interview situations are simulated and analysed afterwards with a view to providing trainee interviewers with some experience and some examples of typical needs for decisions between more depth (obtained by further enquiring) and guaranteeing the range (by introducing new topics or the next question of the interview guide) and with the different solutions at each point. This makes the dilemmas of contradictory targets easier to handle, although they cannot be completely resolved.

Contribution to the general methodological discussion

The four criteria and the problems linked to them can be applied to other types of semi-structured interview without using an advance stimulus and pursuing other research questions. They have become more general criteria for designing and conducting semi-structured interviews and a starting point for describing dilemmas in this method (e.g. in Hopf 1978). Altogether, the concrete suggestions Merton and Kendall made for realizing the criteria and for formulating questions may be used as an orientation for conceptualizing and conducting semi-structured interviews more generally. To focus on a specific object and its meaning as far as possible has become a general aim of semi-structured interviews. The same is the case for the strategies Merton and Kendall have suggested for realizing these aims – mainly to give the interviewee as much scope as possible to introduce his or her views.

Fitting the method into the research process

With this method, subjective viewpoints may be studied in different social groups. The aim may be to generate hypotheses for later quantitative studies, but also the deeper interpretation of experimental findings (see Merton and Kendall 1946, p. 542). The groups investigated are normally defined in advance and the research process is linear in design (see Chapter 4). Research questions focus on the impact of concrete events or the subjective handling of the conditions of one's own activities. Interpretation is not fixed to a specific method. But coding procedures (see Chapter 15) seem to be most appropriate.

Limitations of the method

The specific feature of the focused interview – the use of a stimulus like a film in the interview – is a variation of the standard situation of the semi-structured interview which is hardly ever used but which nevertheless gives rise to some specific problems which need to be considered. Merton and Kendall are concerned less with how the interviewee perceives and assesses the concrete material and more with general relations in the reception of filmed material. In this context, they are interested in subjective views on concrete material. It may be doubted that they obtain the 'objective facts of the case' (1946, p. 541) by analysing this material which can be distinguished from the 'subjective definitions of the situation'. However, they receive a second version of the object in this way. They can relate subjective views of the single interviewee as well as the range of perspectives of the different interviewees to this second version. Further-more, they have a basis for answering questions like: which elements of the interviewee's presentations have a counterpart in the result of the content analysis of the film etc.? Which parts have been left out on his or her side, although they are in the film according to the content analysis? Which topics has the interviewee introduced or added?

A further problem with this method is that it is hardly ever used in its pure and complete form. Its recent relevance is defined rather by its impetus for conceptualizing and conducting other forms of semi-structured interview which have been developed from it and are often used. Further-more, the suggestion to combine open interviews with other methodo-logical approaches to the object under study may be noted. These might provide a point of reference for interpreting subjective viewpoints in the interview. This idea is discussed more generally under the headline of 'triangulation' (see Chapter 18).

THE SEMI-STANDARDIZED INTERVIEW

A specific elaboration of the semi-structured interview is suggested by Scheele and Groeben (1988) in their method for reconstructing subjective theories (see also Groeben 1990). The term 'subjective theory' refers to the fact that the interviewee has a complex stock of knowledge about the topic under study. This knowledge includes assumptions that are explicit and immediate and which he or she can express spontaneously in answering an open question. These are complemented by implicit assumptions. In order to articulate these, the interviewee must be supported by methodological aids, which is why different types of questions (see below) are applied here. They are used to reconstruct the interviewee's subjective theory about the issue under study, e.g. the subjective theories of trust used by counsellors in activities with their clients (see Flick 1989; 1992a). The actual interview is complemented by a graphic representation technique called the 'structure laying technique'. By applying it together with the interviewee, his or her statements from the preceding interview are turned into a structure. Also, this allows their communicative validation, i.e. his or her consent to these statements is obtained.

Example: Subjective theories on trust in counselling

In a study of trust in counselling (Flick 1989), 15 counsellors with different professional backgrounds were interviewed using this method. The interview schedule included topics like the definition of trust, the relation of risk and control, strategy, information and preceding knowledge, reasons for trust, its relevance for psychosocial work, and institutional framework conditions and trust. The interviews showed how subjective theories consisted of stocks of knowledge in store for identifying different types of opening a counselling situation, target representations of ideal types of counselling situations and their conditions, and ideas of how at least to approximately produce such conditions in the current situation. Analysing counselling activities showed how counsellors act according to these stocks of knowledge and use them for coping with current and new situations.

Elements of the semi-standarized interview

During the interviews, the contents of the subjective theory are reconstructed. The interview guide mentions several topical areas. Each of these is introduced by an open question and ended by a confrontational question. *Open questions*[2] may be answered on the basis of the knowledge the interviewee has immediately at hand.

Example: Subjective definition of trust in counselling

As a response to the question 'Could you please tell me briefly what you relate to the term "trust", if you think of your professional practice?', an interviewee gave as her definition:

> If I think of my professional practice – well . . . very many people ask me at the beginning whether they can trust me in the relationship, and – because I am a representing a public agency – whether I really keep confidential what they will be telling me. Trust for me is to say at this point quite honestly how I might handle this, that I can keep it all confidential up to a certain point, but if they tell me any jeopardizing facts that I have difficulties with then I will tell them at that point. Well, this is trust for me: to be frank about this and the point of the oath of secrecy, that actually is the main point.

Additionally, *theory-driven, hypotheses-directed questions* are asked. These are oriented to the scientific literature about the topic or are based on the researcher's theoretical presuppositions ('Is trust possible among strangers or do the people involved have to know each other?'). In the interview, the relations formulated in these questions serve the purpose of making the interviewee's implicit knowledge more explicit. The assumptions in these questions are designed as an offer to the interviewee, which he or she might take up or refuse 'according to whether they correspond to his or her subjective theory or not' (Scheele and Groeben 1988, pp. 35–6).

The third type of questions – *confrontational questions* – respond to the theories and relations the interviewee has presented up to that point in order to critically re-examine these notions in the light of competing alternatives. It is stressed that these alternatives have to stand in 'real thematical opposition' to the interviewee's statements in order to avoid the possibility of their integration into the interviewee's subjective theory. Therefore, the interview guide includes several alternative versions of such confrontational questions. Which one is used concretely depends on the view of the issue developed in the interview up to that point.

Conducting the interview here is characterized by introducing topical areas and by the purposive formulation of questions based on scientific theories on the topic (in the hypotheses-directed questions) (Box 8.3).

The structure laying technique (SLT)

In a second meeting with the interviewee, no more than one or two weeks after the first interview, the SLT is applied. In the meantime the interview just outlined has been transcribed and roughly content analysed. In the second meeting, the interviewee's essential statements are presented to him or her as concepts on small cards for two purposes. The first is to assess the contents: the interviewee is asked to recall the interview and check if its contents are correctly represented on the cards. If this is not the case, he or she may reformulate, eliminate and/or replace statements with other more appropriate statements. This assessment regarding the contents, i.e. the communicative validation of the statements by the interviewee, is finished for the moment. The second purpose is to structure the remaining concepts in a form similar to scientific theories by applying the SLT rules. For this purpose, the interviewee is given a short paper introducing the SLT, in order to familiarize him or her with the rules for applying it and – as far as necessary and possible – with the way of thinking it is based on. Also given in the paper is a set of examples.[3] Figure 8.1 shows an excerpt from an example of applying the technique and some of the possible rules for representing causal relations among concepts, such as 'A is a precondition for B' or 'C is a promoting condition of D'.

The result of such a structuring process using the SLT is a graphic representation of a subjective theory. At the end, the interviewee compares his or her structure with the version the interviewer has prepared between

> **Box 8.3 Example questions from the semi-standardized interview**
>
> - Could you please tell me briefly what you relate to the term 'trust' if you think of your professional practice?
> - Could you tell me what are the essential and the decisive features of trust between client and counsellor?
> - There is a proverb: 'Trust is good, control is better.' If you think of your work and relations to clients, is this your attitude when you approach them?
> - Can counsellors and clients reach their goals without trusting each other?
> - Will they be ready to trust each other without a minimum of control?
> - How do people that are ready to trust differ from people who are not willing to trust?
> - Are there people who are more easily trusted than others? How do those trustworthy people differ from the others?
> - Are there activities in your work which you can practise without trust between you and your client?
> - If you think of the institution you work in, what are the factors which facilitate the development of trust between you and your clients? What are the factors that make it more difficult?
> - Does the way people come to your institution influence the development of trust?
> - Do you feel more responsible for a client if you see that he or she trusts you?
>
> *Source*: Flick 1989

the two meetings. This comparison – similar to the confrontational questions – serves the purpose of making the interviewee reflect again on his or her views in the light of competing alternatives.

Problems in applying the method

The main problem in both parts of the method is how far the interviewer manages to make the procedure plausible to his or her partner and deals with irritations which may be caused by confrontational questions. The careful introduction of alternative viewpoints (e.g. 'One could perhaps see the problem you just mentioned in the following way: . . .') is a way of handling such annoyances. The rules of the SLT and the way of thinking they are based on can produce irritations, because it is not always standard procedure for people to put concepts into formalized relations in order to

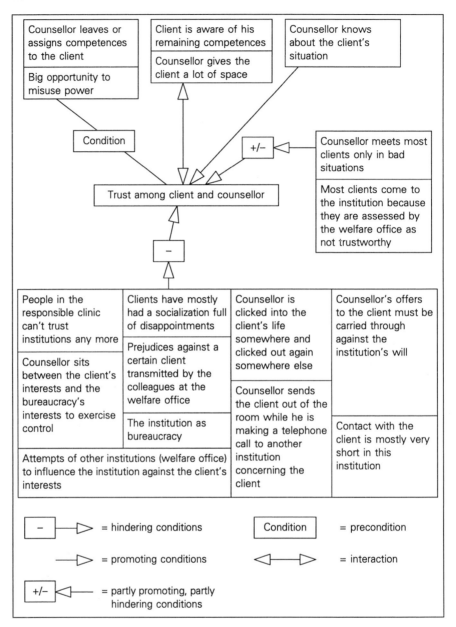

FIGURE 8.1 *Excerpt from a subjective theory on trust in counselling*

visualize their interconnections. Therefore, it is suggested that it is made clear to the interviewee that applying the SLT and its rules by no means should be understood as a performance test, but that they should rather be used playfully. After initial inhibitions have been overcome, in most cases it is possible to produce in the interviewee the necessary confidence in applying the method.

Contribution to the general methodological discussion

The general relevance of this approach is that the different types of questions allow the researcher to deal more explicitly with the presuppositions he or she brings to the interview in relation to aspects of the interviewee. The 'principle of openness' in qualitative research (Hoffmann-Riem 1980) has often been misunderstood as encouraging an attitude of diffuseness. Here this principle is transformed into a dialogue between positions as a result of the various degrees of explicit confrontation with topics. In this dialogue, the interviewee's position is made more explicit and may also be further developed. The different types of questions, which represent different approaches to making implicit knowledge explicit, may point the way to the solution of a more general problem of qualitative research. A goal of semi-structured interviews in general is to reveal existing knowledge in a way that can be expressed in the form of answers and so become accessible to interpretation.

The structure laying technique also offers a model for structuring the contents of interviews in which different forms of questions have been used. That this structure is developed with the interviewee during data collection, and not merely by the researcher in the interpretation, makes it an element of the data. Whether the shape Scheele and Groeben suggest for this structure, and the suggested relations, correspond with the research issue can only be decided in an individual case. In summary a methodological concept has been proposed here which explicitly takes into account the reconstruction of the object of research (here a subjective theory) instead of propagating a more or less unconditional approach to a given object.

Fitting the method into the research process

The theoretical background to this approach is the reconstruction of subjective viewpoints. Presuppositions about their structure and possible contents are made. But the scope of this method for shaping the contents of the subjective theory remains wide enough for the general target of formulating grounded theories to be realized as well as the use of case-oriented sampling strategies. Research questions that are pursued with this method concentrate partly on the content of subjective theories (e.g. psychiatric patients' subjective theories of illness) and partly on how they are applied in (e.g. professional) activities.

Limitations of the method

The fastidious details of the method (types of questions, rules of the SLT) need to be adapted to the research question and the potential interviewees by reducing the rules suggested by Scheele and Groeben, and perhaps also by abandoning confrontational questions (e.g. in interviews with patients on their subjective theories of illness). Therefore, in a large part of the research on subjective theories, only a short version of the method is applied. Another problem is the interpretation of the data collected with it, because there are no explicit suggestions for how to proceed. Experience shows that coding procedures fit best (see Chapter 15). Owing to the complex structure of the single case, attempts at generalization face the problem of how to summarize different subjective theories in groups. For research questions related to (e.g. biographical) processes or unconscious parts of actions, this method is not suitable.

THE PROBLEM-CENTRED INTERVIEW

The problem-centred interview suggested by Witzel (1982; 1985) has attracted some interest and been applied mainly in German psychology. In particular, by using an interview guide incorporating questions and narrative stimuli it is possible to collect biographical data with regard to a certain problem. This interview is characterized by three central criteria: *problem centring*, i.e. the 'researcher's orientation to a relevant social problem' (1985, p. 230); *object orientation*, i.e. that methods are developed or modified with respect to an object of research; and finally *process orientation* in the research process and in the understanding of the object of research.

Elements of the problem-centred interview

Witzel names four 'partial elements' for the interview he has conceptualized: 'qualitative interview', 'biographical method', 'case analysis' and 'group discussion' (1985, pp. 235–41). His conception of a qualitative interview comprises a preceding short questionnaire, the interview guide, the tape recording and the postscript (an interview protocol). The interview guide is designed to support the 'narrative string developed by the interviewee himself or herself' (1985, p. 237). But above all, it is used as a basis for giving the interview a new turn 'in the case of a stagnating conversation or an unproductive topic'. The interviewer has to decide on the basis of the interview guide 'when to bring in his or her problem-centred interest in the form of exmanent [i.e. directed] questions in order to further differentiate the topic' (Box 8.4). Four central communicative strategies in the problem-centred interview are mentioned: the conversational entry, general and specific prompting, and *ad hoc* questions (1985, p. 245). In a study on how adolescents found their occupation, Witzel used as a conversational entry: 'You want to become (a car mechanic etc.), how did you arrive at this decision? Please, just tell me that!' (1985, p. 246). General prompting provides further 'material' and details of what has so far been presented. For this purpose, additional questions like 'What happened there in detail?' or

---

Box 8.4   Example questions from the problem-centred interview

1   What comes spontaneously to your mind when you hear the key words 'health risks or dangers'?
2   Which health risks do you see for yourself?
3   Do you do anything to keep yourself healthy?
4   Many people say that our health is impaired by poisons in air, water and food.
  (a)   How do you estimate that problem?
  (b)   Do you feel your health is endangered by environmental pollutants? By which ones?
  (c)   What made you concern yourself with the health consequences of environmental pollutants?
  . . .
11   (a)   How do you inform yourself about the topic 'environment and health'?
  (b)   How do you perceive the information in the media?
  How credible are scientific statements in this context?
  What about the credibility of politicians?

Source: Ruff 1990

'Where do you know that from?' are used. Specific prompting deepens the understanding on the part of the interviewer by mirroring (summarizing, feedback, interpretation by the interviewer) what has been said, by questions of comprehension and by confronting the interviewee with contradictions and inconsistencies in his statements. Here, 'it is important that the interviewer makes clear his or her substantial interest and is able to maintain a good atmosphere in the conversation' (1985, p. 249).

Example: Subjective theories of illness in pseudo-croup

In a study analysing the subjective theories of illness[4] of parents of 32 children who got ill from 'pseudo-croup' (a strong cough in children, caused by environmental pollution), Ruff (1991; 1993) conducted problem-centred interviews. The interview guide included the following 'key questions':

- How did the first illness episode occur and how did the parents deal with it?
- What do the parents see as the cause of their children's illness?
- What are the consequences of the parents' view of the problem for their everyday life and further planning of their life?
- According to the parents' judgement, which environmental pollutants carry risks for their children's health? How do they deal with them? (1991, p. 103)

As a main finding, it was stated that about two-thirds of the interviewed parents assumed a relation between their children's illness of the respiratory tract and the air pollution in their subjective theories of illness. Although air pollution was mostly seen as only one reason among possible others and the causal assumptions are linked with high uncertainty, the majority of these parents had adapted their everyday lives and also partly the planning of their further lives to that new view of the problem (1991, pp. 109–10).

Contribution to the general methodological discussion

For a general discussion beyond his own approach, Witzel's suggestion to use a short questionnaire together with the interview is fruitful. It enables the researcher to collect the data (e.g. demographic data) which are less relevant than the topics of the interview itself before the actual interview. This allows the researcher to reduce the number of questions and – what is particularly valuable in a tight time schedule – to use the short time of the interview for more essential topics. Contrary to Witzel's suggestion to use this questionnaire before the interview, it would seem to make more sense to use it at the end in order to prevent its structure of questions and answers from imposing itself on the dialogue in the interview.

As a second suggestion, the postscript may be carried over from Witzel's approach into other forms of interviews. Immediately after the end of the interview the interviewer should note his or her impressions of the communication, of the interviewee as a person, of himself or herself and his or her behaviour in the situation, external influences, the room in which the interview took place etc. (see Chapter 14). Thus context information, which might be instructive, is documented. This may be helpful for the later interpretation of the statements in the interview and allow the comparison of different interview situations. With regard to the tape recording of interviews suggested by Witzel for the better contextualization of statements, this has already been established for a long time in using semi-structured interviews. The different strategies for deeper inquiries to the interviewee's answers that are suggested by Witzel (general and specific promptings) are another suggestion which might be carried over to other interview forms.

Fitting the method into the research process

The theoretical background of the method is the interest in subjective viewpoints. The research is based on a processual model with the aim of developing theories (see Chapter 4). Research questions are oriented to knowledge about facts or socialization processes. The selection of interviewees should proceed gradually (see Chapter 7) in order to realize the process orientation of the method. This approach is not committed to any special method of interpretation but mostly to coding procedures and qualitative content analysis (see Chapter 15) is mainly used.

Limitations of the method

The combination of narratives and questions suggested by Witzel is aimed at focusing the interviewee's view of the problem around which the interview is centred. At some points, Witzel's suggestions of how to use the interview guide give the impression of an over-pragmatic understanding of how to handle the interview situation. So he suggests introducing questions to shortcut narratives about an 'unproductive topic' (1985, p. 237). Witzel includes group discussions and 'biographical method' with the aim of integrating the different approaches. As the author discusses these parts under the headline of 'partial elements of the problem-centred interview' (1982, p. 74; 1985, p. 235), the role of the group discussion, for example, remains unclear here: it might be added as a second or additional step, but a group discussion cannot be part of an interview with one person. There have been reservations about the criterion of problem centering. Hopf (1991) criticizes that this criterion seems not very useful to distinguish this method from others as most interviews are focusing on special problems. However, the name and the concept of the method make the implicit promise that it is – perhaps more than other interviews – centred around a given problem. This makes the method often especially attractive for beginners in qualitative research. Witzel's suggestions for the interview guide (1985, pp. 236–7; 1982, pp. 90–1) stress that it should comprise areas of interest but does not mention concrete types of questions to include. Although instructions about how to shape deeper inquiries to interviewee's answers are given to the interviewer with the 'general and specific promptings', applications of the method, however, have shown that these instructions do not prevent the interviewers from the dilemmas between depth and range mentioned above for the focused interview.

The semi-structured interviews discussed up to now have been presented in greater detail with regard to methodological aspects. The focused interview has been described because it was the driving force behind such methods in general and because it offers some suggestions for how to realize semi-structured interviews. The semi-standardized interview includes different types of questions and is complemented by ideas about how to structure its contents during data collection. The problem-centred interview offers additional suggestions about how to document the context and how to deal with secondary information. In what follows, some other types of semi-structured interviews which have been developed for specific fields of application in qualitative research are briefly discussed.

THE EXPERT INTERVIEW

Meuser and Nagel (1991) discuss expert interviews as a specific form of applying semi-structured interviews. In contrast to biographical interviews, here the interviewee is of less interest as a (whole) person than in his or her capacity of being an expert for a certain field of activity. He or she is integrated into the study not as a single case but as representing a group (of specific experts – see also Chapter 7). The range of potentially relevant information provided by the interviewee is restricted much more than in other interviews. Therefore, the interview guide here has a much stronger directive function with regard to excluding unproductive topics. Corresponding to this peculiarity, Meuser and Nagel discuss a series of problems and sources of failing in expert interviews. The main question is whether or not the interviewer manages to restrict and determine the interview and the interviewee to the expertise of interest. Meuser and Nagel (1991, pp. 449–50) name as versions of failing:

- The expert blocks the interview in its course, because he or she proves to be not an expert for this topic as previously assumed.

- The expert tries to involve the interviewer in ongoing conflicts in the field and talks about internal matters and intrigues in his or her work field instead of talking about the topic of the interview.

- He or she often changes between the roles of expert and private person, so that more information results about him or her as a person than about his or her expert knowledge.

- As an intermediate form between success and failure, the 'rhetoric interview' is mentioned. In this, the expert gives a lecture on his or her knowledge instead of joining the question–answer game of the interview. If the lecture hits the topic of the interview, the latter may nevertheless be useful. If the expert misses the topic, this form of interaction makes it more difficult to return to the actual relevant topic.

Interview guides have a double function here: 'The work which goes into developing an interview guide ensures that the researcher does not present him or herself as an incompetent interlocutor . . . The orientation to an interview guide also ensures that the interview does not get lost in topics that are of no relevance and permits the expert to extemporize his or her issue and view on matters' (1991, p. 448).

In this field of application, various problems of semi-structured interviews in general are highlighted. Problems of directing arise here more intensely, because the interviewee is less interesting as a person than in a certain capacity. The need for the interviewer to make clear in the interview that he or she is also familiar with its topic is in general a condition for successfully conducting such interviews. The interpretation of expert interviews mainly aims at analysing and comparing the content of the expert knowledge. Cases are integrated into the study according to the pattern of gradual sampling.

THE ETHNOGRAPHIC INTERVIEW

In the context of field research, participant observation is mainly used. In applying it, however, interviews also play a part (Spradley 1980). A particular problem is how to shape conversations arising in the field into interviews in which the unfolding of the other's specific experiences is aligned with the issue of the research in a systematic way. The local and temporal framework is less clearly delimited than in other interview situations. There, time and place are arranged exclusively for the interview. Here, opportunities for an interview often arise spontaneously and surprisingly from regular field contacts. Explicit suggestions for conducting such an ethnographic interview are made by Spradley:

> It is best to think of ethnographic interviews as a series of friendly conversations into which the researcher slowly introduces new elements to assist informants to respond as informants. Exclusive use of these new ethnographic elements, or introducing them too quickly, will make interviews become like a formal interrogation. Rapport will evaporate, and informants may discontinue their cooperation. (1979, pp. 58–9)

According to Spradley (1979, pp. 59–60), ethnographic interviews include the following elements which distinguish them from such 'friendly conversations':

- a specific request to hold the interview (resulting from the research question);

- ethnographic explanations, in which the interviewer explains the project (why an interview at all) or the noting of certain statements (why he or she notes what); these are completed by everyday language explanations (with the aim that informants present relations in their language), interview explanations (making clear why this specific form of talking is chosen, with the aim that the informant gets involved) and explanations for certain (types of) questions, introducing the way of asking explicitly;

- ethnographic questions, i.e. descriptive questions, structural questions (answering them should show how informants organize their knowledge about the issue) and contrast questions (they should provide information about the meaning dimensions used by informants to differentiate objects and events in their world).

With this method, the general problem of making and maintaining interview situations arises in an emphasized way because of the open framework. The characteristics Spradley mentions for designing and explicitly defining interview situations apply also to other contexts in which semi-structured interviews are used. In these, some of the clarifications may be made outside the actual interview situation. Nonetheless, the explicit clarifications outlined by Spradley are helpful in any case for producing a reliable working agreement (see Legewie 1987) for the interview which guarantees that the interviewee really joins in. The method is mainly used in combination with field research and observational strategies (see Chapter 12).

SEMI-STRUCTURED INTERVIEWS: PROBLEMS OF MEDIATION AND STEERING

So far various versions of the semi-structured interview[5] as one of the methodological bases of qualitative research have been discussed. It is characteristic of these interviews that more or less open questions are brought to the interview situation in the form of an interview guide. It is hoped that these questions will be answered freely by the interviewee. The starting point of the method is the assumption that inputs that are characteristic for standardized interviews or questionnaires, and which restrict when, in which sequence or how topics should be dealt with, obscure rather than illuminate the subject's viewpoint. On the way to securing topically relevant, subjective perspectives, some problems also arise in the semi-structured interview: problems of mediating between the input of the interview guide and the aims of the research question on the one hand, and the interviewee's style of presentation on the other. Thus, the interviewer can and must decide during the interview when and in which sequence to ask which questions. Whether a question perhaps has already been answered *en passant* and may be left out can only be decided *ad hoc*. The interviewer also faces the question of if and when to inquire in greater detail and to support the interviewee in roving far afield, or when rather to return to the interview guide when the interviewee is digressing. The term 'partly standardized interview' is also used with respect to choice in the actual conduct of the interview – the choice between trying to mention certain topics given in the interview guide, and at the same time being open to the interviewee's individual way of talking about these topics and other topics relevant for him or her. These decisions, which can only be taken in the interview situation itself, require a high degree of sensitivity to the concrete course of the interview and the interviewee. Additionally they require a great deal of overview of what has already been said and its relevance for the research question in the study. Here a permanent mediation between the course of the interview and the interview guide is necessary. Hopf (1978) warns against applying the interview guide too bureaucratically. This might restrict the benefits of openness and contextual information because the interviewer is sticking too rigidly to the interview guide. This might encourage him or her to interrupt the interviewee's accounts at the wrong moment in order to turn to the next question instead of taking up the topic and trying to get deeper into it. According to Hopf (1978, p. 101), there may be several reasons for this:

- the protective function of the interview guide for coping with the uncertainty due to the open and indeterminate conversational situation;

- the interviewer's fear of being disloyal to the targets of the research (e.g. because of skipping a question);

- finally, the dilemma between pressure of time (due to the interviewee's limited time) and the researcher's interest in information.

Therefore detailed interview training has proved to be necessary, in which the application of the interview guide is taught in role plays. These simulated interview situations are recorded (if possible on videotape). Afterwards they are evaluated by all the interviewers taking part in the study: for interview mistakes, for how the interview guide was used, for procedures and problems in introducing and changing topics, the interviewer's non-verbal behaviour and his or her reactions to the interviewee. This evaluation is made in order to make different interviewers' interventions and steering in the interviews more comparable. This allows one to take up so-called 'technical' problems (how to design and conduct interviews) and to discuss solutions to them in order to further back up the use of interviews.

The advantage of this method is that the consistent use of an interview guide increases the comparability of the data and that their structuration is increased as a result of the questions in the guide. If concrete statements about an issue are the aim of the data collection, a semi-structured interview is the more economic way. If the course of a single case and the context of experiences is the central aim of the research, narratives of the development of experiences should be considered as the preferable alternative.

NOTES

1 The examples are taken from Merton and Kendall (1946).
2 The examples are taken from Flick (1989).
3 A complete rule paper can be found in Scheele and Groeben (1988, pp. 53–62). Experience shows that it has to be adapted to one's own research question and be tailored to the interviewees, mainly concerning the examples used.
4 Whereas the method described before was developed especially for reconstructing subjective theories, the problem-centred interview is used for this purpose as well. Thus, it is rather coincidental that subjective theories are the object in both examples.
5 As a further variant, the biographical interview (Fuchs 1984) should be mentioned, in which biographical data are collected using an interview guide. The main part of this research is based on narratives and will be discussed in Chapter 9.

FURTHER READING

The focused interview

The first text is the classic text on the focused interview. The other two texts offer recent developments and applications of this strategy.

Merton, R.K., Kendall, P.L. (1946), The Focused Interview. *American Journal of Sociology*, 51, pp. 541–57.

Merton, R.K. (1987), The Focused Interview and Focus Groups: Continuities and Discontinuities. *Public Opinion Quarterly*, 51, pp. 550–6.

Oerter, R., Oerter, R., Agostiani, H., Kim, H.-O., Wibowo, S. (1996). The Concept of Human Nature in East Asia: Etic and Emic Characteristics. *Culture & Psychology*, 2, pp. 9–51.

The semi-standardized interview

The first two texts outline methodological strategies for realizing the aims of this kind of method, whereas the third gives an introduction to the theoretical background and assumptions they are based on.

Dann, H.D. (1990), Subjective Theories: A New Approach to Psychological Research and Educational Practice. In: Semin, G.R., Gergen, K.J. (eds), *Everyday Understanding: Social and Scientific Implications*, pp. 204–26. London: Sage.

Flick, U. (1992a), Triangulation Revisited: Strategy of or Alternative to Validation of Qualitative Data. *Journal for the Theory of Social Behavior*, 22, pp. 175–97.

Groeben, N. (1990), Subjective Theories and the Explanation of Human Action. In: Semin, G.R., Gergen, K.J. (eds), *Everyday Understanding: Social and Scientific Implications*, pp. 19–44. London: Sage.

The problem-centred interview

The first text is an example of the application of the method, which is outlined in the second.

Ruff, F.M. (1993), Les Nuisances environnementales portent atteinte à la santé: Un nouveau schème explicatif. In: Flick, U. (ed.), *La Perception quotidienne de la santé et de la maladie*, pp. 123–42. Paris: L'Harmattan.

Witzel, A. (1985), Das problemzentrierte Interview. In: Jüttemann, G. (ed.), *Qualitative Forschung in der Psychologie*, pp. 227–55. Weinheim: Beltz.

The ethnographic interview

The first text is an outline of the method and the second puts it in the framework of participant observation.

Spradley, J.P. (1979), *The Ethnographic Interview*. New York: Holt, Rinehart and Winston.

Spradley, J.P. (1980), *Participant Observation*. New York: Holt, Rinehart and Winston.

Mediation and steering

The first text is typical for a more attitudinal approach to interviewing, whereas the other two treat more concrete and also technical problems.

Fontana, A., Frey, J.H. (1994), Interviewing: The Art of Science. In: Denzin, N., Lincoln, Y.S. (eds), *Handbook of Qualitative Research*, pp. 361–76. London: Sage.

Kvale, S. (1996), *InterViews: An Introduction to Qualitative Research Interviewing*. London: Sage.

Smith, J.A. (1995), Semi-Structured Interview and Qualitative Analysis. In: Smith, J.A., Harré, R., Langenhove, L.v. (eds), *Rethinking Methods in Psychology*, pp. 9–26. London: Sage.

NARRATIVES AS DATA

CONTENTS

An alternative to approaching individual worlds of experience through the openness that can be achieved in semi-structured interviews is to use the narratives[1] produced by interviewees as a form of data. The starting point here is a basic scepticism about how far subjective experiences may be tapped in the question–answer scheme of traditional interviews, even if this is handled in a flexible way. Narratives, on the other hand, allow the researcher to approach the interviewee's experiential world in a more comprehensive way, this world being structured in itself. A narrative is characterized as follows:

> First the initial situation is outlined ('how everything started'), then the events relevant to the narrative are selected from the whole host of experiences and presented as a coherent progression of events ('how things developed'), and finally the situation at the end of the development is presented ('what became)'. (Hermanns 1991, p. 183)

The narrative interview introduced by Schütze (1977; 1983; see also Riemann and Schütze 1987) is a particularly good example of this type of approach. With the attention it attracted (especially in the German-speaking areas) it has intensified the interest in qualitative methods as a whole. Narratives as a mode of knowledge and of presenting experiences are also increasingly analysed in psychology (e.g. Bruner 1990; 1991; Flick 1996; Sarbin 1986; Wiedemann 1986). Two methods which use narratives in this way are discussed in this chapter.

THE NARRATIVE INTERVIEW

The narrative interview is mainly used in the context of biographical research (for overview see Bertaux 1981; Denzin 1988; Kohli and Robert 1984; Krüger and Marotzki 1994). The method was developed in the context of a project on local power structures and decision processes. Its basic principle of collecting data is described as follows:

> In the narrative interview, the informant is asked to present the history of an area of interest, in which the interviewee participated, in an extempore narrative . . . The interviewer's task is to make the informant tell the story of the area of interest in question as a consistent story of all relevant events from its beginning to its end. (Hermanns 1991, p. 183)

Elements of the narrative interview

The narrative interview is begun using a 'generative narrative question' (Riemann and Schütze 1987, p. 353) which refers to the topic of the study and is intended to stimulate the interviewee's main narrative. The latter is followed by the stage of narrative enquiries in which narrative fragments which were not exhaustively detailed before are completed. The last stage of the interview is the 'balancing phase, in which the interviewee may also be asked questions that aim at theoretical accounts of what happened and at balancing the story, reducing the "meaning" of the whole to its common denominator' (Hermanns 1991, p. 184). At this stage the interviewee is taken as an 'expert and theoretician of himself or herself' (Schütze 1983, p. 285).

If a narrative is to be accomplished which is relevant to the research question, the generative narrative question has to be formulated broadly but at the same time sufficiently specifically for the interesting experiential domain to be taken up as a central theme. The interest may refer to the informant's life history in general. In this case the generative narrative question is rather unspecified, for example: 'Then, I would like to ask you to begin with your life history' (Riemann 1987, p. 46). Or it may aim at a specific, temporal and topical aspect of the informant's biography, e.g. a phase of professional reorientation and its consequences. An example of such a generative question is shown in Box 9.1.

It is important to check that the generative question really is a narrative question. In the example given by Hermanns in Box 9.1 there are clear hints on the course of events to be told, which includes several stages and the explicit request for a narration and for detailing it.

If the interviewee begins a narrative after this question, it is crucial for the quality of the data that this narrative is not interrupted or obstructed by the interviewer, for example with questions (e.g. 'Who is this about?'), directive interventions (e.g. 'Could this problem not have been managed in a

---

Box 9.1 Example of a generative narrative question in the narrative interview

I want to ask you to tell me how the story of your life occurred. The best way to do this would be for you to start from your birth, with the little child that you once were, and then tell all the things that happened one after the other until today. You can take your time in doing this, and also give details, because for me everything is of interest that is important for you.

Source: Hermanns 1991, p. 182

---

different way?) or evaluations ('That was a good idea of yours!'). Instead, the interviewer, as a listener, must signal (e.g. by reinforcing 'hm's) that he or she empathizes with the narrated story and the perspective of the narrator and is trying to understand it. Thus, he or she supports and encourages the narrator to continue his or her narrative until its end.

The end of the story is indicated by a 'coda', e.g. 'I think I've taken you through my whole life' (Riemann and Schütze 1987, p. 353), or 'That was pretty well it by and large. I hope that has meant something to you' (Hermanns 1991, p. 184). In the next stage of narrative enquiries, fragments of narratives that have not been further carried out yet or passages that have remained unclear are taken up again by the interviewer with a another generative narrative question (e.g. 'You told me before how it came about that you moved from X to Y. I did not quite understand how your disease went on after that. Could you please tell me that part of the story in a little more detail?'). In the balancing phase, more and more abstract questions are asked which aim for description and argumentation. Riemann (1987, p. 49) suggests first to ask 'how' questions and then only afterwards to complement them with 'why' questions aiming at explanations.

A main criterion for the validity of the information is whether the interviewee's account is primarily a narrative. Although to some extent descriptions of situations and routines or argumentations may be incorporated in order to explain reasons or goals, the dominant form of presentation should be a narrative of the course of events (if possible from the beginning to the end) and of developmental processes. This distinction is clarified by Hermanns who uses the following example:

My attitude towards nuclear plants cannot be narrated, but I could tell the story about how my present attitude came about: 'Well, I walked – it must have been 1972 – across the site at Whyl, all those huts there and I thought – well that is great, what these people have got going here, but with their concern about nuclear energy they are kind of mad. I was strongly M/L at that time.'[2]

That the method works and that, especially in the main narrative, it provides richer versions of an event or of experiences than other forms of presentation, are argued to be the consequence of one main reason: the narrator becomes entangled in certain constraints ('threefold narrative zugzwangs'). This entangling starts as soon as he or she has got involved in the situation of the narrative interview and started the narrative. The constraints are the *constraint of closing gestalt*, the *constraint of condensing*, and the *constraint of detailing*. The first makes a narrator bring to an end a narrative he or she has already begun. The second requires that only what is necessary for understanding the process in the story becomes part of the presentation. The story is condensed not only because of limited time but also so that the listener is able to understand and follow it. The result of the constraint of detailing is that only those background details and relationships necessary for understanding the story are provided in the narrative. Through these narrative constraints, the narrator's control, which dominates in other forms of oral presentation, is minimized to such an extent that awkward topics and areas are also mentioned:

> The narrator of unprepared extempore narratives of his or her own experiences is driven to talk also about events and action orientations which he or she prefers to keep silent about in normal conversations and conventional interviews owing to his or her awareness of guilt or shame or his or her entanglements of interests. (Schütze 1976, p. 225)

Thus, a technique for 'eliciting . . . narratives of topically relevant stories' (Schütze 1976) was created. This technique provides data that other forms of interviewing cannot provide for three reasons. First, the narrative takes on a certain independence during its recounting. Second, 'people "know" and are able to present a lot more of their lives than they have integrated in their theories of themselves and of their lives. This knowledge is available to informants at the level of narrative presentation but not at the level of theories' (Hermanns 1991, p. 185). Finally, an analogous relationship between the narrative presentation and the narrated experience is assumed: 'In the retrospective narrative of experiences, events in the life history (whether actions or natural phenomena) are reported on principle in the way they were experienced by the narrator as actor' (Schütze 1976, p. 197).

Example: Excerpt from a narrative interview
As an illustration, the following is taken from the beginning of a biographical main narrative of a mental patient (E) (Riemann 1987, pp. 66–8). References to villages and areas are replaced by general words in double brackets ((. . .)). Words in italics are strongly emphasized; a slash indicates the interruption of a word by another; and the interviewer's reinforcing signals ('hmh', 'Oh yes') are represented exactly at the position they occurred:

1 E Well, I was born in ((area in the former East Germany))
2 I hmh
3 E actually in (( )) which is a purely Catholic, purely/mainly

```
 4        Catholic district of ((area, western part)
 5  I                        Oh yes
 6  E    ((town))
 7  I    hmh
 8  E    My father uh . . . was captain
 9  I    hmh
10  E    and . . . uh was already county court judge . . .
11       and then was killed in the war.
12  I    hmh
13  E    My mother got stuck alone with my elder brother/he is three years
14       older than me and uh – fled with us.
15  I    hmh
16  E    About the journey I don't know anything in detail, I only remember –
17       as a memory, that I once uh sat in a train and felt terrible/uh
18       terrible thirst or anyhow hunger
19  I    hmh
20  E    and that then somebody came with a pitcher and a cup for us
21       uh poured coffee and that I felt that to be very refresh-
22  I                                                              hmh
23  E    -ing.
24       But other memories are also related to that train which
25       maybe point uh to *very much* later, well, when I
26  I                                                  hmh
27  E    came into psychiatry, see.
28       Namely, uh – that comes up again as an image from time to time.
29       And we had laid down in that train to go to sleep
30       and I was somehow raised . . . uh to be put to sleep
31  I    hmh
32  E    And I must have fallen down in the night without waking
33       up.
34  I    hmh
35  E    And there I rem/remember that a uh female, not my
36       mother, a female person took me in her arms and smiled
37       at me.
38  I    hmh
39  E    Those are my earliest memories.
40  I    hmh.
```

This narrative continues over another 17 pages of transcript. The interview is continued in a second meeting. A detailed case analysis is presented by Riemann (1987, pp. 66–200).

In the narrative interview, on the one hand, the expectation is that factual processes will become evident in it, that 'how it really was' will be revealed, and this is linked to the nature of narrative data. On the other hand, analysing such narrated life histories should lead to a general theory of biographical processes. Schütze (1983) calls this 'processual structures of the individual life course'. In some areas, such typical courses have been demonstrated empirically, as in the following.

Example: Professional biographies of engineers

Hermanns (1984) has applied this method to around 25 engineers in order to elaborate the patterns of their life histories – patterns of successful professional courses and patterns of courses characterized by crises. The case studies showed that at the beginning of his or her professional career, an engineer should go through a phase of seeking to acquire professional competencies. The central theme of the professional work of the following years should result from this phase. If one fails with this, the professional start turns into a dead-end. From the analyses, a series of typical fields for the engineer's further specialization resulted. A decisive stage is to build up 'substance' (i.e. experience and knowledge), for example by becoming an expert in a technical domain. Other types of building up substance are presented by Hermanns. The next stage of an engineer's career is to develop a biographical line in the occupation, i.e. to link oneself to a professional topic for a longer time and construct a basis from which he or she can act. Lines can be accelerated by successes, but also may 'die', for example by losing the basis because the competence for securing the line is missing, because the topic loses its meaning in some crisis, or because a new line emerges. Professional careers fail when one does not succeed in constructing a basis, developing and securing a line, building up competence and substance, when one of the central professional tasks distilled from the analysis of professional biographies is not managed successfully.

This example shows how patterns of biographical courses can be elaborated from case studies of professional biographies. These patterns and the stages of the biographical processes contained in them can be taken as points of reference for explaining success and failure in managing the tasks of successful biographies.

Problems in conducting the interview

One problem in conducting narrative interviews is the systematic violation of the role expectations of both participants: first, expectations relating to the situation of an 'interview', because (at least for the most part) questions in the usual sense of the word are not asked; and second, expectations linked to the situation of 'everyday narration', because the space awarded to the interviewee for the production of his or her narrative is rarely given in everyday life. These violations of situational expectations often produce irritations in both parties which prevent them from settling down into the interview situation. Furthermore, although being able to narrate may be an everyday competence, it is mastered to varying degrees. Therefore, it is not always the most appropriate social science method: 'We must assume that not every interviewee is capable of giving narrative presentations of his or her life. We meet reticent, shy, uncommunicative or excessively reserved people not only in everyday social life but also in biographical interviews' (Fuchs 1984, p. 249). Additionally, Matthes (1984) sees problems in applying this method in foreign cultures, because the validity of the narrative schema dominant in Western culture cannot simply be presumed for other, non-Western cultures.

Because of these problems, interview training which focuses on active listening, i.e. signalling interest without intervention, and on how to maintain the relationship with the interviewee is again necessary. This training should be tailor made for the concrete research question and the specific target group whose narratives are sought. For this, role plays and rehearsal interviews are again recommended. The recordings of these should be systematically evaluated by a group of researchers for problems in conducting the interview and with the interviewer's role behaviour. A precondition for successfully conducting the interview is to explain the specific character of the interview situation to the interviewee. For this purpose it has proved useful to pay special attention to explaining, in detail, targets and procedures during the phase of recruiting interviewees.

Contribution to the general methodological discussion

The narrative interview and the methodology attached to it highlight the fact that qualitative interviews should be responsive to the structure and gestalt of how experiences are made. In stressing narratives as a gestalt that includes more than statements and reported 'facts', a model for reconstructing the internal logic of processes has been presented. This also provides a solution to the dilemma of the semi-structured interview: how to mediate between freedom to unfold subjective viewpoints and the thematical direction and limitation of what is mentioned. This solution includes three elements:

- The primary orientation is to provide the interviewees with the scope to tell their story for perhaps several hours, and to require them to do so.

- Concrete, structuring or thematically deepening interventions in the interview are postponed until its final part, in which the interviewer may take up topics broached before and ask more direct questions. The restriction of the structuring role of the interviewer to the end of the interview and to the beginning is linked to this.

- The generative narrative question serves not only to stimulate the production of a narrative, but also to focus the narrative on the topical area and the period of the biography with which the interview is concerned.

The methodological discussion so far has dealt mainly with questions of how interviewers should behave to keep a narrative going once it is stimulated, and to enable it to be finished with the least disturbance possible. But the argument that a good generative narrative question highly structures the following narrative has not yet fully been taken into account. Imprecise and ambiguous generative narrative questions often result in narratives which remain general, disjointed and topically irrelevant. Therefore, this method is not the completely open interview that it is often erroneously presented as being in textbooks (e.g. Lamnek 1989, p. 90). However, the structuration by the interviewer is more clearly localized than in other methods – in its limitation to the beginning and the end of the interview. In the framework thus produced, the interviewee is allowed to unfold his or her view unobstructed by the interviewer as far as possible. Thus, this method has become a way of exploiting the potential of narratives as a source of data for social research.

Fitting the method into the research process

Although dependent on the method used for interpretation, the theoretical background of studies using narrative interviews is mainly the analysis of subjective views and activities. Research questions pursued from within this perspective contextualize biographical processes against the background of concrete and general circumstances (e.g. life situations such as a phase of professional orientation and a certain social context and biographical period, e.g. the post-war period in Germany). The procedure is mainly suitable for developing grounded theories (see Chapter 4). A gradual sampling strategy according to the concept of theoretical sampling (see Chapter 7) seems to be most useful. Special suggestions for interpreting narrative data gathered using this method have been made which take into account their formal characteristics as well as their structured (see Chapter 16). The goal of analysis is the development of typologies of biographical courses as an intermediate step on the way to theory building (see Chapter 18).

Limitations of the method

One problem linked to the narrative interview is the following assumption: that it allows the researcher to gain access to factual experiences and events. This assumption is expressed in putting narrative and experience in an analogous relationship. However, what is presented in a narrative is constructed in a specific form during the process of narrating, and memories of earlier events may be influenced by the situation in which they are told. These are further problems which obstruct the realization of some of the claims to the validity of the data which are linked to the narrative interview (see Flick 1996). Furthermore, it is necessary to critically ask another question before applying the method: is it as appropriate for one's own research question, and above all for the interviewees, to rely on the effectiveness of narrative constraints and entanglements in a narrative, as it was during the developmental context of the method? The local politicians Schütze originally interviewed with this method probably had different reasons for and better skills at concealing awkward relations than other potential interviewees. In the latter case, using this kind of strategy for eliciting biographical details also raises questions of research ethics.

A more practical problem is the sheer amount of textual material in the transcripts of narrative interviews. Additionally these are less obviously structured (by topical areas, by the interviewer's questions) than semi-structured interviews. At the very least it is more difficult to recognize their structure. The sheer mass of unstructured texts produces problems in interpreting them. Südmersen (1983) thus wrote an article with the title 'Help, I am Stifled by Texts!' on this problem (see Chapter 16). The consequence is often that only a few but extremely voluminous case studies result (e.g. in Riemann 1987). Therefore, before choosing this method it should be decided beforehand whether it is really the course (of a life, a patient's career, a professional career) which is central to the research question. If it is not, the purposive topical steering allowed by a semi-structured interview may be the more effective way to achieve the desired data and findings.

Critical discussions provoked by this method (Bude 1985; Denzin 1988; Gerhardt 1985) have clarified the limits of narratives as a data source. These limits may be based on the issue of the interview in each case: 'It is always only "the story of" that can be narrated, not a state or an always recurring routine' (Hermanns 1991, p. 183). In the face of these limits of narratives it should be settled, before applying this method, whether narratives are appropriate as the only approach to the research question and the potential interviewees, and whether and with which other sorts of data they should be combined.

THE EPISODIC INTERVIEW

The starting point for the episodic interview (Flick 1996) is the assumption that subjects' experiences of a certain domain are stored and remembered in forms of narrative-episodic and semantic knowledge. Whereas episodic knowledge is organized closer to experiences and linked to concrete situations and circumstances, semantic knowledge is based on assumptions and relations which are abstracted from these and generalized. For the former, the course of the situation in its context is the main unit around which knowledge is organized. In the latter, concepts and their relation among each other are the central units (Figure 9.1).

To access both forms of knowledge about a domain, a method has been designed which collects and analyses narrative-episodic knowledge using narratives, whilst semantic knowledge is made accessible by concrete pointed questions. However, it is not so much a time-saving, pragmatic jumping between the data types 'narrative' and 'answer' which is intended but rather the systematic link between forms of knowledge that both types

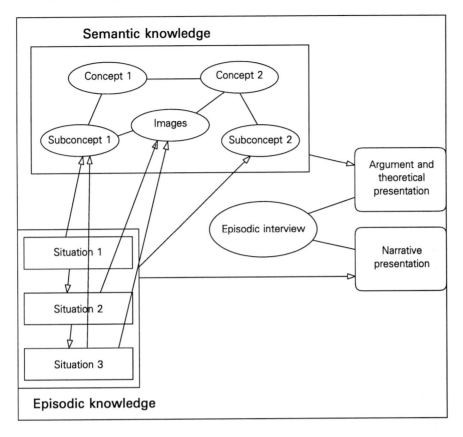

FIGURE 9.1 *Forms of knowledge in the episodic interview*

of data can make accessible. The episodic interview yields context-related presentations in the form of a narrative, because these are closer to experiences and their generative context than other presentational forms. On the other hand, they make the processes of constructing realities more readily accessible than approaches which aim at abstract concepts and answers in a strict sense. But the episodic interview is not an attempt to artificially stylize experiences as a 'narratable whole'. Rather it starts from episodic-situative forms of experiential knowledge. Special attention is paid in the interview to situations or episodes in which the interviewee has had experiences that seem to be relevant to the question of the study. Both the form of the presentation (description or narrative) of the situation and the selection of other situations can be chosen by the interviewee according to aspects of subjective relevance. In several domains, the episodic interview facilitates the presentation of experiences in a general, comparative form and at the same time it ensures that those situations and episodes are told in their specificity. Therefore it includes a combination of narratives oriented to situative or episodic contexts and argumentations that peel off such contexts in favour of conceptual and rule-oriented knowledge. The interviewee's narrative competence is used without relying on zugzwangs and without forcing the interviewee to finish a narrative against his or her intentions.

Elements of the episodic interview

The central element of this form of interview is the periodical invitation to present narratives of situations[3] (e.g. 'If you look back, what was your first encounter with television? Could you please recount that situation for me?'). Also chains of situations may be mentioned ('Could you please recount how your day yesterday went off, and where and when technology played a part in it?'). An interview guide is prepared in order to orient the interviewer to the topical domains for which such a narrative is required. In order to familiarize the interviewee with this form of interview its basic principle is first explained (e.g.: 'In this interview, I will ask you repeatedly to recount situations in which you have had certain experiences with technology in general or with specific technologies'). A further aspect is the interviewee's phantasies concerning expected or feared changes ('Which developments do you expect in the area of computers in the near future? Please imagine and tell me a situation which would make this evolution clear for me!'). Such narrative incentives are complemented by questions asking for the interviewee's subjective definitions ('What do you link to the word "television" today?') and for abstractive relations ('In your opinion, who should be responsible for change due to technology, who is able to or should take the responsibility?') as the second large complex of questions aimed at accessing semantic parts of everyday knowledge.

Example: Technological change in everyday life

In a comparative study (Flick 1996) 27 episodic interviews on the perception and evaluation of technological change in everyday life were conducted. In order to be able to analyse different perspectives on this issue, information engineers, social scientists and teachers were interviewed as members of professions dealing with technology in different degrees (as developers of technology, as professional and everyday users of technology). The interview mentioned the following topical fields: the interviewee's 'technology biography' (his or her first encounter with technology that is remembered, his or her most important experience linked to technology) and his or her technological everyday life (how yesterday went off with regard to where and when technology played a part in it; domains of everyday life like work, leisure, household and technology).

As a response to the narrative incentive 'If you try to recall, what was your first encounter with technology? Could you please recount that situation?', for example the following situation was recounted:

> I was a girl, I am a girl, let's say, but I was always interested in technology, I have to say, or and, well I was given puppets as usual. And then sometime, my big dream, a train set, and uh yeah that train, I wound it up and put it on the back of my sister's head, and then the little wheels turned, and the hair got caught up in the train wheels, and then it was over with the technology, because then my sister had to go to the hairdresser, the train had to be taken to pieces, it was most complicated, she

had no more hair on her head, everybody said 'Oh how awful', I cried because my train was taken to pieces. That was already the end of the technology. Of course, I did not know at all what had happened, I did not realize at all what would happen. I don't know what took me, why I had the devil in me. She was sitting around and I thought, 'put the train on her head.' How long I actually played with the train before, I don't really know. Probably not very long, and it was a great train. Yeah, then it was over for a while. That was an experience, not a very positive experience.

Another example is the following situation, which is remembered as a first encounter with technology:

Yes, electric lights on the Christmas tree, I knew that already from that time, yeah and that has impressed me deeply, I saw those candles at other children's houses and actually, nowadays I would say, that this is much more romantic, much more beautiful, but at that time, of course, it was impressive, if I turned a candle, everything went off, yes, and when I wanted, and that was just the case on the first Christmas holiday, it's a holiday, the parents sleep longer, and the children of course are finished sleeping very early, they go out to the Christmas tree to continue playing with the gifts, which had had to be stopped on Christmas Eve, and I could then turn on the candles again and everything shone again, and with wax candles this was not the case.

A large part of the interview focused on the use of various exemplary technologies which determine changes in everyday life in an extraordinary way (computer, television). For these examples, definitions and experiences were mentioned. As a response to the question 'What do you link to the word "computer" today?', a female information engineer gave the following definition:

Computer, of course I must have an absolutely exact conception of that . . . Computer, well, uh, must have a processor, must have a memory, can be reduced to a Turing machine. These are very technical details, that means a computer can't do anything except go left, go right and write on a tape, that is a model of the computer. And I don't relate more to it at all at first. This means, for me, a computer is a completely dull machine.

Consequences of technological change in different areas (e.g. family life, children's life etc.) were focused across the different technologies. In each of these areas, narrative incentives were complemented by conceptual-argumentative questions (Box 9.2). A context protocol was written for every interview. The interviews showed the common aspects of the different views, so that in the end an everyday theory of technological change could be formulated across all cases. They also showed group-specific differences in the views, so that every group-specific accentuation of this everyday theory could be documented.

Problems in conducting the interview

The general problem of interviews generating narratives – that some people have greater problems with narrating than others – is also the case here. But it is qualified here, because a single overall narrative is not requested – as in the narrative interview – but rather several delimited narratives are

---

Box 9.2   Example questions from the episodic interview

- What does technology mean for you? What do you associate with the word 'technology'?
- When you look back, what was your first experience with technology? Could you please tell me about this situation?
- If you look at your household, what part does technology play in it and what has changed in it? Please tell me a situation typical for that!
- On which occasion did you first have contact with a computer? Could you please tell me about that situation?
- Have your relations with other people changed due to technologies? Please tell me a typical situation!
- Please recount how your day yesterday went off and when technologies played a part in it!
- Which parts of your life are free of technology? Please tell me about a typical situation!
- What would life without technology look like for you? Please tell me about a situation of this type, or a typical day!
- If you consider the life of (your) children today and compare it with your life as a child, what is the part played by technology in each case? Please tell me a about situation typical for that, which makes this clear for you and me!
- What do you link to the word 'television' today? Which device is relevant for that?
- What part does TV play in your life today? Please tell me about a typical situation!
- What determines if and when you watch TV? Please tell me a situation typical for that!
- If you look back, what was your first encounter with TV? Please tell me about that situation!
- On which occasion did TV play its most important role in your life? Please tell me about that situation!
- Are there areas in your life in which you feel fear when technology enters? Please tell me about a situation typical for that!
- What gives you the impression that a certain technology or a device is outdated? Please tell me about a typical situation!

Source: Flick 1996

---

stimulated. The problem of how to mediate the principle of recounting certain situations to the interviewee has to be handled carefully in order to prevent situations (in which certain experiences have been had) from being mentioned but not recounted. As in other forms of interview, it is an essential precondition that the interviewer has really internalized the principle of the interview. Therefore, careful interview training using concrete examples is necessary here as well. This should focus on how to handle the interview guide and, above all, how to stimulate narratives and – where necessary – how to phrase deepening inquiries.

Contribution to the general methodological discussion

Episodic interviews seek to exploit the advantages of both the narrative interview and the semi-structured interview. They use the interviewee's competence to present experiences in their course and context as narratives. Episodes as an object of such narratives and as an approach to the experiences relevant for the subject under study allow a more concrete approach than does the narrative of the life history. On the other hand, and in contrast to the narrative interview, routines and normal everyday phenomena can be analysed with this procedure. For a topic like technological change, these routines may be as instructive as the particulars of the interviewee's history with technology. In the episodic interview, the range of experiences is not confined to those parts that can be presented in a narrative. In orienting to a series of key questions concerning the situations to be recounted and the concepts to be defined, the interviewer has more options to intervene in the course of the interview in order to direct it. Thus, the extremely one-sided and artificial situation given in the narrative interview here is replaced by a more open dialogue, in which narratives are used as only one form of data. By linking narratives and question–answer sequences this method realizes the triangulation of different approaches as the basis of data collection.

Fitting the method into the research process

The theoretical background of studies using the episodic interview is the social construction of reality during the presentation of experiences. The method was developed as an approach to social representations. Therefore, research questions have mainly up to now focused on group-specific differences in experiences and everyday knowledge. The comparison between certain groups is the goal of sampling cases (see Chapter 7). The connection between a linear and a circular understanding of the research process underlies its application. The data from episodic interviews should be analysed with the methods of thematic and theoretic coding (see Chapter 15).

Limitations of the method

Apart from the problems already mentioned in conducting episodic interviews, their application is limited to the analysis of everyday knowledge of certain objects and topics and interviewees' own history with them. As with other interviews, it gives access neither to activities nor to interactions. However, these can be reconstructed from the participants' viewpoints and group-specific differences in such experiences may be clarified.

NARRATIVES BETWEEN BIOGRAPHY AND EPISODE

Interviews primarily aiming at interviewees' narratives collect data in the form of a more or less comprehensive and structured whole – as a narrative of life histories or of concrete situations in which certain experiences have been had. Thus they are more sensitive and responsive to interviewees' viewpoints than other interviews in which concrete topics and the way these should be treated are pre-structured very much by the questions that are asked. Procedures generating narratives, however, are also based on interviewers' inputs and ways of structuring the situation of collecting data. Which form of narrative should be preferred as a source of data – the comprehensive biographical narrative in the narrative interview, or the narrative of details that are linked to situations in the episodic interview – can only be decided with regard to the research question and the issue under study. Such decisions should not be made on the basis of the fundamentally postulated strength of one method compared with all other methods of collecting data, as the programmatic discussions around the narrative interview sometimes suggest. An alternative to mythologizing narratives in such a programmatic way is to reintroduce a dialogue between the interviewer and the interviewee in the episodic interview. A second alternative is to stimulate this dialogue among the members in a family in joint narratives of family histories. These will be discussed in the second part of the next chapter.

NOTES

1   Sometimes also in semi-structured interviews, narratives are integrated as an element (e.g. in the problem-centred interview). In case of doubt, if they are unproductive, they are subordinated to the interview guide. More generally, Mishler (1986, p. 235) has studied what happens when interviewees in the semi-structured interview start to narrate, how these narratives are treated and how they are suppressed rather than taken up.
2   Whyl is a place where a nuclear power plant was planned and built and where big anti-nuclear demonstrations took place in the 1970s, with lots of people camping on the site of the planned plant. M/L was a quite influential Marxist–Leninist political group at that time, which was not supporting this kind of demonstration.
3   The following examples of questions are taken from Flick (1996).

FURTHER READING

The narrative interview

The first two texts deal with the topic of biographical research, whereas the third introduces the method into English language.

Bertaux, D. (ed.) (1981), *Biography and History: The Life History Approach in Social Sciences.* Beverley Hills, CA: Sage.

Denzin, N.K. (1988), *Interpretive Biography.* London: Sage.

Riemann, G., Schütze, F. (1987), Trajectory as a Basic Theoretical Concept for Analyzing Suffering and Disorderly Social Processes. In: Maines, D. (ed.), *Social Organization and Social Process – Essays in Honor of Anselm Strauss*, pp. 333–57. New York: Aldine de Gruyter.

The episodic interview

In these texts, some applications and the methodological background of the episodic interview can be found.

Flick, U. (1994a), Social Representations and the Social Construction of Everyday Knowledge: Theoretical and Methodological Queries. *Social Science Information*, 33, pp. 179–97.

Flick, U. (1995a), Social Representations. In: Harré, R., Smith, J., Langenhove, L.v. (eds), *Rethinking Psychology*, pp. 70–96. London: Sage.

Flick, U. (1996), *Psychologie des technisierten Alltags.* Opladen: Westdeutscher Verlag.

Narratives between biography and episode

To enter into a discussion of these questions more deeply, these two works of Bruner are very instructive.

Bruner, J. (1987), Life as Narrative. *Social Research*, 54, pp. 11–32.

Bruner, J. (1991), The Narrative Construction of Reality. *Critical Inquiry*, pp. 1–21.

10

GROUP PROCEDURES

Semi-structured and narrative interviews were developed starting from a critique of standardized interview situations. The scepticism about this type of interview situation was partly based on the argument of its artificiality, because the interviewee is separated from all everyday relations during the interview. Also the interaction in the standardized interview is not comparable in any way with everyday interactions. Particularly when studying opinions and attitudes about taboo subjects it was repeatedly suggested that the use of the dynamics of a group discussing such topics was more appropriate than a clear and well-ordered interview situation. These methods have been discussed as group interviews, group discussions or focus groups. In contrast to the situation of monological narration produced in the narrative interview, processes of constructing social reality are referred to that take place in common narratives of family members for example. By thus extending the scope of data collection, it is attempted to further contextualize the data collected and to create an interactional situation that comes closer to everyday life than the (often one-off) encounter of interviewer and interviewee or narrator permits.

GROUP INTERVIEWS

Beginning with Merton et al. (1956), group interviews have been conducted in a number of studies (Fontana and Frey 1994; Merton 1987). Patton, for example, defines the group interview as follows:

> A focus group interview is an interview with a small group of people on a specific topic. Groups are typically six to eight people who participate in the interview for one-half to two hours. (1990, p. 335)

Several procedures are differentiated, which are more or less structured and moderated by an interviewer. In general, the interviewer should be 'flexible, objective, empathic, persuasive, a good listener' (Fontana and Frey 1994, p. 365). Objectivity here mainly means the mediation between the different participants. According to Merton et al. (1956), the interviewer's main tasks are to prevent single participants or partial groups from dominating the interview and thus the whole group with their contributions. Furthermore, the interviewer should encourage reserved members to become involved in the interview and give their views and should try to obtain answers from the whole group in order to cover the topic as far as possible. Finally, he or she must balance his or her behaviour between (directively) steering the group and (non-directively) moderating it.

Patton sees the focus group interview as a 'highly efficient qualitative data-collection technique [which provides] some quality controls on data collection in that participants tend to provide checks and balances on each other that weed out false or extreme views . . . and it is fairly easy to assess the extent to which there is a relatively consistent, shared view . . . among the participants' (1990, pp. 335–6). He also discusses some weaknesses of the method such as the limited number of questions it is possible to address and the problems of taking notes during the interview. He therefore suggests the employment of pairs of interviewers, one of whom is free to document the responses while the other manages the interview and the group. In contrast to other authors Patton underlines the fact that: 'The focus group interview is, indeed, an *interview*. It is not a discussion. It is not a problem solving session. It is not a decision making group. It is an *interview*' (1990, p. 335).

In summary, the main advantages of group interviews include that they are low cost and rich in data, that they stimulate the answerers and support them in remembering events, and that they can lead beyond the answers of the single interviewee.

GROUP DISCUSSIONS

Apart from the saving of time and money made by interviewing a group of people at the same time instead of interviewing different individuals at different times, the elements of group dynamics and of discussion among the participants are highlighted when group discussions are conducted. Blumer, for example, holds that:

> A small number of individuals, brought together as a discussion or resource group, is more valuable many times over than any representative sample. Such a group, discussing collectively their sphere of life and probing into it as they meet one another's disagreements, will do more to lift the veils covering the sphere of life than any other device that I know of. (1969, p. 41)

Although partly starting from a comparable critique of standardized interviews, group discussions have been used as an explicit alternative to open interviews in the German-speaking area. They have been proposed as a method of interrogation since the studies of the Frankfurt Institute for Social Research (Pollock 1955). In contrast to the group interview already mentioned, the stimulation of a discussion and the dynamic developing in it are used as the central sources of knowledge here. The method attracted a lot of interest and is left out of hardly any textbook, although more recently it has only been applied in fields like marketing research. One problem of the method is that different reasons are discussed for using it. In these discussions there is also the problem of contradictory understandings of what an appropriate group is like. However, it is up to the researcher actually using the method to decide on the 'right' conception, i.e. the one which is best fitted to the research object. The alternatives to be found in the literature will be discussed here briefly.

Reasons for using group discussions

Group discussions are used for various reasons. Pollock prefers them to single interviews because 'studying the attitudes, opinions and practices of human beings in artificial isolation from the contexts in which they occur should be avoided' (1955, p. 34). The starting point here is that opinions which are presented to the interviewer in interviews and surveys are detached from everyday forms of communication and relations. Group discussions on the other hand correspond to the way in which opinions are produced, expressed and exchanged in everyday life. Another feature of group discussions is that corrections by the group concerning views that are not correct, not socially shared or extreme are available as means for validating statements and views. The group becomes a tool for reconstructing individual opinions more appropriately. Krüger (1983), however, studies the group opinion, i.e. the participants' consensus negotiated in the discussion about a certain issue. Mangold (1973) takes the group opinion as an empirical issue, which is expressed in the discussion but exists independently of the situation and applies for the group outside the situation. Another aim of group discussions is the analysis of common processes of problem solving in the group. Therefore a concrete problem is introduced and the group's task is to discover, through discussion of alternatives, the best strategy for solving it (Dreher and Dreher 1982). Thus approaches which take group discussions as a medium for better analysing individual opinions can be differentiated from those which understand group discussions as a medium for a shared group opinion which goes beyond individuals. However, studying processes of negotiating or solving problems in groups should be separated from analysing states like a given group opinion which is only expressed in the discussion.

Forms of groups

A brief look at the history of and the methodological discussion about this procedure shows that there have been different ideas about what a group is. A common feature of the varieties of group discussions is, as against using the purposive questioning of one person, to use as a data source the discussion on a specific topic in a natural group (i.e. existing in everyday life) or an artificial group (i.e. put together for the research purpose according to certain criteria). Nießen, for example, suggests the use of real groups, i.e. groups 'that are concerned by the issue of the group discussion also independently of the discussion and as a real group including the same members as in the research situation' (1977, p. 64). He mentions as a reason for this that 'real groups start from a history of shared interactions in relation to the issue under discussion and thus have already developed forms of common activities and underlying patterns of meaning' (1977, p. 66).

Furthermore, there is a distinction between homogeneous and heterogeneous groups. In homogeneous groups, members are comparable in the essential dimensions related to the research question and have a similar background. In heterogeneous groups, members should be different in the characteristics that are relevant for the research question. This is intended to increase the dynamics of the discussion in order that many different perspectives will be expressed and also that individual participants' reserve will be broken down by the confrontation between these perspectives.

Example: Student dropouts

In a study of the conditions and the subjective experience of students dropping out of studies, a homogeneous group would consist of students of the same age, from the same discipline and who dropped out of their studies after the same number of terms. If the concrete question focuses on gender differences in the experiences and the reasons for not completing one's studies, a homogeneous group is put together comprising only female students, with male students being put into a second group. A heterogeneous group should include students of various ages, of both genders, from different disciplines (e.g. psychology and information sciences) and from different terms (e.g. dropouts from the first term and from shortly before the end of their studies). The expectation linked to this is that the different backgrounds will lead to intensified dynamics in the discussion, which will reveal more aspects and perspectives of the phenomenon under study.

However, in a homogeneous group the members may differ in other dimensions, which were not considered as relevant for the composition of the group. In the previous example this was the dimension of the students' current living situation – alone or with their own family. Another problem is that heterogeneous groups in which the members differ too much may only find a few starting points for a common discussion. If the conditions of studying the various disciplines are so different there may be little that the student dropouts can discuss in a concrete way with each other and the discussion may end up in exchanging only general statements. These considerations should make it clear that the juxtaposition of 'homogeneous' and 'heterogeneous' is only relative. Groups normally comprise five to ten members. Opinions about the best size of a group diverge.

The role of the moderator

Another aspect which is treated differently in the various approaches is the role and function of the moderator in the discussion. In some cases, the group's own dynamic is trusted so much that moderation by a researcher is abandoned altogether in order to prevent any biasing influence on the discussion in process and content that may arise as a result of his or her interventions. However, it is more often the case that the moderation of the discussion by a researcher is found to be necessary for pragmatic reasons. Here three forms are distinguished (see Dreher and Dreher 1982, pp. 150–1). *Formal direction* is limited to control of the agenda of the speakers and to fixing the beginning, course and end of the discussion. *Topical steering* additionally comprises the introduction of new questions and steering the discussion towards a deepening and extension of specific topics and parts. Beyond this, *steering the dynamics* of the interaction ranges from reflating the discussion to using provocative questions, polarizing a slow discussion or accommodating relations of dominance by purposively addressing members remaining rather reserved in the discussion. Another possibility is the use of texts, images etc. to further stimulate the discussion or topics to be dealt with during the discussion. However, these interventions should only support the dynamics and the functioning of the group and the discussion to a large extent should be allowed to find its own dynamic level: 'It generally may be stated for the tasks of the moderator that he or she should disturb the participants' own initiative as little as possible and leave it a scope which is as free as possible, so that the discussion keeps going first through the exchange of arguments' (1982, p. 151).

From the alternatives available concerning the aims, the kind and composition of the group, and the function of the moderator, a combination is chosen for the particular application, as the following example illustrates.

Example: Work situation and future of employees

Krüger has studied 'restrictive contexts of actions for a professional future' and conducted eight group discussions with 'bank employees on the lowest hierarchical level, i.e. officials in charge from specific departments of the credit business . . . They were real groups because the group members came from one department and knew each other. The group was homogeneous; superiors were not involved in order to exclude any inhibiting impact on the discussion from these' (1983, p. 100). An average group included seven participants. Krüger emphasizes the non-directive style of moderating. The moderator should 'always try to stimulate narrative-descriptive statements by pointing out phenomena of the situation that have not (yet) been mentioned' (1983, p. 100). Stimuli for the discussion were given and a protocol of the process was made in order to be able to identify speakers in the transcript later: 'It is essential for the practical conduct of a group discussion that the research question is restricted to a delimited area of experience' (1983, p. 101). In terms of defining cases it was stated: 'The text of each group discussion has to be seen as a case which has to undergo successive stages of interpretation' (1983, p. 101).

Process and elements of group discussions

The way a group discussion should proceed cannot be presented in a single scheme, because it is essentially influenced by the dynamics and the composition of the group. In real or natural groups, the members already know each other and possibly have an interest in the topic of the discussion. In artificial groups, introducing members to one another and enabling members to make one another's acquaintance should be the first step. Roughly, the following steps may be summarized·

- At the beginning, an explanation of the (formal) procedure is given. Here the expectations for the participants are formulated: to be involved in the discussion, maybe to argue certain topics, or (as in Dreher and Dreher 1982) to manage a common task or solve a problem together (e.g. 'We would like you to discuss openly with each other the experiences you have had with your studies and what it was that made you decide not to continue them any further').

- A short introduction of the members to one another and a phase of warming up follows, to prepare the discussion. Here, the moderator should emphasize the common ground of the members in order to facilitate or to reinforce a feeling of being part of the group (e.g. 'As former students of psychology, you all should know the problems, the . . .').

- The actual discussion starts with a 'discussion stimulus' (Krüger 1983, p. 100), which may consist of a provocative thesis, a short film, a lecture on a text or the unfolding of a concrete problem for which a solution is to be found. Here, some parallels to the focused interview can be noted (see Chapter 8 and Merton 1987). In order to stimulate discussions about the change of work and living conditions with workers, Herkommer (1979, p. 263) gave the discussion stimulus shown in Box 10.1.

Box 10.1   Example of a discussion stimulus in a group discussion

The current economic situation in Germany has become more difficult; this is indicated for example by continuously high unemployment, by problems with pensions and social security, and by tougher wage bargaining. From this, a series of problems in occupations and in workplaces has resulted for workers. In general, a decay in the working climate of factories has occurred. But there are also other problems in everyday life and in the family, e.g. in children's school education. With respect to the problems just mentioned, we would like to hear your opinion on the position: 'One day our children will have a better life'!

Source: Herkommer 1979, p. 263

- Particularly in groups with members that did not know each other in advance, phases of strangeness with, orientation to, adaptation to and familiarity with the group as well as conformity and the discussion drying up are gone through (see Mangold 1973, p. 226; Spöhring 1989, p. 223).

Problems in conducting the method

The proclaimed strength of the method compared with interviewing single persons is also the main source of the problems in applying it. The dynamics, which are determined by the individual groups, make it more difficult to formulate distinct patterns of process in discussions and also to clearly define the tasks and multiple behaviours for the moderators beyond the individual group. For this reason it is hardly possible to design relatively common conditions for the collection of data in different groups involved in a study. It is true that the opening of discussions may be shaped uniformly by a specific formulation, a concrete stimulus etc. But the twists and turns of the discussion during its further development can hardly be predicted. Therefore, methodological interventions for steering the group may only be planned approximately and a great deal of the decisions on data collection can only be made during the situation. Similar conditions apply to the decision about when a group has exhausted the discussion of a topic. Here no clear criteria are given, which means that the moderator has to make this decision on the spot.

Problems similar to those that occur in semi-structured interviewing emerge. The problem the researcher faces in mediating between the course of the discussion and his or her own topical input is aggravated by the problem of having to accommodate the developing dynamics of the group and at the same time to steer the discussion in order to integrate all the participants. Thus, it remains difficult to handle the problem that, because of the dynamics of the situation and the group, individual members may dominate while others may refrain from entering into the discussion. In both cases, the result is that some individual members and their views are not available for the later interpretation.

Finally the apparent economics of interviewing several persons at the same time is clearly reduced by the high organizational effort needed to make an appointment at which all members of a group can participate.

Contribution to the general methodological discussion

Group discussions may reveal how opinions are created and above all changed, asserted or suppressed in social exchange. Collecting verbal data may be further contextualized in group discussions. Statements and expressions of opinion are made in the context of a group, and these may be commented upon and become the subject of a more or less dynamic process of discussion. That this dynamic and social negotiation of individual views as an essential element of the social constructionist theoretical approach to reality has been increasingly taken into account in the methodological literature is also a result of the study of the group discussion as a method.

Fitting the method into the research process

The theoretical background to applying the method is often structuralist models (see Chapter 2), starting from the dynamic and from the unconscious in the generation of meanings, this being manifested in group discussions. In more recent applications, the development of theories has been to the fore. Earlier attempts to test hypotheses with this procedure have failed owing to the lack of comparability of the data. The close link between the collection and the interpretation of data suggests a circular concept of the research process (see Chapter 4). Research questions focus on how opinions are produced and how they are distributed or shared in groups. In accessing cases and in sampling, researchers face the problem that the groups in which the individuals are assembled for the data collection become units themselves. Theoretical sampling (see Chapter 7) may focus on the characteristics of the groups in integration (e.g. if groups of psychology students and of medical students have been involved so far, would it be better now to integrate engineering students from technical universities or from colleges?) or may focus on the features of the individual members. In the interpretation of the data, the individual group again is the unit to start from. Sequential analyses (e.g. objective hermeneutics – see

Chapter 16) are suggested which start from the group and the course of discussion in it. In terms of generalizing the findings, the problem arises of how to summarize the different groups.

Limitations of the method

During the interpretation of the data, problems often arise owing to the differences in the dynamics of the different groups and the difficulties of comparing the groups and of identifying the opinions and views of the individual group members within this dynamics: 'As the smallest analytical unit . . . only complete discussion groups or subgroups qualify' (Mangold 1973, p. 222). In order to enable some comparability among the groups and among the members as cases in the whole sample, non-directed groups are now rarely used.

Because of the major effort in conducting, recording, transcribing and interpreting group discussions, their use makes sense mainly for research questions which focus particularly on the social dynamics of generating opinions in groups. Attempts to use group discussions to economize on individual interviewing of many people at the same time has proved less effective. Often this method is combined with other methods, e.g. additional single interviews or observations.

FOCUS GROUPS

Whereas the term 'group discussion' was dominant in earlier studies, especially in the German-speaking area, the method has more recently had some kind of renaissance as 'focus group' in Anglo-Saxon research (for overviews see Lunt and Livingstone 1996; Merton 1987). Focus groups are used especially in marketing and media research. Again the stress is laid on the interactive aspect of data collection:

> The hallmark of focus groups is the explicit use of the group interaction to produce data and insights that would be less accessible without the interaction found in a group. (Morgan 1988, p. 12)

Focus groups are used as a method on their own or in combination with other methods – surveys, observations, single interviews and so on. Morgan sees focus groups as

useful for
- orienting oneself to a new field;
- generating hypotheses based on informants' insights;
- evaluating different research sites or study populations;

- developing interview schedules and questionnaires;
- getting participants' interpretations of results from earlier studies. (1988, p. 11)

Conducting focus groups

A short overview of the literature provides some suggestions for conducting focus groups. The number of groups to be conducted depends on the research question and on the number of different population subgroups required (1988, p. 42). It is generally suggested that it is more appropriate to work with strangers instead of groups of friends or of people who know each other very well, because the level of things taken for granted which remains implicit tends to be higher in the latter (1988, p. 48). On the other hand, it is suggested that one should begin with groups as heterogeneous as possible and then run a second set of groups that are more homogeneous (1988, p. 73). In each case, it is necessary to start the group with some kind of warming up, as in the example in Box 10.2.

As an analytic technique for focus group data, summaries of the contents of the discussions or systematic codings or content analyses are suggested (1988, p. 64).

Box 10.2 Examples for beginning a focus group

Before we begin our discussion it will be helpful for us to get acquainted with one another. Let's begin with some introductory comments about ourselves. X, why don't you start and we'll go around the table and give our names and a little about what we do for a living?

Today we're going to discuss an issue that affects all of you. Before we get into our discussion, let me make a few requests of you. First, you should know that we are tape recording the session so that I can refer back to the discussion when I write my report. If anyone is uncomfortable with being recorded please say so and, of course, you are free to leave. Do speak up and let's try to have just one person speak at a time. I will play traffic cop and try to assure that everyone gets a turn. Finally, please say exactly what you think. Don't worry about what I think or what your neighbour thinks. We're here to exchange opinions and have fun while we do it. Why don't we begin by introducing ourselves?

Source: Stewart and Shamdasani 1990, pp. 92–3

Contribution to the general methodological discussion

Focus groups can be seen and used as simulations of everyday discourses and conversations or as a quasi-naturalistic method for studying the generation of social representations or social knowledge in general (Lunt and Livingstone 1996). The general strength of focus groups is twofold:

> First, focus groups generate discussion, and so reveal both the meanings that people read into the discussion topic and how they negotiate those meanings. Second, focus groups generate diversity and difference, either within or between groups, and so reveal what Billig (1987) has called the dilemmatic nature of everyday arguments. (1996, p. 96)

Limitations of the method

This method faces problems similar to those already mentioned for group discussion. A specific problem is how to document the data in a way that allows the identification of individual speakers and the differentiation between statements of several parallel speakers.

JOINT NARRATIVES

In a similar direction, Hildenbrand and Jahn (1988) extend and develop the narrative approach to data collection. Their starting point was the observation in family studies that families under study jointly narrate and thus restructure and reconstruct domains of their everyday reality. Starting from this observation, the authors stimulate such joint narratives more systematically and use them as data. They take care that all the persons belonging to a household are present in the situation of data collection, which should take place at the family's home: 'At the beginning of the conversation, the family members are invited to recount details and events from their former and current family life. We abandoned the use of an explicit narrative stimulus, because it produces unnecessary restrictions on the variety of topics' (1988, p. 207). The authors also refrain from 'methodologically directed interventions' because the aim is to allow the conversation to be shaped by the family members themselves (1988, p. 207). This is intended to bring the research situation as close as possible to the everyday situation of narratives in the family. Finally, 'by using a checklist, those social data are completed, together with the family, which have not been mentioned during the narrative'. At the end, extended observational protocols are made which refer to the context of the conversation (generative history, living conditions of the family, description of the house and its furniture).

Contribution to the general methodological discussion

With this approach, the situation of the monological narrator is extended. Analyses of the interaction are made which refer to the realization of the narrative and to the way in which the family constructs reality for itself and the listener. This approach has been developed in the context of a specific field of research – family studies.[1] The natural structure of this field or research object is given as a particular reason for the interest in this method. It remains to be seen how this idea of joint narratives can be transferred to other forms of communality. One could imagine using the method to analyse a specific institution, e.g. a counselling service, its history, activities and conflicts, by asking the members of the teams working in it to jointly recount the history of their institution. This would make not only the narrated course of development an analytic issue but also the dynamics of the different views and presentations of the members.

Fitting the method into the research process

The theoretical background of the method is the joint construction of reality. The aim is the development of theories grounded in these constructions (see Chapter 5). The starting point is the single case (a family in Hildenbrand and Jahn 1988), whereafter other cases are included step by step (see Chapter 7). Interpretation of the material proceeds sequentially (see Chapter 16), with the aim of arriving at more general statements from the comparison of cases (see Chapter 18).

Limitations of the method

The method has been developed in the context of a study using several other methods. Its independent use remains to be tested. A further problem is that large textual materials result from a single case. This makes interpretations of single cases very voluminous. Therefore, analyses mostly remain limited to case studies. Finally, the rather far-reaching abstinence from methodological interventions makes it more difficult to purposively apply the method to specific research questions and to direct its application in collecting data. It is possible that not only the strengths but also the problems of the narrative interview are combined with those of group discussions.

The group procedures briefly mentioned here stress different aspects of the task of going beyond interviewing individuals to data collection in groups. Sometimes it is the reduction in time spent interviewing – one group at one time instead of many individuals at different times – which is important. Group dynamics may be attributed as being a helpful or a disturbing feature in realizing the goal of receiving answers from all interviewees. In group discussions, however, it is precisely this dynamic and the additional options of knowledge produced by the group which are given priority. In joint narratives, it is the process of constructing reality as it occurs at this moment in this group which is of particular interest. This process is assumed to occur in a similar form in the family's everyday life and thus also beyond the research situation. In each case, the verbal data gathered are more complex than in the single interview. The advantage of this complexity is that data are richer and more diverse in their content than in an individual interview. The problem of this complexity is that it is more difficult to locate the viewpoints of the individuals involved in this common process of meaning making than in an individual interview.

NOTE

1   A broader interest in collective recounting and remembering is expressed in the work of Hirst and Manier (1996) for families, and in Dixon and Gould (1996) and Bruner and Feldman (1996). The method discussed here gives a concrete procedure for qualitative studies in this area of interest.

FURTHER READING

Group interviews

Both texts deal explicitly with group interviews as a method.

Fontana, A., Frey, J.H. (1994), Interviewing: The Art of Science. In: Denzin, N., Lincoln, Y.S. (eds), *Handbook of Qualitative Research*, pp. 361–76. London: Sage.

Patton, M.Q. (1990), *Qualitative Evaluation and Research Methods* (2nd edn). London: Sage.

Group discussions

Both texts discuss methodological problems and applications of the method.

Mangold, W. (1973), Gruppendiskussionen. In: König, R. (ed.), *Handbuch der empirischen Sozialforschung*, pp. 228–59. Stuttgart: Enke.

Krüger, H. (1983), Gruppendiskussionen: Überlegungen zur Rekonstruktion sozialer Wirklichkeit aus der Sicht der Betroffenen. *Soziale Welt*, 34, pp. 90–109.

Focus groups

The first text discusses recent applications and methodological problems, whereas the other two give general overviews of the method.

Lunt, P., Livingstone, S. (1996), Rethinking the Focus Group in Media and Communications Research. *Journal of Communication*, 46, pp. 79–98.

Morgan, D.L. (1988), *Focus Groups as Qualitative Research*. Newbury Park, CA: Sage.

Stewart, D.M., Shamdasani, P.N. (1990), *Focus Groups: Theory and Practice*. Newbury Park, CA: Sage.

Joint narratives

Each text deals with a field of application of group narratives.

Bruner, J., Feldman, C. (1996), Group Narrative as a Cultural Context of Autobiography. In: Rubin, D. (ed.), *Remembering our Past: Studies in Autobiographical Memory*, pp. 291–317. Cambridge: Cambridge University Press.

Hildenbrand, B., Jahn, W. (1988), 'Gemeinsames Erzählen' und Prozesse der Wirklichkeitskonstruktion in familiengeschichtlichen Gesprächen. *Zeitschrift für Soziologie*, 17, pp. 203–17.

11

VERBAL DATA: AN OVERVIEW

Approaches to verbal data are one of the methodological currents in qualitative research. In these approaches, different strategies are used to realize openness towards the object under study and the views of the interviewee, narrator or participant in discussions. At the same time, the methodological alternatives include specific precautions for structuring the collection of data. Thus, topics referring to the research question should be made an issue in the interview or their treatment should be directed towards a greater depth or towards being more comprehensive. Additionally, aspects of the research question not yet mentioned should be introduced. The different methods alternate between these two goals – openness and structuring. Each method orients to one or the other of these aims. In their central part, at least, narrative interviews are oriented towards openness and scope for the interviewee's presentation. The interviewer's directive interventions should be limited to the generative narrative question and to the stage of narrative enquiries at the end. In semi-structured interviews, on the other hand, the topical direction is given much more preference and the interviews may be focused much more directly on certain topics. Therefore, depending on the goal of the research and on the chosen goal – openness or structuring – specific methods are recommended to a greater or lesser extent for each concrete research question. Four points of reference for such a decision between different methods for collecting verbal data will be outlined in this chapter.

FIRST POINT OF REFERENCE: CRITERIA BASED COMPARISON OF THE APPROACHES

A juxtaposition of the various forms of semi-structured interviews, narrative and group methods may be taken as a first point of reference for deciding between them. As criteria for such a decision, Table 11.1 shows precautions taken in each method for guaranteeing sufficient openness for interviewees' subjective views. Precautions for guaranteeing a sufficient level of structure and depth in dealing with the topical issue in the interview are also listed. Further features shown are each method's contribution to the development of the interview method in general and the fields of application which each was created for or is mainly used in. Finally, the problems of conducting the method and the limits mentioned in the previous chapters are noted for each approach. Thus, the field of methodological alternatives in the domain of verbal data is outlined so that the individual method may be located within it.

SECOND POINT OF REFERENCE: THE SELECTION OF THE METHOD AND CHECKING ITS APPLICATION

The various methodological alternatives aiming at the collection and analysis of verbal data suggest that it is necessary to make a well-founded decision according to one's own study, its research question, its target group etc.: which method to select for collecting data? This decision should be assessed on the basis of the character of the material to be obtained. Not all methods are appropriate to every research question: biographical courses of events may be presented in narratives rather than in the question–answer schema of the semi-structured interview. For studying processes of developing opinions the dynamic of group discussions is instructive, whereas this feature rather obstructs the analysis of individual experiences. The research question and the issue under study are the first anchoring points for deciding for or against a concrete method. Some people are able to narrate, others are not. For some target groups it is a highly strange procedure to reconstruct their subjective theory; others can become involved in the situation without any problem. The (potential) interviewees are the second anchoring point for methodological decisions and for assessing their appropriateness.

TABLE 11.1 *Comparison of methods for collecting verbal data*

Criteria	Semi-structured interviews					Narratives as data		Group procedures		
	Focused interview	Semi-standardized interview	Problem-centred interview	Expert interview	Ethnographic interview	Narrative interview	Episodic interview	Group discussions	Focus groups	Joint narratives
Openness to the interviewee's subjective view by:	• Non-direction by unstructured questions	• Open questions	• Object and process orientation • Room for narratives	• Limited because only interested in the expert, not in the person	• Descriptive questions	• Non-influencing of narratives once started	• Narratives of meaningful experiences • Selection by the interviewee	• Non-directive moderation of the discussion • Permissive climate in the discussion	• Taking the context of the group into account	• Abandonment of narrative stimulus and methodological interventions
Structuring (e.g. deepening) the issue by:	• Giving a stimulus • Structured questions • Focusing on feelings	• Hypothesis-directed questions • Confrontational questions	• Interview guide as basis for turns and ending unproductive presentations	• Interview guide as instrument for structuring	• Structural questions • Contrastive questions	• Generative narrative questions • Part of narrative questioning at the end • Balancing part	• Connection of narratives and argumentations • Suggestion of concrete situations to be recounted	• Dynamics developing in the group • Steering with a guide	• Using an interview guide to direct the discussion	• Dynamics of joint narrative • Checklist for demographic data • Observation protocol
Contribution to the general development of the interview as a method	• Four criteria for designing interviews • Analysing the object as a second data sort	• Structuring the contents with structure laying technique • Suggestions for explicating implicit knowledge	• Short questionnaire • Postscript	• Highlighting of direction: limitation of the interview to the expert	• Highlighting the problem of making interview situations	• Localization of structuring the interview at the beginning and the end • Testing narratives as instrument	• Systematic link of narrative and argumentation as data sorts • Purposive generative narrative question	• Alternative to single interview owing to group dynamics	• Simulation of the way discourses and social representations are generated in their diversity	• Combination of narrative and interaction analyses • Stressing the constructive part in narratives

Domain of application	• Analysis of subjective meanings	• Reconstruction of subjective theories	• Socially or biographically relevant problems	• Expert knowledge in institutions	• In the framework of field research in open fields	• Biographical courses	• Change, routines and situations in everyday life	• Opinion and attitude research	• Marketing and media research	• Family research
Problems in conducting the method	• Dilemma of combining the criteria	• Extensive methodological input • Problems of interpretation	• Unsystematic change from narrative to question–answer schema	• Role diffusion of the interviewee • Blocking by the expert	• Mediation between friendly conversation and formal interview	• Extremely unilateral interview situation • Problems of the narrator • Problematic zugzwangs	• Explication of the principle • Handling the interview guide	• Mediation between silent and talkative people • Course can hardly be planned	• How to sample groups and members	• Abandonment of topically focusing the narrative
Limitations of the method	• Assumption of knowing objective features of the object is questionable • Hardly any application in its pure form	• Introducing a structure • Need to adapt the method to the issue and the interviewee	• Problem orientation • Unsystematic combination of most diverse partial elements	• Limitation of the interpretation on expert knowledge	• Mainly sensible in combination with observation and field research	• Supposed analogy of experience and narrative • Reducing the object to what can be recounted	• Limitation on everyday knowledge	• High organizational effort • Problems of comparability	• Documentation of data • Identification of single speakers and several speakers at the same time	• Abandonment of steering • Own standing as a single method? • Extension of case analyses
References	Merton and Kendall (1946)	Groeben (1990); Scheele and Groeben (1988)	Ruff (1991); Witzel (1982; 1985)	Meuser and Nagel (1991)	Spradley (1979)	Hermanns (1991); Riemann and Schütze (1987); Schütze (1983)	Flick (1994a; 1995a; 1996)	Blumer (1969); Bohnsack (1991); Krüger (1983)	Lunt and Livingstone (1996); Merton (1987); Morgan (1988)	Hildenbrand and Jahn (1988)

But, such differences in becoming involved in specific interview situations are not only individual differences. If one takes into account the research question and the level of statements the study is aiming at, then the relation between method, subject(s) and issue may be regarded systematically. The criterion here is the appropriateness of the chosen method and of its application. However, questions concerning this should be asked not only at the end of the data collection when the interviews or discussions have been conducted, but also earlier on in the procedure after one or two trial interviews or discussions. One aspect for checking the appropriateness of the methodological selection is to examine if and how far the method has been applied in its own terms. For example, has a narrative interview really been started with a generative narrative question? Have changes of topics and new questions been introduced only after the interviewee had had enough time and scope to deal with the preceding topic in sufficient detail in a semi-structured interview?

The analysis of the initial interviews may show that it is not only the interviewees who have more problems with certain methods than with others. Interviewers may also have more problems in applying a certain method than other methods. One reason for this is that it may be over-challenging the interviewer's ability to decide when and how to return to the interview guide if the interviewee deviates from the subject or to deploy the necessary active listening skills in the narrative interview. Thus, how far an interviewer and method match should also be checked. If problems emerge at this level, there are two possible solutions. Careful interview training may be given (for this see the sections on the focused and semi-standardized interview in Chapter 8 and on the narrative and episodic interviews in Chapter 9) in order to reduce these problems. If this is not sufficient, changing the method should be considered. A basis for such decisions may be provided by analysing the interaction in the situation of collecting data for the scope allowed to the interviewee by the interviewer and for how clearly the roles of both have been defined. A final factor to be considered in choosing a method and in assessing it relates to how the data are to be interpreted later and at which level of generalization the findings will be obtained.

Suggestions for making the decision about which method of data collection to use and for assessing the appropriateness of this decision are given in the checklist in Table 11.2.[1]

THIRD POINT OF REFERENCE: APPROPRIATENESS OF THE METHOD TO THE ISSUE

The impression is sometimes given in methodological discussions that certain procedures are the 'ideal way' to study the issue, or indeed the only practicable and methodologically legitimate way. In such discussions, one

TABLE 11.2 *Checklist for selecting an interview type and evaluating its application*

1 *Research question*
   Can the interview type and its application address the essential aspects of the research question?
2 *Interview type*
   The method must be applied according to the methodological precautions and targets. There should be no jumping between interview types, except when this is grounded in the research question or theoretically.
3 *Interviewer*
   Is the interviewer able to apply the interview type? What are the consequences of his or her own fears and uncertainties in the situation?
4 *Interviewee*
   Is the interview type appropriate to the target group of the application? How can one take into account the fears, uncertainties and expectations of (potential) interviewees?
5 *Scope allowed to the interviewee*
   Can the interviewee present his or her view in the framework of the questions?
   Can he or she assert his or her view against the framework of the questions?
6 *Interaction*
   Has the interviewer conducted the type of interview correctly?
   Has he or she left enough scope for the interviewee?
   Did he or she fulfil his or her role? (Why not?)
   Were the interviewee's role, the interviewer's role and the situation clearly defined for the interviewee?
   Could the interviewee fulfil his or her role? (Why not?)

Analyse the breaks in order to validate the interview between the first and second interview if possible!

7 *Aim of the interpretation*
   Delimited and clear answers or complex, multifold patterns, contexts etc.?
8 *Claim for generalization*
   The level on which statements should be made:
   • For the single case (the interviewed individual and his or her biography, an institution and its impact, etc.)?
   • With reference to groups (about a profession, a type of institution, etc.)?
   • General statements?

central feature of qualitative research is ignored: methods should be selected and evaluated according to their appropriateness to the subject under study (see Chapter 1). One exception to this is studies that explore certain methods mainly in order to obtain findings about their conduct, conductability and problems. Then, the object of research has only an exemplary status for answering such methodological questions. In all other cases, the decision to use a certain method should be regarded as subordinate: the issue, research question, individuals studied and statements striven for are the anchoring points for assessing the appropriateness of concrete methods in qualitative research.

FOURTH POINT OF REFERENCE: FITTING THE METHOD
INTO THE RESEARCH PROCESS

Finally, a selected method should be checked for how it fits into the research process. The aim is to find out if the procedure for collecting data suits the procedure for interpreting them. Thus it does not make sense to use the narrative interview during the data collection in order to allow the presentation a wide scope, if the data received then undergo a content analysis using only categories derived from the literature and paraphrases of the original text (for this see Chapter 15). It also does not make sense to want to interpret an interview which stresses the consistent treating of the topics in the interview guide with a sequential procedure (see Chapter 16) which is concerned to uncover the development of the structure of the presentation. In a similar way, the compatibility of the procedure for collecting data with the method of sampling cases (see Chapter 7), the theoretical background of one's own study (see Chapter 2) and the understanding of the research process as a whole (e.g. developing theories versus testing hypotheses: see Chapter 4) should be checked.

The starting points for this assessment are provided by the paragraphs about the fitting of the method into the research process given in the sections about each method. They outline the method's inherent understanding of the research process and its elements. The next step is to check how far the design of one's own study and its understanding of the single steps are compatible with the method's inherent understanding.

Thus, four points of reference for deciding on a concrete method are outlined, which also can and should be applied to procedures not primarily aimed at visual data (see Chapter 13) and alternatives for interpretation (see Chapter 17). In addition to the appropriateness of the methods used for the object under study (see Chapter 1), it is above all the orientation to the process of research (see Chapters 18 and 20) which becomes an essential criterion to evaluate methodological decisions.

NOTE

1 For more clarity, only the term 'interview' is used. If it is replaced by 'group discussion', the same questions may be asked and answers may be found in the same way.

PART 4
VISUAL DATA

$\boxed{12}$

VISUAL DATA METHODS

Methodological discussions about the role of observation as a sociological research method have been central to the history of qualitative research. This is particularly so in the United States. Different conceptions of observation and of the observer's role can be found in the literature. There are studies in which the observer does not become part of the observed field, e.g. in the tradition of Goffman (1961). These studies are complemented by approaches which try to accomplish the goal of gaining an insider's knowledge of the field through the researcher's increasing assimilation as a participant in the observed field. Second-hand observation – using photographs, films or videos – has recently also attracted more and more attention.

In general, these approaches stress that practices are only accessible through observation, and that interviews and narratives merely make the accounts of practices accessible instead of the practices themselves. The claim is often made for observation that it enables the researcher to find out how something factually works or occurs. Presentations in interviews, on the other hand, comprise a mixture of how something is and of how something should be, which still needs to be untangled.

OBSERVATION

Besides the competencies of speaking and listening which are used in interviews, observing is another everyday skill which is methodologically systematized and applied in qualitative research. Not only visual perceptions but also those based on hearing, feeling and smelling are integrated (Adler and Adler 1994). According to Friedrichs (1973, pp. 272–3) observational procedures may be generally classified along five dimensions. One may differentiate:

- Covert versus overt observation: how far is the observation revealed to those who are observed?

- Non-participant versus participant observation: how far does the observer become an active part of the observed field?

- Systematic versus unsystematic observation: is a more or less standardized observation scheme applied or does the observation remain rather flexible and responsive to the processes themselves?

- Observation in natural versus artificial situations: are observations done in the field of interest or are interactions 'moved' to a special place (e.g. a laboratory) to give a better observability?

- Self-observation versus observing others: mostly other people are observed, so how much attention is paid to the researcher's reflexive self-observation for further grounding the interpretation of the observed?

This general classification can also be applied to observation in qualitative research, except that here data are in general collected from natural situations. In this chapter, the method of non-participant observation is discussed first. This form refrains from interventions in the field – in contrast to interviews and participant observations. The expectations linked to this are outlined as follows: 'Simple observers follow the flow of events. Behaviour and interaction continue as they would without the presence of a researcher, uninterrupted by intrusion' (Adler and Adler 1994, p. 378).

Here, the typology of participant roles developed by Gold (1958) is taken as a starting point to define the differences from participant observation. Gold distinguishes four types of participant roles:

- the complete participant;
- the participant-as-observer;
- the observer-as-participant;
- the complete observer.

The last maintains distance from the observed events in order to avoid influencing them. This may be partly accomplished by replacing the actual observation in the situation by videotaping. Alternatively, attempts may be made to distract the attention of those under observation from the researcher in order that they become oblivious to the process of observation as quickly and as completely as possible. In this context, covert observation is applied, in which observed persons are not informed about being observed. This procedure, however, is ethically contestable, especially if the field can be easily observed and there are no practical problems in inform- ing the observed or obtaining their consent. Often, however, this kind of observation is practised in open spaces – e.g. in train stations or public places, in cafés with frequently changing custom – where this agreement cannot be obtained.

Phases of observation

Authors like Adler and Adler (1994), Denzin (1989b) and Spradley (1980) name as phases of such an observation:

- the selection of a setting, i.e. where and when the interesting processes and persons can be observed;
- the definition of what is to be documented in the observation and in every case;
- the training of the observers in order to standardize such focuses;
- descriptive observations which provide an initial general presentation of the field;
- focused observations which concentrate more and more on aspects that are relevant to the research question;
- selective observations which are intended to purposively grasp only central aspects;
- the end of the observation, when theoretical saturation has been reached (Glaser and Strauss 1967), i.e. further observations do not provide any further knowledge.

Problems in conducting the method

A main problem here is to define a role for the observer which he or she can take, and which allows him or her to stay in the field or at its edge and observe it at the same time (see the discussion of participant roles in Chapter 6). The more public and unstructured the field is, the easier it will be to take a role that is not conspicuous and does not influence the field.

The easier a field is to overlook, the more difficult it is to participate in it without becoming a member.

Example: Finding a role in observation

In the 1960s, Humphreys (1975) conducted an observational study of the sexual behaviour of homosexuals. This study led to a debate on the ethical problems of observations in this and comparable fields which continued for a long time. He observed in public toilets which were meeting places in the homosexual subculture. As homosexuality was still illegal at that time, toilets offered one of the few possibilities for clandestine meetings. Adler and Adler (1994) mention this study as an example of observation without participation, because Humphreys conducted his observation explicitly from the position of the sociologist as a voyeur so as not to become a member of the observed events and yet to be accepted as an observer. In order to do this Humphreys took the role of somebody (the 'watchqueen') whose job it was to ensure that no strangers approached the events. In this role, he could observe all that was happening without being perceived as interfering and without having to take part in the events:

> Outwardly I took on the role of a voyeur, a role which is excellently suitable for sociologists and which is the only role of a watchdog, which is not of a manifest sexual nature . . . In the role of the watchqueen-voyeur, I could freely move in the room, walk from window to window and observe everything without my subjects becoming suspicious and without disturbing the activities in any other way. (Humphreys 1973, p. 258)

The dilemmas of observation are described here in three respects: the researcher must find a way into the field of interest; he or she wants to observe in a way that influences the flow of events as little as possible; and in sanctioned, forbidden, criminal or dangerous activities in particular, the problem arises of how to observe them without the researcher becoming an accomplice. A solution is applied by Niemann for observing the leisure activities of adolescents at leisure sites: 'The observations were covert in order to avoid influencing the behaviour of the adolescents that was typical for a specific site' (1989, p. 73).

Example: Leisure behaviour of adolescents

Here, juveniles were observed 'parallel at two times of measurement' in two discotheques, ice stadiums, shopping malls, summer baths, football clubs, concert halls etc. in various situations in the sites. The situations were selected randomly (1989, p. 76), and 'developmental tasks' specific to these situations (e.g. realizing the goal of integration in the peer group) were documented on protocol sheets. In order to better prepare the researcher a period of training in observational techniques was given prior to the actual research, in which different and independent observations of a situation were analysed for their correspondence with the aim of increasing the latter. An observational manual was applied in order to make the notes more uniform: 'Observations of situations in principle were given a protocol only after they finished . . . mostly based on free notes on little pieces of scrap paper, beer mats or cigarette boxes.

Here, however, there was a danger of bias and imprecise representations which would interfere with the goal of minimizing the influence on the adolescents' behaviour' (1989, p. 79). The attempt to avoid reactivity, i.e. feedback of the procedure of observation on the observed, here determines the data collection, which in this case was complemented by interviews with single juveniles.

Merkens characterizes this strategy of 'non-participant field observation' as follows:

> The observer here tries not to disturb the persons in the field by striving to make himself as invisible as possible. His interpretations of the observed occur from his horizon . . . The observer constructs meanings for himself, which he supposes direct the actions of the actors in the way he perceives them. (1989, p. 15)

Influences on the behaviour of the participants in the field may be avoided but at a price which decisively constricts the interpretation of the data, which has to be undertaken from an external perspective on the field under study.

Contribution to the general methodological discussion

In order to increase the expressiveness of the data gathered in this way, triangulation of observations with other sources of data and also the employment of different observers have been suggested. Gender differences are a crucial aspect here. Particularly in observing in public places, the possibilities for access and moving about are much more restricted for women owing to particular dangers for them compared with men. On the other hand, women's perceptions of such restrictions and dangers are much more sensitive, which makes them observe differently and notice different things compared with male observers. This shows the 'gendered nature of fieldwork' (Lofland, quoted in Adler and Adler 1994, p. 385), and this is the reason for the suggested use of mixed gender teams in observational studies. A further suggestion is the painstaking self-observation of the researcher while entering the field, during the course of the observation and when looking back on its process in order to integrate implicit impressions, apparent incidentals and perceptions in the reflection of the process and results.

Fitting the method into the research process

The theoretical background here is the analysis of the production of social reality from an external perspective. The goal is (at least often) the testing of theoretical concepts for certain phenomena on the basis of their occurrence and distribution (see Chapter 4). Research questions aim at descriptions of the state of certain life worlds (e.g. adolescents in Berlin). The selection of situations and persons occurs systematically according to criteria of representativeness and random sampling (see Chapter 7). Data analyses are based on counting the incidence of specific activities by using procedures of categorizing (see Chapter 15).

Limitations of the method

All in all, this form of observation is an approach to the observed field from an external perspective. Therefore it should be applied mainly to the observation of public spaces, in which the number of the members cannot be limited or defined. Furthermore it is an attempt to observe events as they occur naturally. How far this aim can be fulfilled remains doubtful, because the act of observation influences the observed in any case. Sometimes the argument is made for the use of covert observation, which eliminates the influence of the researcher on the field; however, this is highly problematic with respect to research ethics. Furthermore the researcher's abstinence from interacting with the field leads to problems in analysing the data and in assessing the interpretations, because of the systematic restraint on disclosing the interior perspective of the field and of the observed persons. This strategy is associated more with an understanding of methods based on quantitative and standardized research.

PARTICIPANT OBSERVATION

A form of observation which is more commonly used in qualitative research is participant observation. A definition has been given by Denzin:

> participant observation will be defined as a field strategy that simultaneously combines document analysis, interviewing of respondents and informants, direct participation and observation, and introspection. (1989b, pp. 17–18)

The main features of the method are that the researcher dives headlong into the field, observes from a member's perspective but also influences what is observed owing to his or her participation. The differences from non-participant observation and its aims, as just discussed, are elucidated in the seven features of participant observation listed by Jorgensen:

1 a special interest in human meaning and interaction as viewed from the perspective of people who are insiders or members of particular situations and settings;
2 location in the here and now of everyday life situations and settings as the foundation of inquiry and method;

3 a form of theory and theorizing stressing interpretation and understanding of human existence;
4 a logic and process of inquiry that is open-ended, flexible, opportunistic, and requires constant redefinition of what is problematic, based on facts gathered in concrete settings of human existence;
5 an in-depth, qualitative, case study approach and design;
6 the performance of a participant role or roles that involves establishing and maintaining relationships with natives in the field; and
7 the use of direct observation along with other methods of gathering information. (1989, pp. 13–14)

Here, the openness in collecting data based solely on communicating with the observed is highlighted as essential. This method is often used for studying subcultures (for an overview see Girtler 1991).

Phases of participant observation

Participant observation should be understood as a process in two respects. First, the researcher should increasingly become a participant and gain access to the field and to persons (see below). Second, the observation should also move through a process of becoming increasingly concrete and concentrated on the aspects that are essential for the research questions. Thus, Spradley (1980, p. 34) distinguishes three phases of participant observation:

1 *descriptive observation*, at the beginning, which serves to provide the researcher with an orientation to the field under study and provides non-specific descriptions, and which is used to grasp the complexity of the field as far as possible and to develop at the same time more concrete research questions and lines of vision;

2 *focused observation*, in which the perspective increasingly narrows on those processes and problems which are most essential for the research question;

3 *selective observation*, towards the end of the data collection, which is rather focused on finding further evidence and examples for the types of practices and processes found in the second step.

Sometimes observation sheets and schemes are used which are more or less structured. More often, protocols of situations are produced (see Chapter 14) which are as detailed as possible in order to obtain 'thick descriptions' (Geertz 1973) of the field. Whether the use of field notes is to be preferred to the use of structured protocol sheets, which concretely define those activities and situational features to be documented in every case, depends both on the research question and on the phase in the research process in which observations are made. The more a protocol sheet differentiates between aspects, the more those aspects integrated become voluminous and the greater is the danger that those aspects not contained in the sheet are neither perceived nor noted. Therefore, descriptive observation should refrain from using heavily structured sheets in order to prevent the observer's attention from being restricted and from limiting his or her sensitivity to the new. In selective observation, however, structured protocol sheets may be helpful for grasping fully the relevant aspects elaborated in the phase before. However, participant observations are confronted with the problem of the observer's limited observational perspective, as not all aspects of a situation can be grasped (and noted) at the same time. Bergmann holds: 'We have only a very limited competence of remembering and reproducing amorphous incidents of an actual social event. The participant observer thus has no other choice than to note the social occurrences which he was witness to mainly in a typifying, resuming, reconstructive fashion' (1985, p. 308). The question of whether to work with overt observation (where the observed know that they are observed) or with covert observation arises here as well, but less as a methodological than as an ethical question.

Example: Boys in white

Becker et al. (1961) studied a state medical school in order 'to discover what a medical school did to students other than give them a technical education. We assumed that students left medical school with a set of ideas about medicine and medical practice that differed from the ideas they entered with . . . We did not know what perspectives a student acquired while in school' (Becker and Geer 1960, p. 269). For this purpose, over a period of one or two months, participant observations in lectures, practical exercises, dormitories, and all departments of the hospital were carried out which sometimes extended to the whole day. The orientations that were found were examined for the degree to which they were collectively held, which means how far they were valid for the studied groups as a whole as against only for single members.

Problems in conducting the method

One problem is how to delimit or select observational situations in which the problem under study becomes really 'visible'. According to Spradley, social situations generally may be described along nine dimensions for observational purposes:

1. *space*: the physical place or places
2. *actor*: the people involved
3. *activity*: a set of related acts people do
4. *object*: the physical things that are present
5. *act*: single actions that people do
6. *event*: a set of related activities that people carry out

7 *time*: the sequencing that takes place over time
8 *goal*: the things people are trying to accomplish
9 *feeling*: the emotions felt and expressed. (1980, p. 78)

If it is not possible to observe the whole day in an institution, for example, the problem of selection arises. How can one find those situations in which the relevant actors and interesting activities can be assumed to take place? At the same time, how can one select situations which are as different from one another as possible, from the range of an average day's events, in order to increase the variation and variety of what is actually observed?

Another problem is how to access the field or the studied subculture. In order to solve this, key persons are sometimes used, who introduce the researcher and make contacts for him or her. It is sometimes difficult, however, to find the right person for this job. On the other hand, the researcher should not leave him or herself too much at the mercy of key persons, but should take care as to how far he or she accepts their perspective uncritically and should be aware of the fact that they may only be providing the researcher with access to a specific part of the field. Finally, a key person may even make it more difficult to gain access to the field under study or to approach certain persons within it, for example if he or she is an outsider in the field.[1]

Going native

In participant observation, even more than in other qualitative methods, it becomes crucial to gain as far as possible an internal perspective on the studied field and to 'systematize the status of the stranger' (Flick 1991b, pp. 154–5) at the same time. Only the achievement of the latter enables one to view the particular in what is everyday and routine in the field. To lose this critical external perspective and to unquestioningly adopt the viewpoints shared in the field is known as 'going native'. The process of going native, however, is discussed not only as a researcher's fault but also as an instrument for reflecting on one's own process of becoming familiar and for gaining insights into the field under study which would be inaccessible by maintaining distance. However, the goal of the research is not limited to becoming familiar with the self-evidence of a field. This may be sufficient for a successful participation but not for a systematic observation. Researchers who seek to obtain knowledge about relations in the studied field which transcends everyday understanding also have to maintain the distance of the 'professional stranger' (see Agar 1980). Thus, Koepping underlines the fact that, for participant observation, the researcher

> as social figure must have exactly those features that Simmel has elaborated for the stranger: he has to dialectically fuse the two functions in himself, that

of commitment and that of distance . . . [The researcher therefore tries to realize] what is outlined by the notion of participation in observation, the task of which is to understand through the eyes of the other. In participating the researcher methodologically authenticates his theoretical premise and furthermore he makes the research subject, the other, not an object but a dialogical partner. (1987, p. 28)

Example: Participant observation in intensive care units

Before carrying out participant observation in intensive care units, Sprenger (1989, pp. 35–6) first had to run through a 'basic lesson in intensive care medicine' in order to become familiar with the terminology (syndromes, treatment concepts etc.) in the field. In collecting data, observational guides were used, which were geared to the different scenarios that were to be analysed (e.g. the doctoral round, visits by family members). During the data collection, a weekly exchange with a 'professional consulting group' (doctors, nurses) and the 'systematic variation of the observational perspective', i.e. 'observations centring on physicians, nurses or patients . . . and scene oriented observations (doctoral rounds, washing, setting a catheter etc.)' (1989, p. 36), served to widen the perspective on the field under study. Special problems (here as well) resulted from the selection of an appropriate location and the 'right' moment for observing, as the following notes about the researcher's experience may clarify:

> In the room there is a relative hurry, permanently something has to be done, and I am successfully overrun by nurse I.'s whisky business. (No minutes at the 'nurses' desk'.) After the end of the shift I remark after leaving the ward that I was a quasi-trainee today. The reason is for me mainly related to the moment of my arrival in the ward. Afterwards I consider it ineffective to burst into the middle of a shift. To participate in the handing over, in the beginning of the shift, means for us as well as for the nurses the chance to adapt to each other. I did not find any time today to orient myself calmly, there was no phase of feeling or growing into the situation, which would have allowed me a certain sovereignty. So I unexpectedly slipped into the mechanisms of the little routines and constraints and before I could get rid of them, my time was gone. (1989, p. 46)

This scene elucidates two aspects. The choice of the moment or of the actual beginning of an observational sequence determines essentially what can be observed and above all how. In addition it becomes clear here that especially in very hectic settings the observer's 'inundation' by the events leads to her functionalization as 'quasi-trainee' for managing the events. Such 'participation in activity processes' can lead to 'observation obstacles', against which Sprenger suggests a remedy:

> This problem of being inundated by the field events is virulent during the whole course of the research, but may be controlled quite well. In addition to choosing the optimal beginning for the observation, as already mentioned in the presented protocol, defining the observational goals and leaving the field intentionally as soon as the researcher's observational capacity is exhausted have proved very effective control strategies. However, this requires the researcher to learn about his or her own capacity limits. (1989, p. 47)

This example shows that steering and planning the observation as well as reflecting on one's own resources may reduce the danger, just outlined, of the researcher being absorbed by the field as well as the danger of 'going native' and therefore of adopting perspectives from the field unreflexively.

In terms of Gold's (1958) typology of observer roles, the role of the participant-as-observer best fits the method of participant observation. Linked to the approach of diving headlong into the field is the often experienced sense of a culture shock on the part of the observer (see Denzin 1989b, pp. 164–5). This is particularly obvious in ethnographic field studies in foreign cultures. But this phenomenon also occurs in observations in subcultures or generally in strange groups or in extreme situations such as intensive medicine: familiar self-evidence, norms and practices lose their normality, and the observer is confronted with strange values, self-evidence and so on. These may seem hard to understand at first but he or she has to accept them to be able to understand them and their meaning. In particular in participant observation the researcher's action in the field is understood not only as a disturbance but also as an additional source of or as corner-stones for knowledge: 'Fortunately, the so-called "distuburbances" created by the observer's existence and activities, when properly exploited, are the cornerstones of a scientific behavioral science, and not – as is currently believed – deplorable *contretemps*, best disposed of by hurriedly sweeping them under the rug' (Devereux 1967, p. 7).

Contribution to the general methodological discussion

All in all, participant observation elucidates the dilemma between increasing participation in the field, from which understanding alone results, and the maintenance of a distance, from which understanding becomes merely scientific and verifiable. Furthermore, this method still comes closest to a conception of qualitative research as a process, because it assumes a longer period in the field and in contact with persons and contexts to be studied, whereas interviews mostly remain one-off encounters. Strategies like theoretical sampling (see Chapter 7) can be applied here more easily than in interview studies. If it becomes evident that a specific dimension, a particular group of persons, concrete activities etc., is needed for completing the data and for developing the theory, the researcher is able to direct his or her attention to them in the next observational sequence. For interviews, on the other hand, this is rather unusual and needs detailed explanation if the researcher wants to make a second appointment. Furthermore, in participant observation, the interaction with the field and the object of research may be realized most consistently. Also, by integrating other methods, the methodical procedures of this strategy may be especially well adapted to the research issue. Methodological flexibility and appropriateness to the object under study are two main advantages of this procedure.

Fitting the method into the research process

The theoretical background is above all more recent versions of symbolic interactionism (see Chapter 2). In terms of pursuing the goal of developing theories about the research object (see Chapter 4), questions of how to access the field become a decisive methodological problem (see Chapter 6). Research questions (see Chapter 5) focus on the description of the field under study and of the practices in it. In the main, step-by-step strategies of sampling (see Chapter 7) are applied. Interpretations are carried out by using coding strategies as well as sequentially (see Chapters 15, 16).

Limitations of the method

One problem with this method is that not all phenomena can be observed in situations. That biographical processes are difficult to observe is readily understood. But also comprehensive knowledge processes are not accessible to observation. Events or practices that seldom occur – although they are crucial to the research question – can be captured only with luck or if at all by a very careful selection of situations of observation. As a way of solving these problems, often additional interviews of participants are integrated into the research programme which allow the reconstruction of biographical processes or stocks of knowledge which are the background of practices that can be observed. Therefore the researchers' knowledge in participant observation is based only in part on the observation of actions. A large part is grounded in participants' verbal statements about certain relations and facts. In order to be able to use the strengths of observation compared with interview studies and to assess how far this strength applies for the data received, Becker and Geer (1960, p. 287) suggest the scheme in Table 12.1 for locating the data.

They are interested in answering the question of how likely it is that an activity or an attitude that is found is valid for the group they studied in general or only for individual members or specific situations. They start from the notion that attitudes deduced from activities in the group are most likely shared by the group, because otherwise the activities would have been corrected or commented on by the other members. Statements within the group are more likely to be seen as shared attitudes rather than a member's statements in face-to-face contact with the observer. Spontaneous activities and statements seem more reliable than those responding to an observer's intervention, e.g. a direct question. The most important thing again is to answer the question of how likely the observed activities and statements are to occur independently of the researcher's observation and participation.

Another problem arises out of the advantages of the methods that were discussed with key phrases like flexibility and appropriateness to the object of research. Participant observation can hardly be standardized and formalized beyond a general research strategy, and it does not make sense to see

TABLE 12.1 *Dependability of observations*

		Volunteered	**Directed by the observer**	**Total**
Statements	To observer alone			
	To others in everyday conversations			
Activities	Individual			
	Group			
altogether				

Source: Becker and Geer 1960, p. 287

this as a goal for further methodological developments (Lüders 1995). Correspondingly the methodological discussions have stagnated in recent years. Attempts to codify participant observation in textbooks are based on the discussions of the early 1970s (e.g. Lamnek 1989) or else are reported from the workshop of observation (e.g. Aster et al. 1989; Girtler 1991).

ETHNOGRAPHY

In recent discussions, interest in the method of participant observation has faded more and more into the background, while the more general strategy of ethnography, in which observation and participation are interwoven with other procedures, has attracted more attention:

> The ethnographer participates, overtly or covertly, in people's daily lives for an extended period of time, watching what happens, listening to what is said, asking questions; in fact collecting whatever data are available to throw light on the issues with which he or she is concerned. (Hammersley and Atkinson 1983, p. 2)

Features of ethnographic research

The concrete definition and formulation of methodological principles and steps are subordinated to practising a general research attitude in the field which is observed, or more generally studied. However, in a more recent overview, Atkinson and Hammersley (1994, p. 248) note several substantial features of ethnographic research, as shown in Box 12.1.

Data collection here is most consistently subordinated to the research question and the circumstances in the respective field. Methods are

---

Box 12.1 Features of ethnographic research

- A strong emphasis on exploring the nature of a particular social phenomenon, rather than setting out to test hypotheses about them.
- A tendency to work primarily with 'unstructured' data, that is, data that have not been coded at the point of data collection in terms of a closed set of analytic categories.
- Investigation of a small number of cases, perhaps just one case, in detail.
- Analysis of data that involves explicit interpretation of the meanings and functions of human actions, the product of which mainly takes the form of verbal descriptions and explanations, with quantification and statistical analysis playing a subordinate role at most.

Source: Atkinson and Hammersley 1994, p. 248

---

subordinated to practice (for the plurality of methods in this context see also Hitzler and Honer 1991). Lüders sees the central defining features of ethnography as follows:

> first [there is] the risk and the moments of the research process which cannot be planned and are situative, coincidental and individual . . . Second, the researcher's skilful activity in each situation becomes more important . . . Third, ethnography . . . transforms into a strategy of research which includes as many options of collecting data as can be imagined and are justifiable. (1995, pp. 320–1)

Methodological discussions focus less on methods of data collection and interpretation than on questions of how to report findings in a field (see Chapter 19). However, methodological strategies applied in the fields under study are still very much based on observing what is going on in the field by participating in the field. Interviews and the analysis of documents are integrated into this kind of participatory research design where they hold out the promise of further knowledge.

Problems in conducting the method

Methods define which aspects of the phenomenon are especially relevant and deserve particular attention. At the same time they give an orientation for the researcher's practice. In ethnography, both are given up in favour of a general attitude towards the research through the use of which the researcher finds his or her own way in the life world under study.

Using their approach of a life world ethnography, Hitzler and Honer (e.g. 1991) study different 'small life worlds' of do-it-yourselfers, members of parliaments and body builders. This study is characterized as follows: 'The methodological stress of this investigation was laid on analysing documents and especially on observing participation. Complementary semi-structured interviews with the aim of generating narratives were also conducted' (1991, p. 384). Also central to the data collection is the development of a special 'intensive interview'. The programmatic openness and flexibility regarding methodological determinations and the plurality of methods are relativized again by this.

Contribution to the general methodological discussion

Special attention has been attracted by ethnography in recent years owing to two sets of circumstances. First, in this context, an extensive debate about the presentation of observation has begun (Berg and Fuchs 1993; Clifford and Marcus 1986) which has not been and will not be without consequences for other domains of qualitative research (see Chapter 19 for this). Second, the recent methodological discussion about qualitative methods in general in the Anglo-Saxon area (e.g. in the contributions to Denzin and Lincoln 1994a; or in Hammersley 1990; 1992; Lincoln and Guba 1985) has been strongly influenced by strategies and discussions in ethnography. Ethnography has been the most powerful influence on the transformation of qualitative research into some kind of postmodern research attitude as opposed to the more or less codified application of specific methods. In addition, ethnography has been rediscovered in developmental and cultural psychology (cf. the volume of Jessor et al. 1996) and has stimulated a new interest in qualitative methods in this area.[2]

Fitting the method into the research process

Ethnography starts from the theoretical position of describing social realities and their making (see Chapter 2). It aims at developing theories (see Chapter 4). Research questions focus mainly on detailed descriptions of case studies (see Chapter 5). Entering the field has central importance for the empirical and theoretical disclosure of the field under study and is not simply a problem which has to be solved technically (see Chapter 6). Sampling strategies generally orient to theoretical sampling or procedures based on this (see Chapter 7). Interpretations are mainly done using sequential and coding analyses (see Chapters 15 and 16).

Limitations of the method

In the discussion about ethnography, methods of data collection are treated as secondary to strategies of participation in the field under study, the interpretation of data and above all styles of writing and the question of authority and authorship in the presentation of results (see Chapter 19 for this in greater detail). This approach may be interpreted (in a positive way) as showing flexibility towards the subject under study but it also holds the danger of a methodological arbitrariness. The concretely applied methods make ethnography above all a strategy which uses the triangulation (see Chapter 18) of various methodological approaches in the framework of realizing a general research attitude.

PHOTOS AS INSTRUMENT AND OBJECT OF RESEARCH

Recently, a certain revival of second-hand observation, both as topic and as method, can be noted, i.e. the use of visual media for research purposes. Photographs, films and video are increasingly used as genuine forms and sources of data (see Becker 1986a; Billman-Mahecha 1990; Denzin 1989b; Harper, 1994; Petermann 1991; for a discussion of the use of video cameras for recording conversations or interviews see Chapter 14). Photography, in particular, has a long tradition in anthropology and ethnography. Bateson and Mead's (1942) study of the 'Balinese character' is repeatedly treated as classic (cf. Wolff 1991 for an overview of the study).

Example: Bateson and Mead's study of the 'Balinese character'
In their investigation of a Balinese mountain village Bateson and Mead collected 25,000 photos, 2000 metres of film, pictures, sculptures and children's drawings. Photos and films are especially important both as data and as an instrument of knowledge: 'For example, they have presented the developed films to the inhabitants of the village and documented their reactions again on films' (Wolff 1991, p. 135). Photographs and films were understood not as mere reproductions of reality but as presentations of reality which are influenced by certain theoretical assumptions. Bateson and Mead were 'aware that photographs and films – not unlike sculptures and drawings – were not mirror images of reality but only presentational forms, which remain blind without analysis' (1991, p. 138). The presentation of the results of the study is essentially determined by the photos and their analysis in so-called image plates. These are groups of photographs together with related (textual) analyses (see Wolff 1991, p. 139 for an example of such an image plate). The images were sorted according to cultural categories assumed to be typical for Bali (such as 'spatial orientation and levels', 'learning', 'integration and disintegration of the body', 'stages of child development'): 'The images were arranged in groups that allowed several perspectives on a single subject to be presented simultaneously, or in sequences that showed how a social event evolved through time' (Harper 1994, p. 404).

In this study, visual material for the complementary documentation of the analysed culture and practices is called into play and contrasted with the presentations and interpretations in textual form in order to extend the integrated perspectives on the subject. It is already taken into account that visual material not only is accomplished against a certain theoretical background, but also is perceived and interpreted from a specific point of view.

The camera as an instrument for collecting data

A visual sociology centred around photo and film has recently been discussed (e.g. in Denzin 1989b, pp. 210–33). The approach was mainly inaugurated by Becker (1986a). Before that Mead (1963) summarized the central purpose of using cameras in social research: they allow detailed recordings of facts as well as providing a more comprehensive and holistic presentation of lifestyles and conditions. They allow the transportation of artefacts and the presentation of them as pictures and also the transgression of borders of time and space. They can catch facts and processes that are too fast or too complex for the human eye. Cameras also allow non-reactive recordings of observations, and finally they are less selective than observations. Photographs are available for reanalysis by others (see also Wuggenig 1990).

Following Barthes (1996), four types of relation between the researcher and the researched may be distinguished. The researcher can show photos (as demonstrator) to a person under study (as spectator) and ask him or her about the material (type I). The operator (who takes the photograph) can use the researched individual as a model (type II). The researcher (as spectator) may ask the subject to show him or her photos concerning a certain topic or period (as demonstrator) (type III). Finally, the researcher (as spectator) may observe the subject (as operator) while he or she takes a picture and conduct an analysis of the choice of subject matter being photographed (type IV: cf. Wuggenig 1990).

More generally, the question discussed is 'how to get information on film and how to get information off film' (Hall 1986, quoted in Denzin 1989b, p. 210). One approach for example is to use the photographs in family albums to analyse the history of the family or subjects documented in them over time. Also, in family or institutional research the integration of their self-presentation in photos and images of their members on the walls in the rooms can reveal social structures in the social field.

In general, several methodological questions have been discussed which centre on the following topics (see Denzin 1989b, pp. 213–14):

- Theoretical presumptions which determine what is photographed and when, which feature is selected from the photograph for analysis, etc. leave their mark on the use of photographs as data or for documentation of relations.

- Cameras are incorruptible in terms of their perception and documentation of the world: they do not forget, do not get tired and do not make mistakes. However, photographs also transform the world which they present into a specific shape.

- Photos tell the truth: however, how far are photos also marked by the interpretations and ascriptions of those who take or regard them?

- Photos (and films) reveal an approach to the symbolic world of the subject and his or her views.

- Photos are only expressive when they are taken at the right moment – when the interesting action occurs and the relevant persons step into the camera's field of vision.

- Not only the participant but also the photographing observer has to find and take a role and an identity in the field.

Using photos in the context of interviews

A different use of the medium of photography is outlined by Dabbs (1982). The persons under study receive cameras and are asked 'to take (or have someone else take) photographs that tell who they are' (1982, p. 55). This may be extended to a photographic diary, in which people capture aspects and events of their daily lives as these unfold. The decision about which of these aspects or events is selected to be photographed is taken not by the researcher but by the subject. What he or she selects and takes as a picture allows the researcher to deduce statements about the views of the subjects towards their own everyday lives. This is especially the case when comparing the perspectives of different subjects in the field expressed in their photographs and the features highlighted in them.

A similar procedure has been applied by Wuggenig (1990, pp. 115–18) in order to study significance in the area of living. People were instructed to use a camera to document their ways of living and the interiors of their apartments typical for people like themselves in 12 photos. The instruction in Box 12.2 was given to them.

In the 'photo elicitation interview' (Harper 1994, p. 410), photos from people's own lives are taken to stimulate interview partners to produce narratives or answers – first about the photo, and then starting from this about their daily life. This procedure may also be seen as a concretization of the focused interview (see Chapter 8). Whereas here visual material is used as a support for conducting the interview, in the following example photographs are used as data in their own right.

Example: Analysis of soldiers' photos
Haupert (1994) analyses soldiers' photos using the method of objective hermeneutics (see Chapter 16) in order to reconstruct biographical processes. Here,

---

Box 12.2   Instruction for the photo interview

What do you like most about your own room and in the flat (or house)? What do you like least about your room and in the flat (or house)? Please photograph first the three motifs you like the most in your room, then the three you like the least. Then please repeat this for the rest of the apartment. It does not matter which room you choose. All in all you can use 12 pictures.

Source: Wuggenig 1990, p. 116

---

photos are not produced for research purposes, but existing photos are analysed for the general relations to the photographed period and the individual fate traced in this material. Photos here have their own special importance as genuine documents. Their analysis can be referred to other forms of data (biographical interview). Photo analysis is explicitly understood and practised as a form of textual analysis (1994, pp. 285–90), i.e. here photos are studied, 'whose textual quality in the sense of social research – although the grammar of the image for the moment remains unclear – . . . can finally be singled out by a programmatic procedure of telling grammatically correct stories which are adequate in meaning and model the contextual framework of the image' (1994, p. 286).

As Morris (1975) made clear, photos have a high iconic quality, which may help to activate people's memories or to stimulate/encourage them to make 'statements about complex processes and situations' (Collier 1957, p. 59).

Problems in the application of the method

Denzin (1989b, pp. 214–15) takes up Gold's typology of observer roles in order to describe the problems associated with finding the most appropriate role for the photographing observer. One problem is the influence of the medium. Photos lose expressiveness when the photographer's efforts to position the subjects to be photographed become too much of an interference (arranged photos) or if the subjects pose for the photos (self-presentation photos). The insights that photos can provide about the everyday life under study will be greatest if the photographing researcher can manage to integrate him or herself with the camera in a way that attracts the least possible attention.

Another problem is the possibility of influencing or manipulating the photographical presentation. Denzin names montage and retouch or the attempt to take artistic photos in this respect, and argues that these techniques may lead to details being left out which are relevant to the research question. Various forms of censorship (by official agencies, by the photographed persons or by the photographer) which may restrict the realization and reliability of photos as social science data are also mentioned by Denzin (1989b, p. 220). Becker discusses this point under the heading of the photographer's control over the final image: 'The choice of film, development and paper, of lens and camera, of exposures and framing, of moment and relations with subjects – all of these, directly under the photographer's control, shape the end product . . . A second influence on the image the photographer produces is his theory about what he is looking at, his understanding of what he is investigating' (1986a, pp. 241– 2). Furthermore, Becker raises the question 'Do photographs tell the truth?', and tries to specify ways of answering it by discussing sampling questions and the problem of reactivity produced by the very act of taking the photographs. A special problem is the question of framing (what is in the picture, what is focused on, what is left out?) and how much the personal aesthetic style of the photographer determines the content of the photo.

Taken together, these problems raise the question of how far the sample of the reality under study contained in the scope of the photo introduces bias into the presentation of reality, and what part the medium of photography plays in the construction of the reality under study.

Another way of using visual data which goes beyond the single photograph or a series of still photographs is to videotape aspects of a specific life world.

Example: Using Video for studying children in their everyday context

In a study of the development of egocentrism in children and changes in their perspectives, Billmann-Mahecha (1990) used videotaping as a method to collect data in an everyday context. After an initial period of participant observation in order to get acquainted with the family, she came back and videotaped a couple of hours of an afternoon in the family and of children's play. Then she sampled appropriate episodes from the video material, transcribed them, and made her own interpretation of them. The next step was to show these episodes to the parents and to interview both about them. These interviews were also transcribed and interpreted. Both perspectives (the researcher's interpretation of the video episodes and the interpretation of the parents' answers) were triangulated on the level of the single case. Then the episodes were analysed on both levels in order to develop a typology of practices and statements of the children in the different episodes.

Fitting the method into the research process

The theoretical background of using photos (and video) is structuralist models such as objective hermeneutics or symbolic interactionism (see Chapter 2) in Denzin's case. Research questions focus on descriptions of aspects of reality contained in the photographs (see Chapter 5). Material is selected in a step-by-step manner (see Chapter 7). Sequential procedures are used for interpretation (see Chapter 16). The analysis of visual material is mostly triangulated with other methods and data (see Chapter 18).

Limitations of the method

Such attempts at a hermeneutic of images (see also Englisch 1991; Müller-Doohm 1993) aim at extending the range of what counts as possible data for empirical social research into the visual domain. However, (at least up to now) procedures of interpretation familiar from analyses of verbal data have been applied to them. In this respect such visual data are also regarded as texts: photos tell a story, visual data are sometimes transformed into text by transcription (see Denzin 1989b, p. 220), content summaries or descriptions of such visual material are made before interpretation is carried out in order to be able to apply textual interpretation methods on visual material. Genuine analytical procedures that directly relate to images still remain to be developed.

FILM ANALYSIS AS AN INSTRUMENT OF RESEARCH

Given that everyday realities are more and more influenced by the images presented on television and in films, the question of what these can tell us about the social construction of reality is seen as more and more significant. Denzin (1989b) analyses Hollywood movies that contain within their scripts social reflections on social experiences (such as alcoholism, corruption and so on), on key moments of history (e.g. the Vietnam War), on certain institutions (e.g. hospitals), on social values (such as marriage and family) and relations, on domains of everyday life and on emotions. These movies and the practices presented can be interpreted on different levels of meaning. Denzin distinguishes 'realistic' and 'subversive readings' (1989b, p. 230). Realistic readings understand a film as a truthful description of a phenomenon, whose meaning can be (completely) disclosed through a detailed analysis of the contents and the formal features of the images. The interpretation serves to validate the truth claims the film makes about reality. Subversive readings on the other hand take into account that the author's ideas of reality influence the film as well as that those of the interpreter will influence its interpretation. The assumption that a correct and complete analysis of film material is possible is abandoned and replaced by the notion of different interpretations of such data. These interpretations of multiple interpreters can be analysed and compared in terms of their different constructions of reality (see Chapter 3).

Steps in conducting a film analysis

For film analyses, Denzin (1989b, pp. 231–2) suggests four steps as a general model:

1   The films are regarded as a whole, and impressions, questions and patterns of meaning are noted which are conspicuous.

2   Research questions to be pursued on the material are formulated. Therefore key scenes are noted.

3   'Structured microanalyses' are conducted of individual scenes and sequences, which should lead to detailed descriptions and patterns in the display (of conflicts etc.) in these excerpts.

4   This search for patterns is extended to the whole film in order to answer the research question. Realistic and subversive readings of the film are contrasted and a final interpretation is written.

This procedure has been applied to several examples.

Example: Alcoholism in Hollywood movies

Using the example of the film *Tender Mercies*, Denzin studies the presentation and treatment of problems like 'alcoholism' and 'families of alcoholics' in order to find out 'how cultural representations form lived experiences' (1989c, p. 37). Therefore, Denzin first studied the 'realistic interpretations' of the film which he derived from reviews and film guides for their 'dominant ideological meanings' (1989c, p. 40). The background assumption is that the interpretations of films and of social problems like alcoholism are often 'patriarchally biased', because they are formulated from a male point of view (1989c, p. 38). Denzin contrasts this with his own 'subversive reading' of the film and the problem, which he conducts from the standpoint of feminism. The focus is shifted from the main male character and his alcohol addiction to the women in his life and to the consequences that the main character's alcoholism has for the women and his family (1989c, p. 46). From this change of perspectives, an analysis of the cultural values and issues to do with the problem of alcoholism, such as family, gender relations and the control of emotions in society, is derived (1989c, p. 49). Finally, the developed readings are assessed against the interpretations of different viewers of the film and the latter are related to the viewers' subjective experiences of the problems that are mentioned (1989c, p. 40).

Problems in conducting the method

The following conclusions may be drawn from this study. Films can be interpreted and analysed from different perspectives. It is the perspective which determines the central focus of the interpretation and its results. The point that Denzin seeks to make is that this is the case not only for the analyses of film reviewers – for whom that won't be news – but also for the analyses social scientists. How far the feminist perspective Denzin takes is the most appropriate one is a question Denzin cannot and does not want to decide with respect to the multiplicity of possible interpretations he highlights.

Using films as data also leads to problems of selection (which films, which scenes are analysed more closely?) and of interpretation (what should attention be paid to in the material?). Additionally the question of working up the data for interpretation arises: should codings, categorizations and interpretations be done directly on the visual material or should transcriptions of dialogues and their contexts be made first thus transforming visual material into text (for this see Denzin 1989b, pp. 220–1)?

Contribution to the general methodological discussion

Using media such as film and photographs as data in qualitative research crosses the boundaries between the various social scientific methods discussed in this book. Compared with interviews, they provide the non-verbal component of events and practices, which could otherwise only be documented in context protocols. Compared with traditional observation, these media offer the advantage of repeated access: whereas the observed situation is irreversibly gone after it is finished, films can be viewed and analysed in unlimited repetition. This may transgress the limitations of perception and documentation which are characteristic of observation (Bergmann 1985). Finally, Petermann (1991) discusses the relation between reality and the presentation of reality in scientific documentary films.

Fitting the method into the research process

The theoretical background of using film materials is Denzin's interpretive interactionism (see Chapter 2). Research questions focus on descriptions of segments of reality contained in the film (see Chapter 5). Concrete examples of these are sampled step by step (see Chapter 7). Interpretation is often carried out using sequential procedures (see Chapter 16).

Limitations of the method

The construction of versions of reality in films is influenced not only by the film maker's perspective and the moment he or she chooses for recording but also by the film's viewers who may interpret the material in many different ways. Film analyses therefore are rarely used as a genuine strategy but rather as an addition to or a part of other methods aimed at analysing verbal data. Up to now, there has been no method of interpretation for such material which deals directly with the visual level. Films are understood as visual texts (Denzin 1989b, p. 228), transformed into text by transcription or by recounting the stories contained in them, and then analysed as such.

NOTES

1 The researcher should reflect on why his or her key person is ready to take this role. Friedrichs and Lüdtke (1973, p. 38) list a range of social positions from which people start to become key persons in participant observation. Most of these positions are characterized by social deficits concerning the social status of the key person in the group or in the field (e.g. the outsider, the novice, the frustrated, people needing loving care, the subordinate). That does not necessarily mean that social acceptance must be the only motive for supporting the researcher in this respect. But the consequences of the key person's motivation and role for the researcher's access and the observation should be taken into account. Thus not only observation *by* key persons but also observation *of* key persons in the field should be integrated as a basis for such reflection.

2 Although there are positions different from postmodern ethnography that are dominant in this context, arguing against 'solipsism and superficiality' and instead making claims for a strategy of 'mind reading', for example Shweder's (1996) concept of 'true ethnography'.

FURTHER READING

Observation

This text gives an overview of non-participant observation in qualitative research.

Adler, P.A., Adler, P. (1994), Observational Techniques. In: Denzin, N., Lincoln, Y.S. (eds), *Handbook of Qualitative Research*, pp. 377–93. London: Sage.

Participant observation

The first text is a classic example of the application of this method, whereas the others are textbooks which discuss the method in greater depth.

Becker, H.S., Geer, B., Hughes, E.C., Strauss, A.L. (1961), *Boys in White: Student Culture in Medical School*. Chicago: University of Chicago Press.

Jorgensen, D.L. (1989), *Participant Observation: A Methodology for Human Studies*. London: Sage.

Spradley, J.P. (1980), *Participant Observation*. New York: Holt, Rinehart and Winston.

Ethnography

The different approaches to ethnography which are characteristic of recent discussions are outlined in the textbook and the handbook chapter by the same authors and also in the reader from cultural psychology.

Atkinson, P., Hammersley, M. (1994), Ethnography and Participant Observation. In: Denzin, N., Lincoln, Y.S. (eds), *Handbook of Qualitative Research*, pp. 236–47. London: Sage.

Hammersley, M., Atkinson, P. (1983), *Ethnography: Principles in Practice*. London: Tavistock.

Jessor, R., Colby, A., Shweder, R.A. (eds) (1996), *Ethnography and Human Development*. Chicago: University of Chicago Press.

Photos

The problems of a visual sociology using photographs as data are discussed in both texts in greater detail.

Becker, H.S. (1986a), *Doing Things Together: Selected Papers*. Evanston, IL: Northwestern University Press.

Denzin, N.K. (1989b), *The Research Act* (3rd edn). Englewood Cliffs, NJ: Prentice-Hall.

Film analysis

The problems of a visual sociology using films as data is discussed in this text in greater detail.

Denzin, N.K. (1989b), *The Research Act* (3rd edn). Englewood Cliffs, NJ: Prentice-Hall.

13

VISUAL DATA: AN OVERVIEW

Visual data are increasingly being rediscovered in qualitative research. There are different reasons for using them instead of or in addition to verbal data. First, there is the desire on the part of the researcher to go beyond the spoken word and the report about actions in favour of analysing the actions themselves as they naturally occur. Second, there is the advantage to be gained from the fact that some forms of observation work without the need for the researcher to make any interventions in the field under study. Finally, there is the possibility of obtaining knowledge through observing by participating and by intervening in the field and then observing consequences in the field.

Observation in its different versions tries to understand practices, inter-actions, and events which occur in a specific context, from the inside as a participant or from the outside as a mere observer. In observation, different starting points are taken to reconstruct the single case: the events in a specific setting, the activities of a specific person, the concrete interaction of several persons together. It is increasingly being taken into account that not only the observer's participation but also the medium of film and the camera as a device have an influence on the events under study and their presentation for the observer. Therefore, observational procedures contribute to the construction of the very reality they seek to analyse – a reality which is already the result of processes of social construction before being observed. Observational methods provide a specific access to trace such construction processes as they occur in interaction. Finally, observational methods also lead to the production of text as empirical material. These texts range from observation protocols, to transcripts of recorded interactions, to verbal descriptions of the events in films or the content of photographs.

FIRST POINT OF REFERENCE: CRITERIA BASED COMPARISON OF THE APPROACHES

The different methods may be juxtaposed by applying the criteria that have already been used for comparing the approaches to verbal data (see Chapter 11). It may also be asked here what precautions are recommended for each procedure to guarantee openness in the research to the perspectives of the subjects who are being observed. Because observations start mostly from interactions and actions, the participants' subjective perspectives are often ascertained in additional interviews. A further aspect for comparing the alternatives is the precautions recommended to guarantee openness in the process of action and interactions during observation in each case. In addition to such efforts at openness, observational methods also include some specific suggestions as to how to structure the data collection in such a way that events and activities relevant to the research question can be grasped in depth. The various approaches to visual data also contribute to developing observation as a general method. Furthermore, they may be characterized by the fields of application in which they are mainly used or for which they were developed. Finally, specific problems in applying them and basic limitations are linked to each of the methods discussed here (see Table 13.1).

The comparison in the table delimits the field of methodological alternatives in the area of observation and facilitates their positioning in this range.

SECOND POINT OF REFERENCE: THE SELECTION OF THE METHOD AND CHECKING ITS APPLICATION

The appropriate method for collecting visual data should be selected on the basis of one's own investigation: its research question, the field which is to be observed and the persons that are most crucial in it. The method selected should be checked against the material obtained. Not every method is appropriate to every research question. Events of the past may best be

TABLE 13.1 *Comparison of methods for collecting visual data*

Visual Data Methods

Criteria	Observation	Participant observation	Ethnography	Use of photos	Film analysis
Openness to observed's subjective view by:	• Integration of interviews	• Integration of interviews • Empathy through participation	• Linking observation and interviewing	• Subject as photographer	• Subversive interpretations focus one protagonist's perspective
Openness to the process of actions and interactions by:	• Not influencing the observed field	• Distance despite participation • Most open observation	• Participation in the life world which is observed	• Documentation in photo series	• Analysis of stories and processes in films
Structuring (e.g. deepening) the analysis by:	• Increased focusing • Selective observation	• Integration of key persons • Increased focusing	• Plurality of the applied methods	• Slice and angle • Photograph at the decisive moment	• Contrasting realistic and 'subversive' interpretations
Contribution to the general development of visual data methods	• Refraining from interventions in the field • Elucidating the gendered nature of fieldwork • Self-observation for reflection	• Elucidating the conflicts between participation and distance	• Highlighting the appropriateness of methods • Sensitizing for problems of description and presentation	• Enriching other methods (observation, interviews)	• Fixing visual data • Documentation and detailed analysis of non-verbal components
Area of application	• Open fields • Public places	• Delimited fields • Institutions	• Everyday life worlds	• Strange cultures • Biographic experiences	• Social problems • Cultural values
Problems in conducting the method	• Agreement of (unknown) people observed in public places	• Going native • Problems of access • Inundation of the observer	• Unspecified research attitude instead of using specific methods	• Selectivity of the medium and its application	• Interpretation at the level of the image or at the level of the text
Limitations of the method	• Covert observation as a problem of ethics	• Relation between statements and actions in the data	• Limited interest in methodological questions	• Photo analysis as text analysis?	• No specific method for analysing filmed data
Reference	Adler and Adler (1994)	Denzin (1989b); Spradley (1980)	Jessor et al. (1996); Lüders (1995)	Becker (1986a); Harper (1994)	Denzin (1989b)

analysed by using those visual materials that emerged at the time the events took place. Photos open a path in this direction. How a society defines cultural values and handles social problems in general (i.e. across various situations) may be studied by analysing films shown in cinema and television. How such values and problems are concretely treated in situations of interaction may become clear in observing the fields and persons to whom they are relevant. But observation only has access to the actions realized in the situation, and the social and individual biographical background, knowledge or attention can only be reconstructed in a mediated way from them. If the situation, the field and the members can be sufficiently confined, the additional options of knowledge resulting from the researcher's participation in the field under study should be integrated. Non-participant observation mainly makes sense where the field cannot be delimited in a way that makes participation possible or where the actions to be observed prevent participation owing to the dangers linked to them or their illegality.

Beyond the research question, the persons to be observed are a second consideration for deciding between methods of collecting visual data. Some people are more irritated and embarrassed by mere observation than by the researcher's temporary participation in their daily life, whereas others have problems with the disturbance created by the presence of the participant observer in the domain of interest. Some researchers have bigger problems in finding their way in the studied field, whereas others have more problems with the withdrawal in mere observation. With respect to the participants in the study, clarifying the situation and the researchers' procedures and checking the appropriateness of the selected method for this concrete purpose may be helpful. For the observers and for solving their problems, observational training may be offered. Observed situations can be analysed in order to find out if the relevant aspects have been taken into account or not. Field contacts should be analysed additionally for problems in orienting and staying in the field. If this training does not solve the researcher's problems in the field, the choice of method or the choice of observer should be reconsidered. The analysis of the first observation should also concentrate on the question of how far the selected method has been applied according to its rules and aims. For example, have observational sheets been applied as exactly and as flexibly as the method requires? Has the necessary distance been maintained by the researcher in his or her participation? Did the participation correspond in extension and intensity to the goals of the research? Here also it should be taken into account, in selecting and assessing a method, what kind of statements will be obtained at the end and at what level of generalization. Only by taking these factors into account is it possible to specify what a good observation is (Table 13.2).

By using the questions in Table 13.2, the appropriateness of the method and of its application can be assessed from different angles. The assessment this allows should be done after the first field contacts and repeatedly in the further proceeding of the observation.

TABLE 13.2 *Checklist for selecting a visual data method and evaluating its application*

---

1 *Research question*
   Can the method of observation and its application address the essential aspects of the research question?

2 *Form of observation*
   The method must be applied according to the methodological rules and goals. There should be no jumping between the forms of observation except when it is grounded in the research question and/or theoretically.

3 *The observer*
   Is the observer able to apply the method? What part do his or her own fears and uncertainties play in the situation?

4 *The observed*
   Is the form of observation appropriate to the target group?
   How can the fears, uncertainties and expectations of (potential) participants in the study be taken into account?

5 *Field*
   Is the form of observation appropriate to the field under study? How are its accessibility and realizability and ethical problems taken into account?

6 *Scope for the observed*
   How are the perspectives of the persons that are observed and their variability taken into account? Do the members' perspectives have a chance of asserting themselves against the methodological framework of the study (e.g. are the observational sheets flexible enough for the unexpected)?

7 *Course of the observation*
   Did the observer realize the form of observation? Did he or she leave enough scope to the members? Did he or she manage his or her roles? (Why not?)
   Was the observed's role, the observer's role and the situation defined clearly enough for the observed? Could they fulfil their role? (Why not?)

Analyse the breaks in order to validate the observations between the first and second field contact if possible!

8 *Aim of the interpretation*
   Clearly defined actions or complex, multifold patterns, contexts etc.?

9 *Claim for generalization*
   The level on which statements should be made:
   • For the single case (the observed individual and his or her action, an institution and the relations in it, etc.)?
   • Referring to groups (findings about a profession, a type of institution, etc.)?
   • General statements?

THIRD POINT OF REFERENCE: APPROPRIATENESS OF THE METHOD TO THE ISSUE

There is no generally valid ideal method for collecting visual data. The research question and the issue under study should determine whether participant observation or a film analysis is applied. Because 'pure' observation can only provide insights that are limited to actions and interactions in concrete situations, the extension to participation in the events to be observed and to parallel conversations with the persons in the field is the more appropriate way of getting to grips with the subjective perspectives and the life world of the participants. The problem of appropriateness of methods is solved in the field of observation particularly by combining different methods in ethnographic studies.

FOURTH POINT OF REFERENCE: FITTING THE METHOD INTO THE RESEARCH PROCESS

Locating observational methods in the research process is a fourth point of reference. The data collection has to be cross-checked with the method of interpretation that is used, to find out if the effort to realize openness and flexibility towards the issue under study is comparable in both cases. On the one hand, it does not make much sense to design the observation in the field so that it is free of methodological restrictions and is as flexible and comprehensive as possible, if afterwards the data are exclusively analysed with categories that have been derived from existing theories (see Chapter 15). On the other hand, it has proved extremely difficult to analyse data that are only documented in field notes with sequential methods (see Chapter 16) like objective hermeneutics (for this problem see Reichertz 1989). Methods of interpretation located between these two poles – e.g. theoretical coding (see Chapter 15) – are more appropriate for these data. In a similar way, the form and design of observation has to be cross-checked with the method of sampling fields and situations and with the theoretical background of one's own study.

Starting points for this cross-checking can be found in the considerations about fitting the method into the research process given for each method in the preceding chapter. The understanding of the research process outlined in these considerations should be compared with the understanding of the research process on which one's own study and its design are based.

Thus, the choice of the concrete method may be taken and assessed with respect to its appropriateness to the subject under study and to the process of research as a whole.

PART 5
FROM TEXT TO THEORY

14

DOCUMENTATION OF DATA

The preceding chapters have dealt with each of the two main ways in which data are collected or produced in qualitative research. However, before analysing the data generated in these ways, they have to be documented and edited. In the case of interview data, an important part of this editing process is to record the spoken words and then to transcribe them. For observations, the most important task is to document actions and interactions. In both cases, a contextual enrichment of statements or activities should be a main part of the data collection. This enrichment can be achieved by documenting the process of data collection in context protocols, research diaries or field notes. These procedures transform the studied relations into texts, which are the basis for the actual analyses. In this chapter, the methodological alternatives for documenting collected data are discussed. The data produced as a result of this process are substituted for the studied (psychological or social) relations in order that the next stages of the research process, i.e. interpretation and generalization, may be conducted. The process of documenting the data comprises mainly three steps: recording the data, editing the data (transcription) and constructing a 'new' reality in and by the produced text. All in all, this process is an essential aspect in the construction of reality in the research process.

NEW POSSIBILITIES AND PROBLEMS OF
RECORDING DATA

The more sophisticated (acoustic and audiovisual) possibilities for recording events have had an essential influence on the renaissance and developments of qualitative research over the last 20 years. One condition for this progress was that the use of recording devices (tape and video recorders) has been widespread in daily life itself as well. To some extent, their prevalence has made them lose their unfamiliar character for potential interviewees or for those people whose everyday life is to be observed and recorded through their use. It is these gadgets alone which have made possible some forms of analyses like conversation analysis and objective hermeneutics (see Bergmann 1985 for more details; and see Chapter 16).

Acoustic and visual recordings of natural situations

Using machines for recording makes the documentation of data independent of perspectives – those of the researcher as well as those of the subjects under study. It is argued that that this achieves a naturalistic recording of events or a 'natural design' (Nothdurft 1987): interviews, everyday talk or counselling conversations are recorded on cassettes or videotape. After informing the participants about the purpose of the recording, the researcher hopes that they will simply forget about the tape recorder and that the conversation will take place 'naturally' – even at awkward points.

Presence and influence of the recording

This hope of making a naturalistic recording will be fulfilled above all if the presence of the recording equipment is restricted. In order to get as close as possible to the naturalness of the situation, it is recommended that the use of recording technology is restricted to the collection of data necessary to the research question and the theoretical framework: where videotaping does not document anything essential beyond that obtained with a cassette recorder, the less noticeable machine should be preferred. In any case, the researcher should limit his or her recordings to what is absolutely necessary for his or her research question – in terms of both the amount of data which is recorded and of the thoroughness of the recording.

In research about counselling, for example, the counsellor may be asked to record his or her conversations with clients by using a cassette recorder. In institutions where these kinds of recordings are continuously made, e.g. for purposes of supervision, the fact of recording may have hardly any influence on what is recorded. However, the fact that there may be some influence on the participants' statements must not be ignored. This influence is increased if the researcher is present in the research situation for technical reasons. The greater the effort in videotaping and the more comprehensive the insight it permits into the everyday life under study, the greater may be the possible scepticism and reservations on the part of participants in the study. This makes the integration of the recording procedure in the daily life under study more complicated.

Scepticism about the naturalness of recordings

Correspondingly, thoughtful reflections on the use of recording technology in qualitative research can be found. These forms of recording have replaced the interviewers' or observers' notes – which were the dominant medium in earlier times. For Hopf they provide 'increased options for an intersubjective assessment of interpretations . . . for taking into account interviewer and observer effects in the interpretation . . . and for theoretical flexibility' compared with 'the necessarily more selective memory protocols' (Hopf 1985, pp. 93–4). This new flexibility leads 'to a new type of "qualitative data hoarding" owing to the delays in decisions about research questions and theoretical assumptions which are now possible'.

New questions concerning research ethics, changes in the studied situations caused by the form of recording[1] and a loss of anonymity for the interviewees (see Bergold and Flick 1987, pp. 13–15) are linked to this. The ambivalence Hopf (1985) expresses against the new options for recording qualitative data suggests that it is important to treat this point not as a problem of technical detail but rather in the sense of a detailed 'qualitative technology assessment'; and also, in the considerations about the appropriate method for documentation, to include 'out-of-date' alternatives which were displaced by the new technologies.

FIELD NOTES

The classic medium for documentation in qualitative research has been the researcher's notes (Lofland and Lofland 1984; Sanjek 1990). The notes taken in interviews should contain the essentials of the interviewee's answers and information about the proceeding of the interview. The participant observer repeatedly interrupts his or her participation to note important observations, as the description in Box 14.1 of the classic documentation technique, its problems and the chosen solutions to them makes clear.

Lofland and Lofland (1984) formulate as a general rule that such notes should be made as immediately as possible. The withdrawal necessary for this may introduce a certain artificiality in the relation to interaction partners in the field. Especially in action research, when the researcher takes part in the events in the field and does not merely observe them, it is

---

Box 14.1 Field notes in practice

Our usual practice was to spend limited periods of time in the field, perhaps two or three hours. When we could appropriately leave the field, we headed immediately for a typewriter or Dictaphone. If leaving was impossible, we took brief memory-refreshing notes whenever lulls occurred and recorded them fully as soon thereafter as possible. The recording of field notes presented a number of problems involving discrimination among events seen and heard, as well as an interviewer's impressions or interpretations. As professionals, all of us were mindful of the pitfalls attending recall and the all-too-easy blurring of fact and fancy. We attempted therefore to make these discriminations clearly, either by stating them unmistakably or by developing a notational system for ensuring them. Verbal material recorded within quotations signified exact recall; verbal material within apostrophes indicated a lesser degree of certainty or para-phrasing; and verbal material with no markings meant reasonable recall but not quotation. Finally, the interviewer's impressions or inferences could be separated from actual observations by the use of single or double parentheses. Although this notational system was much used, none of us was constrained always to use it.

Source: Strauss et al. 1964, pp. 28–9

---

additionally difficult to maintain this freedom for the researcher (see Decker 1979). An alternative is to note impressions after ending the individual field contact. Lofland and Lofland (1984, p. 64) recommend that researchers use a 'cloistered rigor' in following the commandment to make notes immediately after the field contact, and furthermore that researchers estimate the same amount of time for carefully noting the observations as for spending on the observation itself. It should be ensured that (maybe much) later a distinction can still be made between what has been observed and what has been condensed by the observer in his or her interpretation or summary of events (see Chapter 18 on procedural reliability of protocols). On the other hand, researchers may develop a personal style of writing notes after a while and with increasing experience.

All in all, the production of reality in texts starts with the taking of field notes. This production is essentially marked by the researcher's selective perception and presentation. This selectivity concerns not only the aspects that are left out but above all those which find their way into the notes. It is only the notation that raises an occurrence out of its everyday course and transitoriness and makes it into an event to which the researcher, interpreter and reader can turn their attention repeatedly. One way of reducing or at least qualifying this selectivity of the documentation is to complement the notes by diaries or day protocols written by the subjects under study in parallel with the researcher's note taking. Thus, their subjective views may be included in the data and become accessible to analysis. Such documents from the subject's point of view can be analysed and contrasted with the researcher's notes. Another way is to add photos, drawings, maps and other visual material to the notes. A third possibility is to use an electronic notebook, a dictating machine or similar for recording the notes.

Correspondingly, Spradley (1980, pp. 69–72) suggests four forms of field notes for documentation:

- condensed accounts in single words, sentences, quotations from conversations etc.;

- an expanded account of the impressions from interviews and field contacts;

- a fieldwork journal, which like a diary 'will contain . . . experiences, ideas, fears, mistakes, confusions, breakthroughs, and problems that arise during fieldwork' (1980, p. 71);

- notes about analyses and interpretations, which start immediately after the field contacts and extend until finishing the study.

RESEARCH DIARY

Especially if more than one researcher is involved, there is a need for documentation of and reflection on the ongoing research process in order to increase the comparability of the empirical proceedings and focuses in the individual notes. One method of documentation is to use continually updated research diaries written by all participants. These should document the process of approaching a field, and the experiences and problems in the contact with the field or with interviewees and in applying the methods. Important facts and matters of minor importance or lost facts in the interpretation, generalization, assessment or presentation of the results, seen from the perspectives of the individual researcher, should also be incorporated. Comparing such documentations and the different views expressed in them makes the research process more intersubjective and explicit. Furthermore, they may be used as 'memos' in the sense of Strauss (1987, in particular Chapter 5) for developing a grounded theory. Strauss recommends making memos during the whole research process which will contribute to the process of building a theory. Documentation of this kind is not only an end in itself or additional knowledge but also serves in the reflection on the research process.

Several methods have been outlined for 'catching' the interesting events and processes, statements and proceedings. In the noting of interventions in the everyday life under study, the researcher should be led in his or her decisions by the following *rule of economy*: to record only as much as is definitely necessary for answering the research question. He or she should avoid any 'technical presence' in the situation of the data collection that is not absolutely necessary for his or her theoretical interests. Reducing the presence of recording equipment, and informing the research partners as much as possible about the sense and purpose of the chosen form of recording, make it more likely that the researcher will 'catch' truly everyday behaviour in natural situations. In the case of research questions where 'out-of-date' forms of documentation such as preparing a protocol of answers and observations are sufficient, it is highly recommended to use these forms. But these protocols should be made as immediate and comprehensive as possible in order mainly to record impressions of the field and resulting questions.

DOCUMENTATION SHEETS

For interviews, it has proved to be helpful to use sheets for documenting the context and the situation of data collection (for this see Flick 1996; Witzel 1985). What information they should concretely include depends on the design of the study, e.g. if several interviewers are involved or if interviews are conducted at changing locations, which supposedly might have influenced the interview. In addition, the research questions determine what should concretely be noted on these sheets. The example in Box 14.2 comes from the study of technological change in everyday life (Flick 1996), in which several interviewers conducted interviews with professionals in different work situations on the influences of technology on childhood, children's education in one's own family or in general, and so on. Therefore, the documentation sheet needed to contain explicit additional contextual information.

TRANSCRIPTION

If data have been recorded using technical media, their transcription is a necessary step on the way to their interpretation. Different transcription systems are available which vary in their degree of exactness (for overview see Ehlich and Switalla 1976; O'Connell and Kowall 1995). A standard has not yet been established. In language analyses the interest often focuses on attaining the maximum exactness in classifying and presenting statements, breaks etc. Here also the question of the appropriateness of the procedure may be asked. Not only does this contribute to the natural science ideals of

---

Box 14.2   Example of a documentation sheet

Information about the Interview and the Interviewee

Date of the interview: . . . .

Place of the interview: . . . .

Duration of the interview: . . . .

Interviewer: . . . .

Identifier for the interviewee: . . . .

Gender of the interviewee: . . . .

Age of the interviewee: . . . .

Profession of the interviewee: . . . .

Working in this profession since: . . . .

Professional field: . . . .

Raised (countryside/city):   . . . .

Number of children: . . . .

Age of the children: . . . .

Gender of the children: . . . .

Peculiarities of the interview: . . . .

. . . .

. . . .

. . . .

. . . .

. . . .

Source: Flick 1996

---

exactness in measurement sneaking into interpretive social science through the back door, but also the formulation of rules for transcription tempts one into some kind of fetishism that no longer has a reasonable relation to the question and the products of the research. Where linguistic and conversation analytic studies focus on the organization of language, this kind of exactness may be justified. In more psychological or sociological questions, however, where linguistic exchange is a medium for studying certain contents, exaggerated standards of exactness in transcriptions are justified only in exceptional cases. It seems more reasonable to transcribe only as much and only as exactly as is required by the research question (Strauss 1987). First, an over-exact transcription of data absorbs time and energy which could be invested more reasonably in their interpretation. Second, the message and the meaning of what was transcribed are sometimes concealed rather than revealed in the differentiation of the transcription and the resulting obscurity of the protocols produced. Thus Bruce (1992, p. 145; quoted in O'Connell and Kowall 1995, p. 96) holds:

> The following very general criteria can be used as a starting point in the evaluation of a transcription system for spoken discourse: manageability (for the transcriber), readability, learnability, and interpretability (for the analyst and for the computer). It is reasonable to think that a transcription system should be easy to write, easy to read, easy to learn, and easy to search.

Beyond the clear rules of how to transcribe statements, turn taking, breaks, ends of sentences etc., a second check of the transcript against the recording and the anonymization of data (names, areal and temporal references) are central features of the procedure of transcription. Transcription in conversation analysis (see Chapter 16) has often been the model for transcriptions in social science. Drew (1995, p. 78) gives a 'glossary of transcription conventions', which may be used after the criteria with regard to the research question mentioned above have been applied (Box 14.3).

Box 14.3 Transcription conventions

[	Overlapping speech: the precise point at which one person begins speaking whilst the other is still talking, or at which both begin speaking simultaneously, resulting in overlapping speech.
(0.2)	Pauses: within and between speaker turns, in seconds.
'Aw:::':	Extended sounds: sound stretches shown by colons, in proportion to the length of the stretch.
<u>Word</u>:	Underlining shows stress or emphasis.
'fishi-':	A hyphen indicates that a word/sound is broken off.
'.hhhh':	Audible intakes of breath are transcribed as '.hhhh' (the number of h's is proportional to the length of the breath).
WORD:	Increase in amplitude is shown by capital letters.
(words. . .):	Parentheses bound uncertain transcription, including the transcriber's 'best guess'.

Source: adapted from Drew 1995, p. 78

REALITY AS TEXT: TEXT AS NEW REALITY

Recording the data, making additional notes and the transcription of the recordings transform the interesting realities into text, and tales from the field result (van Maanen 1988). At the very least, the documentation of processes and the transcription of statements lead to a different version of events. Each form of documentation leads to a specific organization of what is documented. Every transcription of social realities is subject to technical and textual structurations and limitations, which make accessible what was transcribed in a specific way. The documentation detaches the events from their transience (Bergmann 1985). The researcher's personal style of noting things makes the field a presented field; the degree of exactness of the transcription dissolves the gestalt of the events into a multitude of specific details. The consequence of the following process of interpretation is that 'Reality only presents itself to the scientist in substantiated form, as text – or in technical terms – as protocol. Beyond texts, science has lost its rights, because a scientific statement can only be formulated when and in so far as events have found a deposit or left a trace and these again have undergone an interpretation' (Garz and Kraimer 1994, p. 8).

This substantiation of reality in the form of texts is valid in two respects: as a process which opens access to a field and, as a result of this process, as a reconstruction of the reality which has been textualized. The construction of a new reality in the text has already begun at the level of the field notes and at the level of the transcript and this is the only (version of) reality available to the researcher during his or her following interpretations. This should be taken into account in the more or less meticulous handling of the text which is suggested by each method of interpretation.

The more or less comprehensive recording of the case, the documentation of the context of origination and the transcription organizes the material in a specific way. The epistemological principle of understanding may be realized by being able to analyse the presentations or the proceeding of situations from the inside as far as possible. The documentation therefore has to be exact enough to reveal structures in those materials and it has to permit approaches from different perspectives. The organization of the data has the main aim of documenting the case in its specificity and structure. This allows the researcher to reconstruct it in its gestalt and to analyse and break it down for its structure – the rules according to which it functions, the meaning underlying it, the parts that characterize it. Texts produced in this way construct the studied reality in a specific way and make it accessible as empirical material for interpretive procedures.

NOTE

1   According to Bergmann, 'an audiovisual recording of a social event is by no means the purely de-scriptive representation which it may seem to be at first. Owing to its time-manipulative structure it has rather a con-structive moment in

it' (1985, p. 317). Thus after its recording, a conversation can be cut off from its unique, self-contained temporal course and monitored over and over again. Then it may be dissected into specific components (e.g. participants' non-verbal signals) in a way which goes beyond the everyday perceptions of the participants. But this not only allows new forms of knowledge but also constructs a new version of the events. From a certain moment, the perception of these events is no longer determined by their original or natural occurrence but by their artificially detailed display.

FURTHER READING

The second text gives an overview and some critical reflections about transcription, and the others give an orientation for how to work with field notes.

Lofland, J., Lofland, L.H. (1984), *Analyzing Social Settings* (2nd edn). Belmont, CA: Wadsworth.

O'Connell, D., Kowall, S. (1995), Basic Principles of Transcription. In: Smith, J.A., Harré, R., Langenhove, L.v. (eds), *Rethinking Methods in Psychology*, pp. 93–104. London: Sage.

Sanjek, R. (ed.) (1990), *Fieldnotes: The Making of Anthropology*. Albany, NY: State University of New York Press.

CODING AND CATEGORIZING

CONTENTS	

The interpretation of data is at the core of qualitative research – although its importance is seen differently in the various approaches. Sometimes, such as in objective hermeneutics and conversation analysis (see Bergmann 1985; see here Chapter 16), research refrains from using specific methods for data collection beyond making recordings of everyday situations. In these cases, the use of research methods consists of applying methods for the interpretation of text. In other cases it is a secondary step following more or less refined techniques of data collection. This is the case, for example, with qualitative content analysis or with some methods of handling narrative data. In the approach of Strauss (1987), the inter-pretation of data is the core of the empirical procedure, which, however, includes explicit methods of data collection. The interpretation of texts serves to develop the theory and at the same time is the basis for the decision about which additional data should be collected. Therefore the linear process of first collecting the data and later interpreting it is given up in favour of an interwoven procedure. Interpretation of texts may pursue two opposite goals. One is the revealing, uncovering or contextualizing of statements in the text which normally leads to an augmentation of the textual material; for short passages in the original text, page-long interpretations are sometimes written. The other aims at reducing the original text by paraphrasing, summarizing or categorizing. These two strategies are applied either alternatively or successively. In summary we can distinguish two basic strategies in handling texts: on the one hand the coding of the material with the aim of categorizing and/or theory development; and on the other the more or less strictly sequential analysis of the text aiming at reconstructing the structure of the text and of the case. The latter strategy will be the topic of Chapter 16.

THEORETICAL CODING

Theoretical coding is the procedure for analysing data which have been collected in order to develop a grounded theory. This procedure was introduced by Glaser and Strauss (1967) and further elaborated by Glaser (1978), Strauss (1987) and Strauss and Corbin (1990). As already mentioned several times, in this approach the interpretation of data cannot be regarded independently of their collection or the sampling of the material. Interpretation is the anchoring point for making decisions about which data or cases to integrate next in the analysis and how or with which methods they should be collected. In the process of interpretation, different 'procedures' for dealing with text can be differentiated. They are termed 'open coding', 'axial coding' and 'selective coding'. These procedures should be understood neither as clearly distinguishable procedures nor as temporally separated phases in the process. Rather, they are different ways of handling textual material, between which the researcher moves back and forth if necessary and which he or she combines. But the process of interpretation begins with open coding, whereas towards the end of the whole analytical process, selective coding comes more to the fore. Coding here is understood as 'representing the operations by which data are broken down, conceptualized, and put back together in new ways. It is the central process by which theories are built from data' (Strauss and Corbin 1990, p. 57).

According to this understanding, coding includes the constant comparison of phenomena, cases, concepts and so on and the formulation of questions which are addressed to the text. Starting from the data, the process of coding leads to the development of theories through a process of abstraction. Concepts or codes are attached to the empirical material. They are formulated first as closely as possible to the text, and later more and more abstractly. Categorizing in this procedure refers to the summary of such concepts into *generic concepts* and to the elaboration of the relations between concepts and generic concepts or categories and superior concepts. The development of theory involves the formulation of *networks* of categories or concepts and the relations between them. Relations may be elaborated between superior and inferior categories (hierarchically) but also between concepts at the same level. During the whole process, impressions, associations, questions, ideas and so on are noted in *code notes*, which complement and explain the codes that were found, or more generally, in memos.

Open coding

Open coding aims at expressing data and phenomena in the form of concepts. For this purpose, data are first disentangled ('segmented': Böhm et al. 1992). Expressions are classified by their units of meaning (single words, short sequences of words) in order to attach annotations and above all 'concepts' (codes) to them. The example in Box 15.1 of a subjective definition of health and the first codes attached to the text may clarify this procedure (taken from Flick and Niewiarra 1994, p. 23). A slash separates two sections in the interview passage from each other, and each superscript number indicates a section. The notes for each section are then presented: in some cases these led to the formulation of codes and in other cases they were abandoned in the further proceedings as being less suitable.

This procedure cannot be applied to the whole text of an interview or an observation protocol, but rather is used for particularly instructive or perhaps extremely unclear passages. Often, the beginning of a text is the starting point. This procedure serves to elaborate a deeper understanding of the text. Charmaz suggests doing this kind of coding line by line, because it 'also helps you to refrain from inputting your motives, fears or unresolved personal issues to your respondents and to your collected data' (1995, p. 37). She also gives a concrete example of this procedure, as in Box 15.2.

Sometimes hundreds of codes result (Strauss and Corbin 1990, p. 65). The next step in the procedure is to categorize these codes by grouping them around phenomena discovered in the data which are particularly relevant to the research question. The resulting categories are again linked to codes, which are now more abstract than those used in the first step. Codes now should represent the content of a category in a striking way and above all offer an aid to remembering the reference of the category. Possible sources for labelling codes are concepts borrowed from social science literature (constructed codes) or taken from interviewees' expressions (*in vivo* codes). Of the two types of code the latter are preferred because they are closer to the studied material. The categories found in this way are then further developed. To this end the properties belonging to a category are labelled and dimensionalized, i.e. located along a continuum in order to define the category more precisely regarding its content: 'Let us look at the category of "colour". Its properties include shade, intensity, hue and so forth. Each of these properties can be dimensionalized; that is, they vary along continua. Thus colour can vary in intensity from high to low; in hue from darker to lighter; and so forth' (1990, p. 70).

Open coding may be applied in various degrees of detail. A text can be coded line by line, sentence by sentence or paragraph by paragraph, or a code can be linked to whole texts (a protocol, a case etc.). Which of these alternatives is chosen depends on the research question, on the material, on the analyst's personal style and on the stage that the research has reached. It is important not to lose touch with the aims of coding: to break down and understand a text and to attach and develop categories and put them into

---

Box 15.1   Example of segmentation and open coding

Well-I[1]/link[2]/personally[3]/to health[4]/: the complete functionality[5]/ of the human organism[6]/ all[7]/ the biochemical processes[8] of the organism[9]/ included in this[10]/ all cycles[11]/ but also[12]/ the mental state[13]/ of my person[14]/ and of Man in general[15]/. . .

1   Starting shot, introduction.
2   Making connections.
3   Interviewee emphasizes the reference to himself, delimiting from others, local commonplace? He does not need to search first.
4   See 2, taking up the question.
5   Technical, learned, technical textbook expression, model of the machine, norm orientedness, thinking in norms, normative claim (someone who does not fully function is ill).

Codes: functionality, normative claim

6   Distancing, general, contradiction to the introduction (announcement of a personal idea), textbook, reference to Man, but as a machine.

Code: mechanistic image of Man

7   Complete, comprehensive, maximal, no differentiation, equilibrium.
8   Prison, closed system, there is something outside, passive, other directed, possibly an own dynamic of the included.
9   See 6.
10   Textbook category.
11   Comprehensive; model of the machine, circle of rules, procedure according to rules, opposite to chaos.

Code: mechanistic-somatic idea of health

12   Complement, new aspect opposite to what was said before, two (or more) different things belonging to the concept of health.

Code: multidimensionality

13   Mechanistic, negative taste, abuse, static ('what is his state?').
14   Mentions something personal, produces a distance again immediately, talks very neutrally about what concerns him, defence against too much proximity to the female interviewer and to himself.

Code: wavering between personal and general level

15   General, abstract image of Man, norm orientedness, singularity easier to overlook.

Code: distance

Source: Flick and Niewiarra 1994, p. 23

Box 15.2   Example of line-by-line coding

Shifting symptoms, having inconsistent days	If you have lupus, I mean one day it's my liver; one day it's my joints; one day it's my head, and
Interpreting images of self given by others	it's like people really think you're a
Avoiding disclosure	hypochondriac if you keep complaining about different ailments . . . It's like you don't want to say anything because people are going to start
Predicting rejection	thinking, you know, God, don't go near her, all she is – is complaining about this.' And I think
Keeping others unaware	that's why I never say anything because I feel
Seeing symptoms as connected	like everything I have is related one way or
Having others unaware	another to the lupus but most of the people don't know I have lupus, and even those that do
Anticipating disbelief	are not going to believe that ten different
Controlling others' views	ailments are the same thing. And I don't want anybody saying, you know, [that] they don't
Avoiding stigma	want to come around me because I complain.

*Assessing potential losses and
risks of disclosing*

Source: Charmaz 1995, p. 39

---

an order in the course of time. Strauss and Corbin summarize open coding as follows:

> Concepts are the basic building blocks of theory. Open coding in grounded theory method is the analytic process by which concepts are identified and developed in terms of their properties and dimensions. The basic analytic procedures by which this is accomplished are: the asking of questions about the data; and the making of comparisons for similarities and differences between each incident, event and other instances of phenomena. Similar events and incidents are labelled and grouped to form categories. (1990, p. 74)

The result of open coding should be a list of the codes and categories that were attached to the text. This should be complemented by the code notes that were produced for explaining and defining the content of codes and categories, and a multitude of memos which contain striking observations on the material and thoughts that are relevant to the development of the theory.

Not only for open coding but also for the other coding strategies, it is suggested that the researcher addresses the text regularly and repeatedly with the following list of so-called basic questions:

- *What?*　What is it about here? Which phenomenon is mentioned?
- *Who?*　Which persons, actors are involved? Which roles do they play? How do they interact?
- *How?*　Which aspects of the phenomenon are mentioned (or not mentioned)?
- *When? How long? Where?*　Time, course and location.
- *How much? How strong?*　Aspects of intensity.
- *Why?*　Which reasons are given or can be reconstructed?
- *What for?*　With what intention, to which purpose?
- *By which?*　Means, tactics and strategies for reaching the goal. (1990, p. 77; Böhm et al. 1992, p. 28)

By asking these, the text will be disclosed. They may be addressed to single passages, but also to whole cases. In addition to these questions, comparisons between the extremes of a dimension ('flip-flop technique') or with phenomena from completely different contexts and a consequent questioning of self-evidence ('Waving-the-red-flag technique') are possible ways for further untangling the dimensions and contents of a category.

Axial coding

The next step is to refine and differentiate the categories resulting from open coding. From the multitude of categories that were originated, those are selected that seem to be most promising for a further elaboration. These axial categories are enriched by their fit with as many passages as possible. For further refining, the questions and comparisons mentioned above are employed. Finally, the relations between these and other categories are elaborated. Most importantly, relations between categories and their subcategories are clarified or established. In order to formulate such relations, Strauss and Corbin (1990, p. 99) suggest a coding paradigm which may be symbolized as follows in Figure 15.1. This very simple and at the same time very general model serves to clarify the relations between a phenomenon, its causes and consequences, its context and the strategies of those who are involved. The concepts included in each category can become a phenomenon for this category and/or the context or conditions for other categories, and for a third group of categories they may become a consequence. It is important to note that the coding paradigm only names possible relations between phenomena and concepts and is used to facilitate the discovery or establishment of structures of relations between phenomena, between concepts and between categories. Here as well, the questions addressed to the text and the comparative strategies mentioned above are employed once again in a complementary way. The developed relations and the categories that are treated as essential are verified over and over against the text and the data. The researcher moves continuously back and

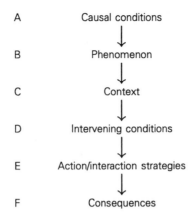

FIGURE 15.1 *The paradigm model*
Source: Strauss and Corbin 1990, p. 99

forth between inductive thinking (developing concepts, categories and relations from the text) and deductive thinking (testing the concepts, categories and relations against the text, especially against passages or cases that are different from those from which they were developed).

Axial coding is summarized as follows:

> Axial coding is the process of relating subcategories to a category. It is a complex process of inductive and deductive thinking involving several steps. These are accomplished, as with open coding, by making comparisons and asking questions. However, in axial coding the use of these procedures is more focused, and geared toward discovering and relating categories in terms of the paradigm model. (1990, p. 114)

In axial coding, the categories that are most relevant to the research question are selected from the developed codes and the related code notes. Many different passages in the text are then sought as evidence of these relevant codes in order to elaborate the axial category on the basis of the questions mentioned above. In order to structure the intermediate results, (means–end, cause–effect, temporal or local) relations are elaborated between the different axial categories by using the parts of the coding paradigm mentioned above.

Selective coding

The third step, selective coding, continues the axial coding at a higher level of abstraction. The aim of this step is to elaborate the core category around which the other developed categories can be grouped and by which they are integrated. In this way, the *story of the case* is elaborated or formulated. At this point, Strauss and Corbin conceive the issue or the central phenomenon of the study as a case and not a person or a single interview. The researcher should keep in mind here that the aim of this formulation is to give a short descriptive overview of the story and the case and should therefore comprise only a few sentences. The analysis goes beyond this descriptive level when the *story line* is elaborated: a concept is attached to the central phenomenon of the story and related to the other categories. In any case the result should be *one* central category and *one* central phenomenon. The analyst must decide between equally salient phenomena and weigh them, so that one central category results together with the sub-categories which are related to it. The core category again is developed in its features and dimensions and linked to (all, if possible) other categories by using the parts and relations of the coding paradigm. The analysis and the development of the theory aim at discovering patterns in the data as well as the conditions under which these apply. Grouping the data according to the coding paradigm allocates specificity to the theory and enables the researcher to say: 'Under these conditions (listing them) this happens; whereas under these conditions, this is what occurs' (1990, p. 131).

Finally, the theory is formulated in greater detail and again checked against the data. The procedure of interpreting data, like the integration of additional material, ends at the point where *theoretical saturation* has been reached, i.e. further coding, enrichment of categories etc. no longer provides or promises new knowledge. At the same time, the procedure is flexible enough that the researcher can re-enter the same source texts and the same codes from open coding with a different research question and aim at developing and formulating a grounded theory of a different issue.

Example: Awareness of dying and awareness contexts

This method was developed (Strauss 1995, p. 70) and applied in a study on the handling of death and dying in hospitals (Glaser and Strauss 1965a). The research question was on what interacting with dying people depends and how the knowledge of a person's imminent death determines the interaction with him or her. More concretely, what was studied were the forms of interaction between the dying and the clinical staff of the hospital, between the staff and the relatives and between the relatives and the dying person. Which tactics are applied in the contact with dying people and what part does the hospital as a social organization play here? The central concept at the end of the analysis was 'awareness contexts'. This concept expresses what each of the interactants knows about a certain state of the patient and what he or she assumes about the other interactants' awareness of his or her own knowledge. This awareness context may change owing to changes in the patient's situation or to new information for one or all of the participants. Four types of awareness were found: *closed awareness* (the patient does not suspect his or her approaching death), *suspicion awareness* (he or she has a suspicion concerning this issue), *awareness of mutual pretence* (everybody knows, but nobody says it openly) and *open awareness* (the patient knows about his or her situation and speaks frankly about it with all others). More generally, the analysis of awareness contexts included their description, and the precondition of the social structure in each context (social relations etc.). It also comprised resulting interactions which included the tactics and counter-tactics of the participants in order to bring about changes in the awareness context and also the consequences of each form of interaction for those who are involved, for the hospital and for further interactions. The analysis was elaborated to a theory of awareness contexts through comparisons with other situations of mutual pretence and differing awareness of those who are involved, into which this typology fits. As examples the authors mention 'buying and selling cars' or 'clowning at the circuses' (1965a, p. 277) etc. By integrating such other fields and the grounded theories developed for them, a formal theory of awareness can be formulated.

An alternative view of the procedure in the development of grounded theory is suggested by Charmaz who, after line-by-line coding at the beginning (see Box 15.2), continues by exploring some of the resulting codes more deeply. In the example given in Box 15.2, these were the two codes printed in italic. Charmaz's second step is called focused coding.

Contribution to the general methodological discussion

This method aims at a consequent breakdown of texts. The combination of open coding with increasingly focused procedures can contribute to the development of a deeper understanding of the content and meaning of the text beyond paraphrasing and summarizing it (which would be the central approaches in the qualitative content analysis which will be discussed later). The interpretation of texts here is methodologically realized and made manageable. This approach allows room for manoeuvre through the different techniques and flexibility in formulating rules. It differs from other methods of interpreting texts because it leaves the level of the pure texts during the interpretation in order to develop categories and relations and thus theories. Finally, the method combines an inductive approach with an increasingly deductive handling of text and categories.

Fitting the method into the research process

The procedure outlined here is the main part of the research process that aims at developing theories (see Chapter 4). In terms of theoretical background, symbolic interactionism has very strongly influenced this approach (see Chapter 2). The material is selected according to theoretical sampling (see Chapter 7). The choice of methods for collecting data is oriented to the research questions and the developmental state of the emerging theory and the blanks still to be filled in it. Which methods should be used for collecting data is not determined beyond that. Generalization aims first at grounded theories which should be related directly to the data and finally at formal theories which are valid beyond the original contexts. The latter are tested by integrating other contexts and the grounded theories developed in them.

Limitations of the method

One problem with this approach is that the distinction between method and art becomes hazy, which makes it in some places difficult to teach as a method. Often, the extent of the advantages and strengths of the method only become clear in applying it. A further problem is the potential endlessness of options for coding and comparisons. Open coding could be applied to all passages of a text, and the categories which are found and which in most cases are very numerous could all be further elaborated. Passages and cases could be endlessly compared with each other. Theoretical sampling could endlessly integrate further cases. The method gives few hints about what the selection of passages and cases should be oriented to and what criteria the end of coding (and sampling) should be based on. The criterion of theoretical saturation leaves it to the theory developed up to that moment, and thus to the researcher, to make such decisions of selection and ending. One consequence is that often a great many codes and potential comparisons result. One pragmatic solution for this potential infinity is to make a break, to balance what was found and to build a list of priorities: which codes should definitely be further elaborated, which codes seem to be less instructive, and which can be left out with respect to the research question? The further procedure may be designed according to this list of priorities. Not only for further grounding such decisions, but also in general, it has proved helpful to analyse texts with this procedure in groups of interpreters and to discuss the results among the members and to mutually check them.

THEMATIC CODING

This procedure has been developed on the background of Strauss (1987) for comparative studies, in which the groups that are studied are derived from the research question and thus defined *a priori*. The research issue is the social distribution of perspectives on a phenomenon or a process. The underlying assumption is that in different social worlds or groups, differing views can be found. In order to assess this assumption and to develop a theory of such groups' specific ways of seeing and experiencing, it is necessary to modify some details of Strauss's procedure in order to increase the comparability of the empirical material. Sampling is oriented to the groups whose perspectives on the issue seem to be most instructive for analysis, and which therefore are defined in advance (see Chapter 7) and not derived from the state of interpretation, as in Strauss's procedure. Theoretical sampling is applied in each group in order to select the concrete cases to be studied. The collection of data is correspondingly conducted with a method which seeks to guarantee comparability by defining topics and at the same time remaining open to the views related to them. This may be achieved for example with the episodic interview, in which topical domains are defined, concerning the situations to be recounted, which are linked to the issue of the study (see Chapter 9), or with semi-structured interviews (see Chapter 8).

The procedure of thematic coding

In the interpretation of the material, thematic coding is applied as a multi-step procedure – again with respect to the comparability of the analyses. The first step addresses the cases involved, which are interpreted in a series of case studies. As a first orientation a short description of each case is produced, which is continuously rechecked and modified if necessary during the further interpretation of the case. This case description includes a statement which is typical for the interview (the motto of the case), a short description of the person with regard to the research question (e.g. age, profession, number of children, if these are relevant for the issue under study) and the central topics mentioned by the interviewee concerning the research issue. After finishing the case analysis, this case profile forms part of the results, perhaps in a revised form. The example in Box 15.3 comes from a comparative study on everyday knowledge about technological change in different professional groups (Flick 1996).

In opposition to Strauss's (1987) procedure a deepening analysis of the single case is carried out which pursues several aims. The meaningful relations in the way the respective person deals with the topic of the study are to be preserved, which is why a case study is done for all cases. In the analysis, a system of categories is developed for the single case. In the further elaboration of this system of categories (similar to Strauss), first open and then selective coding is applied. Selective coding here aims less at developing a grounded core category across all cases than at generating thematic domains and categories for the single case first. After the first case analyses, the developed categories and thematic domains linked to the single cases are cross-checked. A thematic structure results from this cross-check which underlies the analysis of further cases, in order to increase their comparability. The excerpts which are given in Box 15.4 as an example (of such a thematic structure) come from the study on technological change in everyday life previously mentioned.

The structure in Box 15.4 was developed from the first cases and continuously assessed for all further cases. It is modified if new or contradictory aspects emerge. It is used to analyse all cases that are part of the interpretation. For a fine interpretation of the thematic domains, single passages of the text (e.g. narratives of situations) are analysed in greater

---

Box 15.3   Example of a short description of a case

'for me, technology has a tranquillizing side'

The interviewee is a female French information technology engineer, 43 years old and with a son of 15. She has been working for about 20 years in various research institutes. At present, she works in a big institute of social science research in the computer centre and is responsible for developing software, teaching and consulting employees. Technology has to do a lot with security and clarity for her. To mistrust technology would produce problems for her professional self-awareness. To master technology is important for her self-awareness. She narrates a lot using juxtapositions of leisure, nature, feeling and family to technology and work and repeatedly mentions the cultural benefit from technologies, especially from television.

Source: Flick 1996

Box 15.4   Example of the thematic structure of case analyses in thematic coding

1   *First encounter with technology*
2   *Definition of technology*
3   *Computer*
    3.1   Definition
    3.2   First encounter(s) with computers
    3.3   Professional handling of computers
    3.4   Changes in communication due to computers
4   *Television*
    4.1   Definition
    4.2   First encounter(s) with television
    4.3   Present meaning
    . . .
5   *Alterations due to technological change*
    5.1   Everyday life
    5.2   Household equipment

Source: Flick 1996

detail. The coding paradigm suggested by Strauss (1987, pp. 27–8) is taken as a starting point for deriving the following key questions for:

- *Conditions*   Why? What has led to the situation? Background? Course?

- *Interaction among the actors*   Who acted? What happened?

- *Strategies and tactics*   Which ways of handling situations, e.g. avoidance, adaptation?

- *Consequences*   What did change? Consequences, results?

The result of this process is a case-oriented display of the way the case specifically deals with the issue of the study, including constant topics (e.g. strangeness of technology) which can be found in the viewpoints across different domains (e.g. work, leisure, household).

The developed thematic structure also serves for comparing cases and groups, i.e. for elaborating correspondences and differences between the various groups in the study. Thus, the social distribution of perspectives on the issue under study is analysed and assessed. After the case analyses have shown for example that the subjective definition of technology is an essential thematic domain for understanding technological change, it is then possible to compare the definitions of technology and the related codings from all cases.

Example: Subjective definitions of technology and their coding

Two examples of subjective definitions of technology will briefly demonstrate the results of this procedure in one thematic domain. A female information technology engineer from West Germany gave the following answer to a question regarding her definition of technology:

> Technology is for me a machine, somewhere, existing in everyday life, devices for helping people in order to somehow design life either more pleasantly or less pleasantly. What do I link to it? Yes, sometimes something positive, sometimes something negative, depending on what I have experienced with the machine, in contrast perhaps to nature, so nature and technology are in opposition.

Here, on the one hand, it becomes clear that technology equals machines and that an omnipresence of technology is seen. On the other hand, a functional understanding of technology, also a functional evaluation of technology, and finally an explicit juxtaposition of technology and nature are expressed. This definition is coded as 'technology as device'.

A female teacher from France answered the same question as follows:

> For me, technology is something that does not really exist in my life, because if one speaks of technology, I understand it as something scientific . . . Well, if I further reflect, then I say to myself, maybe it is the use of machines whose functioning needs or would need several steps

This is coded as 'technology as unfamiliar science'. This aspect of unfamiliarity could be identified for the other French teachers in this study in general.

TABLE 15.1 *Thematic coding of subjective definitions of technology*

	Information engineers	Social scientists	Teachers
West Germany	• *Technology as device* • Professional technology versus everyday technology	• Technology as necessary means to an end • Dimension 'size' for typification	• Technology as facility • Technology as strange cold world
East Germany	• Technology as device and its vulnerability • Dimension 'functional principle' for typification	• Technology as unfamiliar device • Dimension 'complexity' for typification	• Descriptive definitions of technology • Dimension 'everyday life' versus profession for typification
France	• Technology as the opposite and application of science	• Technology as application of science • Dimension 'everyday life' versus professional for typification	• *Technology as unfamiliar science* • Technology as means to an end • Dimension 'everyday life' versus profession for typification
Specific themes of the professions	• Technology as professional device • Opposition of technology and science • 'Functional principle' for typification	• Application • Technology as means to an end • Typification: complexity and size	• Unfamiliarity with technology • 'Everyday life' versus profession for typification

Codings of technology definitions include two forms of statements: definitions in a descriptive sense (e.g. 'technology as . . .') and the specification of the dimensions used for classifying different technologies and machines (e.g. 'professional technology versus everyday technology'). After coding the subjective definition of technology, the distribution in Table 15.1 results.

Similar codings in the individual groups are summarized and the specific topics of each (professional) group are elaborated. After the constant comparison of the cases on the basis of the developed structure, the topical range in the way the interviewees deal with each theme can be outlined.

Contribution to the general methodological discussion

This procedure specifies Strauss's approach (1987) to studies which aim at developing a theory starting from the distribution of perspectives on a certain issue or process. Group-specific correspondences and differences are identified and analysed. In contrast to Strauss's procedure, case based analyses are conducted in the first step. Only in the second step are group comparisons beyond the single case undertaken. By developing a thematic structure which is grounded in the empirical material for the analysis and comparison of cases, the comparability of interpretations is increased. At the same time, the procedure remains sensitive and open to the specific contents of each individual case and the social group with regard to the issue under study.

Fitting the method into the research process

The theoretical background is the diversity of social worlds as assumed in the concept of social representations (see Chapter 2) or more generally by constructivist approaches (see Chapter 3). Research questions focus on the analysis of the variety and distribution of perspectives on issues and processes in social groups (see Chapter 5). Cases are involved for specific groups (see Chapter 7). In addition, elements of theoretical sampling are used for the selection in the groups. Data are collected with methods that combine structuring inputs and openness with regard to contents (e.g. episodic interviews: see Chapter 9). Generalization is based on comparisons of cases and groups and aims at the development of theories (see Chapter 18).

Limitations of the method

The procedure is above all suitable for studies in which theoretically based group comparisons are to be conducted in relation to a specific issue. Therefore, the scope for a theory to be developed is more restricted than in Strauss's (1987) procedure. The analysis of texts consists of coding statements and narratives in categories, which are developed from the material. It is oriented to elaborating correspondences and differences between the groups defined in advance. These correspondences and differences are demonstrated on the basis of the distribution of codings and categories across the groups that are studied. The analysis above all plunges deep into text and case in the case studies in the first step. If the intermediate step is to be conducted consequently, the procedure may become rather time consuming.

QUALITATIVE CONTENT ANALYSIS

Content analysis is one of the classical procedures for analysing textual material, no matter where this material comes from – ranging from media products to interview data. One of its essential features is the use of categories, which are often derived from theoretical models: categories are brought to the empirical material and not necessarily developed from it, although they are repeatedly assessed against it and modified if necessary. Above all, and contrary to other approaches, the goal here is to reduce the material. Mayring (1983) has developed a procedure for a qualitative content analysis, which includes a procedural model of text analysis and different techniques for applying it.

The procedure of qualitative content analysis

For Mayring, the first step is to define the material, to select the interviews or those parts which are relevant for answering the research question. The second step is to analyse the situation of data collection (How was the material generated? Who was involved? Who was present in the interview situation? Where do the documents to be analysed come from? etc.). In the third step, the material is formally characterized (How was the material documented – recording or protocol? How was it edited – influence of the transcription on the texts? etc.). In the fourth step Mayring defines the direction of the analysis for the selected texts and 'what one actually wants to interpret out of them' (1983, p. 45). The research question is further differentiated on the basis of theories in the next step. For Mayring it is important in this context that the 'research question of the analysis must be clearly defined in advance, must be linked theoretically to earlier research on the issue and generally has to be differentiated in subquestions' (1983, p. 47). This is followed by defining the analytical technique – which of the three techniques Mayring suggests (see below) are applied concretely. Finally, analytic units are defined. Here, Mayring differentiates as units the following. The 'coding unit' defines what is 'the smallest element of material which may be analysed, the minimal part of the text which may fall under a category'. The 'contextual unit' defines what is the largest element in the text which may fall under a category. The 'analytic unit' defines which passages 'are analysed one after the other'. In the last but one step, the actual analyses are conducted before finally their results are interpreted with respect to the research question and questions of validity are asked and answered.

Techniques of qualitative content analysis

The concrete methodical procedure basically includes three techniques. In *summarizing content analysis,* the material is paraphrased, which means that less relevant passages and paraphrases with the same meanings are skipped (first reduction) and similar paraphrases are bundled and summarized (second reduction). This is a combination of reducing the material by skipping statements included in a generalization in the sense of summarizing it on a higher level of abstraction.

Example: Summarizing content analysis

From an interview with an unemployed teacher, the statement 'and actually, quite the reverse, I was well very – very keen on finally teaching for the first time' (Mayring 1983, p. 104) is paraphrased as 'quite the reverse, very keen on practice' and generalized as 'rather looking forward to practice' (1983, p. 59). The statement 'therefore, I have already waited for it, to go to a seminar school, until I finally could teach there for the first time' (1983, p. 104) is paraphrased as 'waited to teach finally' and generalized as 'looking forward to practice'. Owing to the similarity of the two generalizations, the second one then is skipped and reduced with other statements to 'practice not experienced as shock but as big fun' (1983, p. 59). Thus, the source text is reduced by skipping those statements that overlap at the level of the generalization.

The *explicative content analysis* works in the opposite way. It clarifies diffuse, ambiguous or contradictory passages by involving context material in the analysis. Definitions taken from dictionaries or based on the grammar are used or formulated. 'Narrow context analysis' picks up additional statements from the text in order to explicate the passages to be analysed, whereas 'wide context analysis' seeks information outside the text (about the author, the generative situations, from theories). On this basis an 'explicating paraphrase' is formulated and tested.

Example: Explicative content analysis

In an interview, a teacher expresses her difficulties in teaching by stating that she – unlike successful colleagues – was no 'entertainer type' (1983, p. 109). In order to find out what she wishes to express by using this concept, first definitions of 'entertainer' are assembled from two dictionaries. Then the features of a teacher who fits this description are sought from statements made by the teacher in the interview. Further passages are consulted. Based on the descriptions of such colleagues included in these passages, an 'explicating paraphrase can be formulated: an entertainer type is somebody who plays the part of an extroverted, spirited, sparkling and self-assured human being' (1983, p. 74). This explication is assessed again by applying it to the direct context in which the concept was used.

The *structuring content analysis* looks for types or formal structures in the material. Structuring is done on the formal, typifying, scaling level or as regards content:

> According to formal aspects, an internal structure can be filtered out (formal structuring); material can be extracted and condensed to certain domains of content (structuring as regards content). One can look for single salient features in the material and describe them more exactly (typifying structuring); finally, the material may be rated according to dimensions in the form of scales (scaling structuring). (1983, pp. 53–4)

Example: Structuring content analysis

One of the main questions in the project was: 'Did the "shock of the practice" influence the individual's self-confidence?' (1983, p. 88). Therefore, the concept 'self-confidence' (SC) was the subject of a simple scaling, which produced four categories: 'C1, high SC; C2, medium SC; C3, low SC; C4, not inferable' (1983, p. 90). For each degree, a definition is formulated (e.g. for C2: 'I manoeuvred through this somehow, but often it was a tightrope walk': 1983, p. 91). This is completed by formulating rules of coding. These are used to search the text for passages where statements about self-confidence can be found. These classifications finally pass a rating, which for example may aim at an analysis of frequencies of the different degrees in a category. But the fact is, for this form of content analysis: 'For editing the results, no general rule can be defined. It depends on the respective research question' (1983, p. 87).

Contribution to the general methodological discussion

Owing to the schematic elaboration of the proceedings, this procedure seems clearer, less ambiguous and easier to handle than other methods of data analysis. This is also due to the possible reduction of the material outlined above. The many rules that are formulated underline this impression of greater clarity and unambiguity. The approach mainly suits a reductive analysis of large masses of text which is oriented to the surface of these texts. The formalization of the procedure produces a uniform schema of categories, which facilitates the comparison of the different cases to which it is applied throughout. This is an advantage over more inductive and/or case-oriented analytic procedures.

Fitting the method into the research process

The method is not limited to a certain theoretical background. It is mainly used to analyse subjective viewpoints (see Chapters 2, 5), collected with semi-structured interviews (see Chapter 8). The selection of materials mainly follows criteria that are defined in advance, but may also proceed step by step (see Chapter 7).

Limitations of the method

Often, however, the application of the rules given by Mayring proves at least as costly as in other procedures. Particularly owing to the schematization of the proceedings and to the way the single steps are tidied up, the approach is strongly marked by the ideal of a quantitative methodology. The quick and efficient categorizing of the text using categories that are carried over from outside to the text, and based on theories, may obscure the view on the contents of the text rather than facilitate the sounding of the text and its depths and shallows. Interpretation of the text as in other methods is done rather schematically with this method, especially when the technique of explicative content analysis is used, but without really reaching the depths of the text. Another problem is the use of paraphrases, which are used not only to explain the basic text but to replace it – mainly in the summarizing content analysis.

GLOBAL ANALYSIS

A pragmatically oriented supplement to other analytic procedures (mainly theoretical coding or qualitative content analysis) is the global analysis suggested by Legewie (1994). Here the aim is to obtain an overview of the thematic range of the text which is to be analysed.

Steps of the global analysis

As a preparatory step, a clarification of one's own background knowledge and of the research question which is carried to the text is suggested. When reading through the text, key words are noted alongside the transcript and a structuring of the large passages of the text is produced. The next step refines this structure by marking central concepts or statements, and cues for the communicative situation in the generation of each text are identified. Ideas are noted while reading the text. This is followed by the production of a table of contents for the text, which includes the structuring key words noted before with the numbers of the lines to which they refer. Themes (again with the line numbers) are ordered alphabetically, and finally the ideas noted in the different steps are collected in a list. The final step of the global analysis is to summarize the text and to evaluate whether to include it in the actual interpretation or not. The basis for this decision is the viewpoints of the participants, the cues for 'the truth and completeness of the facts that were reported, the appropriateness with respect to the communicative situation, the veracity with respect to the speaker's intentions etc.', and 'indicators for: blanks, biases due to the communicative situation . . . intentional manoeuvres of deception' are sought (Böhm et al. 1992, p. 23). This is completed by noting key words for the entire text and by formulating the consequences of working with the material or of selecting or integrating further texts, cases and information according to theoretical sampling.

Contribution to the general methodological discussion

This form of editing texts before their actual interpretation may be helpful for one's initial orientation to the text and for deciding whether it is worth choosing a certain interview over another one for a detailed interpretation, if the resources (e.g. of time) are limited. Combined with similarly pragmatically oriented analytic procedures of qualitative content analysis, it may give an overview of the material. In theoretical coding, this method may facilitate the finding and assignment of further passages, especially for later steps of axial and selective coding.

Limitations of the method

This method can supplement categorizing methods but cannot replace them. Procedures like objective hermeneutics or conversation analysis which aim at a sequential disclosure of the text (see Chapter 16) will not be compatible with this form of editing the material.

A common feature of the methods discussed in this chapter is that the textual material is analysed by coding. Categories are mostly developed from the text but are also received from the literature. The internal (formal or meaning) structure of the analysed text is not the (main) point of reference for the interpretation. Sooner or later, all these approaches turn to finding evidence for certain categories in the text and to assigning these to the categories. The treatment of the individual case becomes important in different ways. In thematic coding, first a case analysis is produced before the material is analysed across cases. The other procedures take the textual material altogether as a point of reference and develop or apply a system of categories which transcends the single case.

FURTHER READING

Theoretical coding

The first text is not only a good example of the results this strategy is able to produce but also the study for which it was developed. The other texts discuss the method in its various degrees of elaboration.

Glaser, B.G., Strauss, A.L. (1965a), *Awareness of Dying*. Chicago: Aldine.

Glaser, B.G., Strauss, A.L. (1967), *The Discovery of Grounded Theory: Strategies for Qualitative Research*. New York: Aldine.

Strauss, A.L. (1987), *Qualitative Analysis for Social Scientists*. Cambridge: Cambridge University Press.

Strauss, A.L., Corbin, J. (1990), *Basics of Qualitative Research*. London: Sage.

Thematic coding

In these texts, some applications and the methodological back-ground of thematic coding can be found.

Flick, U. (1994a), Social Representations and the Social Construction of Everyday Knowledge: Theoretical and Methodological Queries. *Social Science Information*, 33, pp. 179–97.

Flick, U. (1995a), Social Representations. In: Harré, R., Smith, J., Langenhove, L.v. (eds), *Rethinking Psychology*, pp. 70–96. London: Sage.

Flick, U. (1996), *Psychologie des technisierten Alltags*. Opladen: Westdeutscher Verlag.

Qualitative content analysis

The first text outlines the method in greater detail. The second is an application of the method.

Mayring, P. (1983), *Qualitative Inhaltsanalyse: Grundlagen und Techniken* (2nd edn 1988). Weinheim: Deutscher Studien Verlag.

Ruff, F.M. (1993), Les Nuisances environnementales portent atteinte à la santé – Un nouveau schème explicatif. In: Flick, U. (ed.), *La Perception quotidienne de la santé et de la maladie*, pp. 123–42. Paris: L'Harmattan.

16

SEQUENTIAL ANALYSES

In order to understand and analyse statements it is necessary to take into account the context in which they occur. Context here refers to both the discursive context and the local interactional context. This notion is more or less unarguable in qualitative research. For this reason in qualitative interviews open-ended questions are asked which encourage the respondents to say more rather than less and in so doing to produce enough textual material for the researcher to analyse in terms of contextual considerations. In analysing data, coding is open for this reason, at least in the beginning. The interpretive procedures discussed in the preceding chapter increasingly strip away the gestalt of the text in the course of the rearrangement of statements into categories as a preliminary to analysis and the development of theories. As an alternative to this approach, we find approaches that pay more attention to the gestalt of the text and therefore 'let themselves be guided by the principle of sequential analysis . . . The sequential analysis puts the idea of social order, which reproduces itself in the performance of the interaction, into methodological terms' (Bergmann 1985, p. 313). Such approaches are guided by the assumption that order is produced turn by turn (conversation analysis), that meaning accumulates in the performance of activity (objective hermeneutics) and that contents of interviews are only presented in a reliable way if they are presented in the gestalt of a narrative (narrative analyses). In each case, a specific form of context sensitivity is the methodological principle.

CONVERSATION ANALYSIS

Conversation analysis is less interested in interpreting the content of texts which have been explicitly produced for research purposes, for instance interview responses. Rather it is interested in the formal analysis of everyday situations. Bergmann outlines this approach, which may be considered to be the mainstream of ethnomethodological research, as follows:

> Conversation analysis is the title of an approach of inquiry with the following aim. By way of a strictly empirical analysis of natural texts (priority is given to transcriptions of tape and video recordings of 'natural' interaction), it seeks to specify the formal principles and mechanisms with which actors bring about the meaningful structuration and order of what occurs around them and of what they express and do themselves in the social interaction with others. (1991b, p. 213)

In this way emphasis is placed less on the analysis of the contents of a conversation and more on the formal procedures through which they are mediated and certain situations are produced. One starting point was the work of Sacks et al. (1974) on the organization of turn taking in conversations. Another point of departure was the work of Schegloff and Sacks (1974) in explaining closings in conversations. The central assumptions of conversation analysis are first, that interaction proceeds in an orderly way and that nothing in it should be regarded as random; second, that the context of interaction not only influences this interaction but is produced and reproduced in it; and third, that the decision about what is relevant in social interaction and thus for the interpretation can only be made through the interpretation and not by *ex ante* settings.

Drew (1995, pp. 70–2) has outlined a series of methodological precepts for conversation analysis (CA), shown in Box 16.1.

Research in conversation analysis was at first limited to everyday conversation in a strict sense (i.e. telephone calls, gossip or family conversations in which there is no specific distribution of roles). However, it is now becoming increasingly occupied with specific role distributions and asymmetries like counselling conversation (Wolff 1986), doctor–patient interactions and trials, i.e. conversations occurring in specific institutional contexts. The approach has also been extended to include analysis of written texts, mass media or reports, i.e. text in a broader sense (Bergmann 1991b, p. 218).

The procedure of conversation analysis

The procedure of conversation analysis includes the following steps. First, a certain statement or series of statements is identified in transcripts as a potential element of order in the respective type of conversation. The

---

Box 16.1 Methodological precepts for conversation analytic studies

1   Turns at talk are treated as the product of the *sequential organization* of talk, of the requirement to fit a current turn, appropriately and coherently, to its prior turn.
2   In referring . . . to the observable relevance of error on the part of one of the participants . . . we mean to focus analysis on *participants' analyses of one another's verbal conduct.*
3   By the 'design' of a turn at talk, we mean to address two distinct phenomena: (1) the selection of an activity that a turn is designed to perform; and (2) the details of the verbal construction through which the turn's activity is accomplished.
4   A principal objective of CA research is to identify those *sequential organizations or patterns* . . . which structure verbal conduct in interaction.
5   The recurrences and systematic basis of sequential patterns or organizations can only be demonstrated . . . through collections of cases of the phenomena under investigation.
6   Data extracts are presented in such a way as to *enable the reader to assess or challenge the analysis offered.*

Source: Drew 1995, pp. 70–2

---

second step is to assemble 'a collection of cases', in which this element can be found. It is then specified how this element is used as a means for producing order in interactions and for which problem in the organization of interactions it is the answer. This is followed by an analysis of the methods with which those organizational problems are dealt with more generally (cf. Bergmann 1991b). Thus a frequent starting point for conversation analyses is to enquire into how certain conversations are opened and which linguistic practices are applied for ending these conversations in an ordered way.

Example: Sociopsychiatric counselling

For counselling conversations, it can be shown how entrance into conversation is organized via 'authorized starters' (Wolff 1986, p. 71), regardless of the various conditions under which the individual conversation came about. Their 'task is to mark that point for all who are involved in a comprehensible way, at which organizational principles of everyday conversation (for example to be able to talk about any possible topic) only apply in limited way which is characteristic for that specific type of activity.' In the conversations analysed (Flick 1989), such starters may be designed rather open-endedly (e.g. 'What made you come to us?' or 'And, what is it about?' or 'What is your desire?'). In other cases, they name the (given) topic for the counselling, or specific characteristics in the way the counselling conversation came into being. These openings, which begin the actual counselling relationship and delimit it against other forms of talk, are sometimes linked to explanations about the way the conversation came about. These explanations are specific for the situation (e.g. 'So, your brother gave me a call'). In analyses of the ending of first contacts in counselling processes, it can be shown that on the one hand, a timely ending of the conversation has to be ensured and, on the other hand, the continuation of the relation has to be guaranteed (e.g. 'We have . . . two communities in T-street, which have just been opened. Well, Mr S, we have to wind the whole thing up for today, we must finish it'). In the last example, the ending of the consultation is introduced with a reference to other caring services. This produces continuity in the contact with the client as well doing the work which finishes the conversation 'for today'.

An essential feature of conversation analytic interpretation is the strictly sequential procedure, i.e. ensuring that no later statements or interactions are consulted for explaining a certain sequence. Rather, the order of the occurrence must show itself in understanding it sequentially. The turn-by-turn production of order in the conversation is clarified by an analysis which is oriented to this sequence of turns. Another feature is the emphasis on context. This means that the efforts in producing meaning or order in the conversation can only be analysed as local practices, i.e. only related to the concrete contexts in which they are embedded in the interaction and in which the interaction again is embedded (for example institutionally). Analyses always start from the concrete case, its embedding and its course to arrive at more general statements.

Contribution to the general methodological discussion

Conversation analysis and the empirical results that have been obtained by applying it explain the social production of everyday conversations and specific forms of discourse. The results document the linguistic methods that are used in these discourses. Furthermore, they show the explanatory strength of the analysis of natural situations and how a strictly sequential analysis can provide findings which accord with and take into account the compositional logic of social interaction.

Fitting the method into the research process

The theoretical background of conversation analysis is ethnomethodology (see Chapter 2). Research questions focus on members' formal procedures for constructing social reality (see Chapter 5). Empirical material is selected as a collection of examples of a process to be studied (see Chapter 6). Research avoids using explicit methods for collecting data in favour of recording everyday interaction processes as precisely as possible (see Chapter 14).

Limitations of the method

Formal practices of organizing interaction remain the point of reference for analyses here. Subjective meaning or the participants' intentions are not relevant to the analysis. This lack of interest in the contents of conversations in favour of analysing how the 'conversation machine' (Bergmann 1981) functions, which is at the forefront of many conversation analytic studies, has been criticized repeatedly (e.g. by Coulter 1983; Harré 1998). Another point of critique is that conversation analytic studies often get lost in the formal detail, i.e. they isolate smaller and smaller particles and sequences from the context of the interaction as a whole (for this see Heritage 1985, p. 8; Flick 1989, pp. 180–1). This is enforced by the extreme exactness in producing transcripts.

DISCOURSE ANALYSIS

Discursive psychology as developed by Edwards and Potter (1992), Harré (1998) and Potter and Wetherell (1998) is interested in showing how, in conversations, 'participants' conversational versions of events (memories, descriptions, formulations) are constructed to do communicative interactive work' (Edwards and Potter 1992, p. 16). Although conversation analysis is named as a starting point, the empirical focus is more on the 'content of talk, its subject matter and with its social rather than linguistic organization' (1992, p. 28). This allows the analysis of psychological phenomena like memory and cognition as social and above all discursive phenomena. A special emphasis is on the construction of versions of the events in reports and presentations. The 'interpretative repertoires' which are used in such constructions are analysed. Discourse analytic procedures refer not only to everyday conversations, but also to other sorts of data such as interviews (e.g. in Potter and Wetherell 1998 on the topic of racism) or media reports (in Potter and Wetherell 1998 about the construction of versions in the coverage of the Gulf War).

Example: Racism in New Zealand

Potter and Wetherell (1998) study the social construction of racism in New Zealand using the example of the white majority's treatment of the culture of the Maoris, an indigenous minority. Interviews were conducted with over 80 representatives of the white majority population (professionals from middle income classes like doctors, farmers, managers, teachers and so on). Reports on parliamentary debates and informational material from the mass media were included as well. The results of the study pointed to the existence of different interpretative repertoires such as "Culture As Heritage". In this repertoire the core idea is of Maori culture as a set of traditions, rituals and values passed down from earlier generations. Culture becomes defined in this repertoire as an archaic heritage, something to be preserved and treasured, something to be protected from the rigours of the "modern world", like great works of art or endangered species. Here is a typical example: 'I'm quite, I'm certainly in favour of a bit of Maoritanga it is something uniquely New Zealand, and I guess I'm very conservation minded (yes) and in the same way as I don't like seeing a species go out of existence I don't like seeing (yes) a culture and a language (yes) and everything else fade out' (p. 148). This is opposed for example to the repertoire of 'Culture As Therapy', in which 'culture is constructed as a psychological need for Maoris, particularly young Maoris who have become estranged and need to rediscover their cultural "roots" to become "whole" again' (p. 148).

Contribution to the general methodological discussion

Discourse analytic studies analyse issues which are closer to the topics of social sciences than those of conversation analysis (see Silverman 1993 on this). They combine language analytic proceedings with analyses of processes of knowledge and constructions without restricting themselves to the formal aspects of linguistic presentations and processes.

Fitting the method into the research process

The theoretical background of discourse analysis is social constructionism (see Chapters 2, 3). Research questions focus on how the making of social reality can be studied in discourses about certain objects or processes (see Chapter 5). Empirical material ranges from media articles to interviews (see Chapter 6). Interpretations are based on transcripts of those interviews or the texts to be found (see Chapter 14).

Limitations of the method

Methodological suggestions for how to carry out discourse analyses remain rather imprecise and implicit in most of the literature. Theoretical claims and empirical results are dominant in the works published up to now.

NARRATIVE ANALYSES

Narrative analyses start from a specific form of sequentiality. The individual statement which is to be interpreted is first regarded in terms of whether it is part of a narrative and then analysed. On the one hand, narratives are stimulated and collected in the narrative interview in order to reconstruct biographical processes. On the other hand, life is regarded as narrative (Bruner 1987), in order to analyse the narrative construction of reality (Bruner 1991) without using a procedure of collecting data which explicitly aims at eliciting narratives.

Analysis of narrative interviews for reconstructing events

Schütze has made suggestions for analysing narrative interviews. The 'first analytic step (formal text analysis) is to eliminate all non-narrative passages in the text and then to segment the "purified" narrative text for its formal sections' (Schütze 1983, p. 286). A structural description of the contents follows, which specifies the different parts of narratives ('temporally limited processual structures of the life process' on the basis of formal 'narrative connectors' – Riemann and Schütze 1987, p. 348) such as 'and then' or pauses. The analytic abstraction – as a third step – moves away from the specific details of the life segments in order to elaborate 'the biographical shaping *in toto*, i.e. the life historical sequence of experience-dominant processual structures in the individual life periods up to the presently dominant processual structure' (Schütze 1983, p. 286). Only after this reconstruction of processual patterns do the other non-narrative parts of the interview come into the analysis. Finally, the case analyses produced in this way are compared and contrasted with each other. The aim is less to reconstruct the narrator's subjective interpretations of his or her life than to reconstruct the 'interrelation of factual processual courses' (1983, p. 284).[1]

A different procedure is outlined by Haupert (1991). As a preparation for the actual fine analysis, he first draws up the narrator's short biography, which includes a chronological display of the 'events identified as meaningful' in the life history. This is followed by the segmentation of the interviews according to Schütze's method and by formulating headings for the single sequences. The identification of the 'sequential thematic', and the attachment of quotations explaining it, is the next step. Finally the core of the biography with the central statements of the interview is formulated. Paraphrases of statements from the text and the explication of the contexts of the interviews and the milieus lead to further abstraction. After condensing the case stories to core stories, they are classified in analytic types of processes. These types are attached to life world milieus. This procedure also reconstructs the course of the biography from the course of the narrative. Therefore, here also a sequential analysis is applied.

These reconstructions of factual courses from biographical narratives start from the 'assumption of homology', which according to Bude includes the following premise: 'The autobiographical unprepared extempore narrative is seen . . . as a truly reproductive recapitulation of past experience' (1985, pp. 331–2). Recently, this premise has been questioned more and more, and not only by Bude (see Flick 1996 for an overview). The constructions included in narratives attract more and more attention.

The Analysis of narrative data as life constructions

Accordingly, Bude (1984) outlines a different view on narratives, the data contained in them and thus on their analysis by suggesting the 'reconstruction of life constructions'. Here he takes into account that narratives, like other forms of presentation, include subjective and social constructions in what is presented – life constructions in narrative interviews, for example. In a similar way, authors in psychology like Bruner (1987) understand life histories as social constructions. In their concrete shaping, they draw on basic cultural narratives and life histories offered by the culture. The goal of analysing narrative data is more to disclose these constructive processes and less to reconstruct factual processes. Denzin outlines the procedure for such an interpretation as follows:

> (1) securing the interactional text; (2) displaying the text as a unit; (3) subdividing the text into key experiential units; (4) linguistic and interpretive analysis of each unit; (5) serial unfolding and interpretation of the meanings of the text to the participants; (6) development of working interpretations of the text; (7) checking these hypotheses against the subsequent portions of the text; (8) grasping the text as a totality; and (9) displaying the multiple interpretations that occur within the text. (1989a, p. 46)

For analysing narratives of families and the processes of constructing reality which take place in them (see Chapter 10), Hildenbrand and Jahn (1988, p. 208) suggest the following sequence-analytic procedure. First, the 'hard' social data of the family (birth, marriage, educational situation, stages in professional life etc.) are reconstructed from the narrative. Then they are interpreted with respect to the room for decisions compared with the decisions actually made. From the pattern of decisions which can be elaborated from this, a case structure hypothesis of the studied family is generated and systematically tested in the process of further interpretation. The opening sequence of the narrative in particular and the 'members' self-presentation' which is evident in it are sequence-analytically interpreted. Sampling further cases follows. The case structures elaborated in the analyses can be contrasted, compared, and generalized. The inspiration behind this procedure was the objective hermeneutics of Oevermann et al. (1979) which will be discussed next.

Contribution to the general methodological discussion

Common to all the procedures for analysing narrative data presented here is that in the interpretation of statements they start from the gestalt of the narrative and in so doing they view the statements in the context of the proceeding of the narrative. Furthermore, they include a formal analysis of the material: which passages of the text are narrative passages, which other sorts of text can be identified? The procedures differ in their view of the role of the narrative in the analysis of the studied relations. Schütze sees the narrative presented in the interview as a true representation of the events recounted. The other authors understand and analyse narratives as a special form of constructing events which can also be found in everyday life and knowledge and that this special mode of construction can therefore be used for research purposes particularly well. The combination of a formal analysis with a sequential procedure in the interpretation of constructions of experiences in presentations is a characteristic feature of narrative analysis.

Fitting the method into the research process

The theoretical background is the orientation to the analysis of subjective meaning (see Chapter 2). For this purpose, narrative interviews are used above all for collecting data (see Chapter 9). Research questions focus on the analysis of biographical processes (see Chapter 5). Cases are mainly selected gradually (see Chapter 7), and generalizations aim at developing theories (see Chapter 4). Therefore, case analyses are contrasted with one another (see Chapter 18).

Limitations of the method

In the main those analyses referring to Schütze exaggerate the quality of reality in narratives as data. The influence of the presentation on what is recounted is underestimated while the possible inference from narrative to factual events in life histories is overestimated. Only in very rare examples are narrative analyses combined with other methodological approaches, in order to exceed their limits. A second problem is the degree to which analyses stick to individual cases. The time and effort spent analysing individual cases restricts studies from going beyond a few reconstructions and comparisons. The more general theory of biographical processes which was originally aimed at and promised for quite a while has not yet been realized, although there are instructive typologies in particular domains (e.g. Hermanns 1984).

OBJECTIVE HERMENEUTICS

Objective hermeneutics was conceptualized by Oevermann et al. (1979) originally for analysing natural interactions (e.g. family conversations).

Since its conception, however, the approach has been used to analyse all sorts of other documents including even works of art and photographs (Müller-Doohm 1993). Schneider (1988) has modified this approach for analysing interviews. The general extension of the domain of (possible) objects of enquiry using objective hermeneutics is expressed by the fact that authors understand the 'world as text', as indicated by the title of a recent volume of theoretical and methodological works in this field (Garz 1994). This approach makes a basic distinction between the subjective meaning that a statement or activity has for one or more participants and its objective meaning. The latter is understood by using the concept of a 'latent structure of sense' of an activity. This structure can only be enquired into using the framework of a multi-step scientific procedure of interpretation. Owing to its orientation to such structures the label 'structural hermeneutics' has also been used (e.g. by Schneider 1985).

The procedure of objective hermeneutics

Analyses have to be 'strictly sequential', i.e. following the temporal course of the events or the text. They should be conducted by groups of analysts working on the same text. First, they define what is the case to be analysed and on which level it is to be located: as a statement or activity of a concrete person, or of someone who performs a certain role in an institutional context, or of a member of the human species (Schneider 1985, p. 78). This definition is followed by a sequential *rough analysis* aimed at analysing the external contexts in which a statement is embedded in order to take the influence of such contexts into account. The focus of this rough analysis is mainly on considerations about the nature of the concrete action problem for which the studied action or interaction offers a solution. First, case structure hypotheses, which are falsified in later steps, and the rough structure of the text and the case are developed. The specification of the external context or the interactional embedding of the case serves to answer questions about how the data came about: 'Under the heading of interactional embedding, the different layers of the external context of a protocolled action sequence must be specified with regard to possible consequences and restrictions for the concrete practice of interaction itself, including the conditions of producing the protocol as an interactional procedure' (1985, p. 81).

The central step is the sequential *fine analysis*, which includes interpretations of interactions on nine levels as in Box 16.2 (Oevermann et al. 1979, pp. 394–402). At levels 1 and 3 of the interpretation an attempt is made to reconstruct the objective context of a statement by constructing several possible contexts in thought experiments and by excluding them successively. Here, the analysis of the subjective meanings of statements and actions plays a minor role. Interest focuses on the structures of interactions (cf. Reichertz 1988). The procedure at level 4 is oriented to

---

Box 16.2 Levels of interpretation in objective hermeneutics

0 Explication of the context which immediately precedes an interaction.
1 Paraphrasing the meaning of an interaction according to the verbatim text of the accompanying verbalization.
2 Explication of the interacting subject's intention.
3 Explication of the objective motives of the interaction and of its objective consequences.
4 Explication of the function of the interaction for the distribution of interactional roles.
5 Characterization of the linguistic features of the interaction.
6 Exploration of the interpreted interaction for constant communicative figures.
7 Explication of general relations.
8 Independent test of the general hypotheses which were formulated at the preceding level on the basis of interaction sequences from further cases.

Source: Oevermann et al. 1979, pp. 394–402

---

interpretations using the framework of conversation analysis, whereas at level 5 the focus is on the formal linguistic (syntactic, semantic or pragmatic) features of the text. Levels 6 to 8 strive for an increasing generalization of the structures that have been found: for example, an examination is made of whether communicative figures found in the text can be confirmed as constant figures. These figures and structures are treated as hypotheses and gradually tested in the further material and possibly falsified.

According to Schneider (1985), the elaboration of general structures from interaction protocols can be shown in the following steps in the proceedings of sequential fine analysis. First, the objective meaning of the first interaction is reconstructed, i.e. without taking the concrete contextual conditions into account. Therefore, 'stories about as many contrasting situations which consistently fit a statement are narrated' (Oevermann 1983, p. 236) by the research group. At the next step, the 'general structural features are compared with the concrete contextual conditions in which the analysed statement occurred' (1983, p. 237). The meaning of an action can be reconstructed through the interplay of possible contexts in which it might have occurred and the concrete context in which it really occurred. In thought experiments, the interpreters analyse the implications of the statement first examined for the following interaction. Possible options found in this step can be used as a 'contrasting transparency for specifying the next statement which *really* occurred' (1983, p. 274). By increasingly excluding such alternatives of the proceeding of the interaction, the structure of the case gradually becomes manifest and is finally generalized by testing it against further cases.

Example: Counsellor–client interactions

Sahle (1987) has used this procedure to study the interactions of social workers with their clients. Additionally, she interviewed the social workers. She presents four case studies. In each case, the author has extensively interpreted the opening sequence of the interactions in order to elaborate the 'structure formula' for the interaction, which is then tested against a passage which was randomly sampled from the further text. She derives hypotheses about the professional self-conception of the social workers from the analyses and tests them in the interviews. In a very short comparison, Sahle relates the case studies to each other and finally discusses her results with the social workers that were involved.

Recent developments

This procedure was developed for the analysis of everyday language interactions, which are available in recorded and transcribed form as material for interpretation. The sequential analysis seeks to reconstruct the layering of social meanings from the process of the actions. If the proceedings are available as recordings, they can be analysed step by step from the beginning to the end (at least of the recording). Therefore the analysis always begins with the opening sequence of the interaction. When analysing interviews using this approach, the problem arises that interviewees do not always report events and processes in their chronological order. For example, the interviewee may recount a certain phase in his or her life and and then refer during his or her narrative to events which have to be located earlier. In the narrative interview too, and particularly in the semi-structured interview, events and experiences are not recounted in chronological order. When using sequence-analytic methods for interpreting interviews, first 'the sequential order of the story or the action system under study' has to be reconstructed from the interviewee's statements (Schneider 1988, p. 234). Therefore, the reported events are rearranged in the temporal order in which they occurred. The sequential analysis then is oriented to this order of occurrence and not to the temporal course in the interview: 'The beginning of a sequential analysis is not the analysis of the opening of the conversation in the first interview but the analysis of those actions and events reported by the interviewee which are the earliest "documents" of the case history' (1988, p. 234).

Other recent developments aim at deriving a hermeneutics of images from this approach (Müller-Doohm 1993). Starting from a critique of the increasingly narrow concept of structure in Oevermann's approach (see Reichertz 1988), Lüders (1991) attempts to transfer the distinction between subjective and social meaning to the development of an analysis of interpretive patterns, which also has more interest for subjective viewpoints again.

Contribution to the general methodological discussion

A consequence of this approach is that the sequence-analytical procedure has developed into a programme with clearly demarcated methodological steps. A further consequence of this is that it is made clear that subjective views are only *one* form of access to social phenomena and that meaning is also produced and continued at the level of the social (on this in a different context see Silverman 1993). Finally, the idea of social sciences as textual sciences (Gross 1981) is preserved most consistently here. Another aspect is the call for doing interpretations in groups in order to increase the variation of the versions and perspectives brought to the text and in so doing to use the group to validate interpretations that have been made.

Fitting the method into the research process

The theoretical background of this approach is structuralist models (see Chapter 2). Research questions focus on the explanation of social meanings of actions or objects (see Chapter 5). Sampling decisions are mostly taken successively (step by step) (see Chapter 7). Often, the researcher refrains from using explicit methods for collecting data. Instead, everyday inter-actions are recorded and transcribed, although interviews and occasionally field notes from observational studies are also interpreted using objective hermeneutics. Generalization in this procedure starts from case studies and is sometimes advanced using contrasting cases (see Chapter 18).

Limitations of the method

A problem with this approach is that – because of the great effort involved in the method – it is often limited to single case studies. The leap to general statements is often made without any intermediate steps. Furthermore, the understanding of the method as art, which can hardly be transformed into didactic elaboration and mediation, makes its more general application complicated (for discussions about the crisis of this method see Schneider 1994; for the claim for a hermeneutics of the hermeneutics see Bude 1994; for general scepticism see also Denzin 1988). However a relatively extensive research practice using this approach can be noted in German-speaking countries (cf. Gerhardt 1988).

The common feature of the sequential methods discussed here is that they orient to the temporal-logical structure of the text and take it as a starting point for their interpretation. Thus, they remain oriented more closely to the text than do categorizing methods. The relation of formal aspects and contents is shaped differently. Conversation analysis is mainly interested in formal features of the interaction. Narrative analyses use the formal dis-tinction between narrative and e.g. argumentative passages in interviews for deciding which passages receive interpretive attention and how credible are the contents in them. In interpretations using objective hermeneutics, the formal analysis of the text is a rather secondary level of interpretation. Sometimes, these methods employ hypotheses which have been derived from passages of the text to falsify them against other passages.

NOTE

1   The study of Hermanns (1984) has already been presented briefly in Chapter 9 as an example of a convincing application of this procedure.

FURTHER READING

Conversation analysis

The first three references give an overview of the theoretical and methodological background (ethnomethodology) of the research programme, while the last discusses the more recent state of the art.

Garfinkel, H. (1967), *Studies in Ethnomethodology*. Englewood Cliffs, NJ: Prentice-Hall.

Sacks, H. (1992) *Lectures on Conversation*, Vols 1, 2 (ed. G. Jefferson). Oxford: Blackwell.

Sacks, H., Schegloff, E., Jefferson, G. (1974), A Simplest Systematics for the Organization of Turn Taking for Conversation. *Language*, 4, pp. 696–735.

Drew, P. (1995), Conversation Analysis. In: Smith, J.A., Harré, R., Langenhove, L.v. (eds), *Rethinking Methods in Psychology*, pp. 64–79. London: Sage.

Discourse analysis

These three references give an overview of the research programme.

Edwards, D., Potter, J. (1992), *Discursive Psychology*. London: Sage.

Potter, J., Wetherell, M. (1998), Social Representations, Discourse Analysis and Racism. In: Flick, U. (ed.), *Psychology of the Social*; pp. 138–55. Cambridge: Cambridge University Press.

Potter, J., Wetherell, M. (1995), Discourse Analysis. In: Smith, J.A., Harré, R., Langenhove, L.v. (eds), *Rethinking Methods in Psychology*, pp. 80–92. London: Sage.

Narrative analyses

These three references give an overview of different ways of analysing narratives in their sequential shape.

Bruner, J. (1987), Life as Narrative. *Social Research*, 54, pp. 11–32.

Denzin, N.K. (1988), *Interpretive Biography*. London: Sage.

Riemann, G., Schütze, F. (1987), Trajectory as a Basic Theoretical Concept for Analyzing Suffering and Disorderly Social Processes. In: Maines, D. (ed.), *Social Organization and Social Process: Essays in Honour of Anselm Strauss*, pp. 333–57. New York: Aldine de Gruyter.

Objective hermeneutics

There is hardly any trace of this method in the Anglo-Saxon literature. The first two references are some exceptions, whereas the third one is the classic text which introduced the method to a wider readership.

Denzin, N.K. (1988), *Interpretive Biography*. London: Sage.

Gerhardt, U. (1988), Qualitative Sociology in the Federal Republic of Germany. *Qualitative Sociology*, 11, pp. 29–43.

Oevermann, U., Allert, T., Konau, E., Krambeck, J. (1979), Die Methodologie einer 'objektiven Hermeneutik' und ihre allgemeine forschungslogische Bedeutung in den Sozialwissenschaften. In: Soeffner, H.G. (ed.), *Interpretative Verfahren in den Sozial- und Textwissenschaften*, pp. 352–433. Stuttgart: Metzler.

17

TEXT INTERPRETATION: AN OVERVIEW

Sooner or later in qualitative research texts become the basis of interpretive work and of inferences made from the empirical material as a whole. The starting point is the interpretive understanding of a text, i.e. an interview, a narrative, an observation as these may appear both in a transcribed form and in the form of other documents. In general, the aim is to understand and comprehend each case. However different attention is paid to the reconstruction of the individual case. Content analyses work mainly in relation to categories rather than to cases. For example, the approach adopted by Strauss does not make a principle of a thoroughgoing case analysis. In a similar fashion conversation analyses restrict their focus to the particular socio-linguistic phenomenon under study and dedicate their attention to collecting and analysing instances of this phenomenon as opposed to attempting analyses of complete cases.

In thematic coding, in the analysis of narrative interviews and in objective hermeneutics, on the other hand, the focus is on conducting case studies and only at a later stage is attention turned to comparing and contrasting cases. Global analysis aims at a rough editing of texts to prepare them for later, case-oriented and case-comparing analyses. The understanding of the case in the different interpretive procedures can be located at various points in the range from a 'consequent idiographic' approach to a 'quasi-nomothetic' approach (see Flick 1989, p. 15). The first alternative takes the case as case and infers more or less directly from the individual case (an excerpt of a conversation, a biography or a subjective theory) to general structures or regularities expressed in this case. A particularly good example of this approach is objective hermeneutics and other related approaches of case reconstruction (see Hildenbrand 1991; Kraimer 1998). In the second alternative, several examples are collected and – hence 'quasi-nomothetic' – the single statement is at least partly taken out of its context (the case or the process) and its specific structure in favour of the inherent general structure.

The procedures of text interpretation presented and discussed in detail in the preceding chapters may be more or less appropriate to one's own research question. As an orientation for a decision for or against a specific procedure, four points of reference can again be outlined.

FIRST POINT OF REFERENCE: CRITERIA BASED COMPARISON OF APPROACHES

The different alternatives for coding and sequential interpretation of texts may be compared (see Table 17.1). The criteria suggested for this comparison are as follows. The first is the degree to which precautions are taken in each method to guarantee sufficient openness to the specificity of the individual text with regard to both its formal aspects and its content. A second criterion is the degree to which precautions are taken to guarantee a sufficient level of structural and depth analysis in dealing with the text and the degree to which such structures are made explicit. Further criteria for a comparison are each method's contribution to developing the method of text interpretation in general and the main fields of application they were created for or are used in. The problems in applying each method and each method's limitations mentioned in the preceding chapters are again noted for each approach at the end. This display of the field of methodological alternatives of text interpretation allows the reader to locate the individual methods in it.

SECOND POINT OF REFERENCE: THE SELECTION OF THE METHOD AND CHECKING ITS APPLICATION

As with collecting data, not every method of interpretation is appropriate in each case. A decision between the methodological alternatives discussed here should be grounded in one's own study, its research question and aims and in the collected data and should be reviewed against the material

TABLE 17.1 *Comparison of methods for the interpretation of data*

Criteria	Coding and categorizing				Sequential analyses			
	Theoretical coding	Thematic coding	Qualitative content analysis	Global analysis	Conversation analysis	Discourse analysis	Narrative analysis	Objective hermeneutics
Openness to each text by:	• Open coding	• Principle of case analysis • Short characterization of the case	• Explicating content analysis	• Case-oriented edition of texts	• Sequential analysis of the 'talk-in-interaction'	• Reconstructing participants' versions	• Sequential analysis of the case	• Sequential analysis of the case
Structuring (e.g. deepening) the issue by:	• Axial coding • Selective coding • Basic questions • Constant comparison	• Elaboration of a thematic structure for case analysis • Core and social distribution of perspectives	• Summarizing content analysis • Structuring content analysis	• Overview supports orientation in the search for additional evidence	• Comparative analysis of a collection of cases	• Integration of other forms of texts	• Assessing formal qualities of the text (narrative versus argumentative)	• Group of interpreters • Consulting context • Falsification of hypotheses against the text
Contribution to the general development of interpretation as a method:	• Combination of induction and deduction • Combination of openness and structuring	• Comparison of groups in relation to the issue after case analysis	• Strongly rule based procedure for reducing large amounts of data	• Complementary suggestion for orienting in texts in coding interpretation	• Formal analysis of natural interaction shows how conversation and talk work	• Reorientation of discourse analysis to contents and social science topics	• Concrete model for interpreting narratives	• Transgressing subjective perspectives • Elaboration of a methodology of text interpretation

Domain of application	• Theory building in all possible domains	• Group comparisons	• Large amounts of data from different domains	• Preparation for other procedures	• Formal analysis of everyday and institutional talk	• Analysis of the contents of everyday and other discourses	• Biographical research	• All sorts of texts and images
Problems in application	• Fuzzy criteria for when to stop coding	• Time consuming due to case analysis as intermediate step	• Applying the schematic rules often proves difficult	• Fast overview of the text does not replace and may even impede its fine analysis	• Limitation to formal order and to minimal sequences in conversations	• Hardly developed genuine methodology	• Analyses stick to the case which makes generalization difficult	• Transition from the single case to general statements
Limitations of the method	• Flexibility of methodological rules can be learned mainly through practical experience	• Limited to studies with pre-defined comparative groups	• Strongly oriented to quantitative methodology	• Compatibility with sequential analyses is uncertain	• Limited focus on social science relevant contents	• No concrete definition of the concept of discourse	• Assumption of homology between narrative and reality (in the case of Schütze)	• Concept of structure • Art instead of method
References	Strauss (1987); Strauss and Corbin (1990)	Flick (1995a; 1996)	Mayring (1983)	Legewie (1994)	Bergmann (1991b); Drew (1995)	Harré (1998); Potter and Wetherell (1998)	Hildenbrand and Jahn (1988); Riemann and Schütze (1987)	Oevermann et al. (1979); Schneider (1985; 1988)

to be interpreted. Evaluation of an interpretive method and checking its application should be done as early as possible in the process of interpretation – in case analyses no later than after finishing the interpretation of the first case. A central feature of this evaluation is whether the procedure in itself was applied correctly, e.g. whether the principle of strict sequentiality was kept to or whether the rules on content analysis were applied. The specific problems the individual interpreter has with the attitude of interpretation demanded by the method should be taken into account. If any problems arise at this level, it makes sense to reflect on them and the way the text is handled in a group of interpreters. If it is impossible to remedy them in this way, the researcher should also consider changing the method. Another point of reference for assessing the appropriateness of an interpretive procedure is the level at which results are sought. If large amounts of text are to be analysed with regard to ensuring the representativeness of results on the basis of many interviews, approaches like objective hermeneutics may make the attainment of this goal more difficult or even obstruct it. On the other hand, qualitative content analysis, which would be a more appropriate method for this type of analysis, would not be recommended for deeper case analyses.

Suggestions for deciding on a method of interpretation and for checking the appropriateness of this decision are given in the checklist in Table 17.2.

THIRD POINT OF REFERENCE: APPROPRIATENESS OF THE METHOD TO THE ISSUE

The interpretation of data is often the decisive factor in determining what statements can be made about and which conclusions can be drawn from the empirical material regardless of how it was collected. Here, as with other procedures in qualitative research – despite all the rhetoric surrounding certain approaches – no procedure is appropriate in every case. Procedures like objective hermeneutics were originally developed for the analysis of a specific domain of issues (interaction in families viewed from the perspective of socialization theory: see Oevermann et al. 1979). Over time their field of application has been increasingly extended – both in terms of materials used for analysis (interviews, images, art, television programmes, etc.) and in terms of issues and topics analysed (cf. the contributions in Garz 1994). Similarly, the approach of Strauss and Corbin (1990) is marked by a claim for more and more general applicability, as made clear by the formulation of a very general 'coding paradigm' (see Chapter 15). If the postulated applicability of approaches is extended like this, the criterion of appropriateness to the issue will again need to be taken into account, and in two respects: it should be clarified not only to which issues each method of interpretation is appropriate, but also to which it is *not* appropriate, in order to derive the concrete use of the method in a grounded way.

TABLE 17.2 *Checklist for selecting a method of interpretation and evaluating its application*

1 *Research question*
   Can the method of interpretation and its application address the essential aspects of the research question?
2 *Interpretive procedure*
   The method must be applied according to the methodological precautions and targets. There should be no jumping between forms of interpretation, except when this is based on the research question or theoretically.
3 *Interpreter*
   Is the interpreter able to apply the type of interpretation? What is the effect of his or her own fears and uncertainties in the situation?
4 *Text(s)*
   Is the form of interpretation appropriate to the text or the texts? How is their structure, clarity, complexity taken into account?
5 *Form of data collection*
   Does the form of interpretation fit the collected material and the method of data collection?
6 *Scope for the case*
   Is there room for the case and its specificity in the framework of the interpretation? Can this specificity become clear also against the framework of the interpretation?
7 *Process of the interpretation*
   Did the interpreter apply the form of interpretation correctly? Did he or she leave enough scope for the material?
   Did he or she manage his or her role? (Why not?)
   Was the way of handling the text clearly defined? (Why not?)

Analyse the breaks in order to validate the interpretation(s) between the first and second case if possible!

8 *Aim of the interpretation*
   Delimited and clear answers in their frequency and distribution or complex, multifold patterns, contexts etc.?
   To develop a theory or distribution of viewpoints in social groups?
8 *Claim for generalization*
   The level on which statements should be made:
   • For the single case (the interviewed individual and his or her biography, an institution and its impact etc.)?
   • Referring to groups (about a profession, a type of institution etc.)?
   • General statements?

FOURTH POINT OF REFERENCE: FITTING THE METHOD INTO THE RESEARCH PROCESS

Finally, the selected method should be assessed for its compatibility with other aspects of the research process. Here it should be clarified whether the procedure of interpreting data works well with the strategy of data collection. If, when conducting an interview, great attention was paid to the gestalt of the narrative in the interviewee's presentation, it does not make much sense to apply a content analysis on the data in which only a few categories are used which were defined in advance. Attempts to sequentially analyse field notes with objective hermeneutics have proved impractical and unfruitful. Similarly it needs to be examined whether the method of interpreting data works well with the method of selecting the material (see Chapter 7), whether the theoretical framework of one's own study corresponds to the theoretical background of the interpretive method (see Chapters 2, 3), and whether both understandings of the research process (see Chapter 4) correspond. If the research process is conceptualized in the classical linear way, much is determined at the beginning of the inter-pretation – above all which material was collected and how. In this case the question of selecting and evaluating an interpretive procedure should be answered with regard to these parameters, to which it should correspond. In a research process which is conceptualized in a more circular way, the method of interpretation may determine the decisions made about pro-cedure in the other steps. Here, the collection of data is oriented to the sampling and the method to the needs, which result from the type and the state of interpretation of data (see Chapter 4). At this point it is clear that the evaluation of methodological alternatives and the decision between them should be made with consideration to the process of the research. Suggestions for answering these questions are provided by the paragraphs about fitting the individual method into the research process, and the research questions and the goals of the concrete empirical application.

18

GROUNDING QUALITATIVE RESEARCH

The problem of how to assess qualitative research has not yet been solved. It is repeatedly taken up as an argument in order to raise general questions about the legitimacy of this kind of research.

SELECTIVE PLAUSIBILIZATION

Thus one critique often expressed is that the interpretations in and results of qualitative research are made transparent and comprehensible for the reader only by the interweaving of 'illustrative' quotations from interviews or observation protocols. Especially where the researcher uses this as 'the only instrument for documenting his statements', Bühler-Niederberger (1985, p. 475) critically holds that 'the credibility passed on by this is not sufficient.' Why this is the case is clarified by Girtler, although involuntarily, in a very illustrative way:

> If I now prepare the publication about my research . . . I finally present what is characteristic. In order to make vivid and provable these characteristics or

the characteristic rules from which I 'understand' the social practice to be studied or which I use to explain it, I quote the corresponding passages from my observational protocols or interviews. Of course I quote only those passages which I believe illustrate the characteristics of the everyday world under study. (1984, p. 146)

This procedure, which may also be labelled 'selective plausibilization' (Flick 1989), cannot solve the problem of comprehensibility in an adequate way. Above all it remains unclear how the researcher handles cases and passages which he or she 'believes' are not so illustrative of the characteristics, or cases and passages which may even be deviant or contradictory.

The different facets of the problem mentioned here can be summarized as 'grounding qualitative research'. Essentially, three topics fall under this heading:

- What criteria should be used to assess the procedure and results of qualitative research in an appropriate way?

- What degree of generalization of the results can be obtained each time and how can one guarantee generalization?

- Especially in more recent discussions about these topics, the question of how to present procedures and results of qualitative research has become increasingly important (see Chapter 19).

Concerning the criteria for assessing the procedure and results of qualitative research, the following alternatives are discussed in the literature. The first is to apply classical criteria like validity and reliability to qualitative research or to reformulate them in an adequate way for this purpose. The second is to develop new, 'method-appropriate criteria' (Flick 1987), which do justice to the specificity of qualitative research because they have been developed from one of its specific theoretical backgrounds and take the peculiarity of the qualitative research process into account. A third version engages with the discussion about how is it still possible at all to ask about validity, given the crises of representation and legitimation mentioned by Denzin and Lincoln (1994b, p. 11). This last version surely will neither contribute to further establishing the credibility of qualitative research nor contribute to its results being considered as relevant in any way to the community. Therefore, attention will be given here to the first two ways. In terms of the use of classical criteria, the discussion concentrates on reliability and validity (Kirk and Miller 1986).

RELIABILITY

In order to specify the sense of reliability as a criterion for assessing qualitative research, Kirk and Miller (1986) discuss three forms. *Quixotic reliability* they see as the attempt to specify how far a particular method can continuously lead to the same measurements or results. This form of specifying reliability is rejected by the authors as trivial and misleading. Especially in field research, statements or observations which are stereotypically repeated are viewed as an indicator for a purposively shaped version of the event rather than as a clue for how it 'really' was. *Diachronic reliability* Kirk and Miller discuss as the stability of measurements or observations in their temporal course. What becomes problematic here is the precondition that the phenomenon under study in itself may not undergo any changes, so that this criterion is effective. Qualitative studies are seldom engaged in such unchanging objects. *Synchronic reliability* is for Kirk and Miller the constancy or consistency of results obtained at the same moment but by using different instruments. Kirk and Miller emphasize here that this criterion is most instructive when it is *not* fulfilled. The question then follows as why this is the case, and also questions concerning the different perspectives on the issue resulting from different methods applied by several researchers.

Procedural reliability

Reliability receives its importance as a criterion for assessing qualitative research only against the background of a specific theory of the issue under study and about the use of methods (1986, p. 50). But researchers can go different ways in order to increase the reliability of data and interpretations. In ethnographic research, in terms of which Kirk and Miller discuss these criteria, the quality of recording and documenting data becomes a central basis for assessing their reliability and that of succeeding interpretations. One starting point for examining this is the field notes in which researchers document their observations. In order to increase the reliability of such data, a more or less general standardization of notes is suggested, especially if several observers are collecting the data. The four forms of field notes, which have already been discussed in Chapter 14 on documentation (see also Spradley 1979), are one approach to this structuring. For increasing their reliability, Kirk and Miller (1986, p. 57) suggest conventions for note taking, which are further developed by Silverman (1993, p. 147). These are shown in Table 18.1.

The underlying idea is that the conventionalization of notes increases the comparability of the perspectives which have led to the corresponding data. In particular, the separation of concepts of the observed from those of the observers in the notes makes reinterpretation and assessment by different analysts possible. Transcription rules, which clarify procedures for transcribing conversations, have a similar function to notes conventionalized in such a way.

For interview data, reliability can be increased by interview training for the interviewers and by checking the interview guides or generative questions in test interviews or after the first interview (Silverman 1993, p. 148; see Chapter 11 here). For observations, the requirement to train the

TABLE 18.1 *Conventionalization of field notes*

Sign	Convention	Use
" "	Double quotation marks	Verbatim quotes
' '	Single quotation marks	Paraphrases
( )	Parentheses	Contextual data or fieldworker's interpretations
< >	Angled brackets	Emic concepts (of the member)
/ /	Slash	Etic concepts (of the researcher)
_____	Solid line	Beginning or end of a segment

Source: adapted from Kirk and Miller 1986; Silverman 1993

observers before they enter the field and to regularly evaluate the observing can be added. In the interpretation of data, training and reflexive exchange about the interpretive procedures and about the methods of coding can increase the reliability. From analysing the opening sequence of a narrative, a hypothesis about the case structure can be derived and falsified against following sequences (Hildenbrand and Jahn 1988). This is another way to arrive at reliable interpretations. Assessing categories developed in open coding with other passages has a similar function in the approach of Strauss (1987). In each of these examples, the attempt is made to check the reliability of an interpretation by testing it concretely against other passages in the same text or against other texts.

In general, the discussion about reliability in qualitative research comes down to the need for explication in two respects. First, the genesis of the data needs to be explicated in a way that makes it possible to check what is a statement of the subject on the one hand and where the researcher's interpretation begins on the other. Second, procedures in the field or interview and with the text need to be made explicit in training and rechecking in order to improve the comparability of different interviewers' or observers' conduct. Finally, the reliability of the whole process will be increased by documenting it. Thus, the criterion of reliability is reformulated in the direction of checking the dependability of data and procedures, which can be grounded in the specificity of the various qualitative methods. Other understandings of reliability, such as frequently repeated data collection leading to the same data and results, should be rejected. If this form of reliability is used it may be more convenient to mistrust rather than to trust the dependability of the data (Kirk and Miller 1986, p. 42).

VALIDITY

In the discussions about grounding qualitative research, validity receives more attention than reliability (e.g. in Hammersley 1990; 1992; Kvale 1989; 1991; Wolcott 1990a). The question of validity can be summarized as 'a question of whether the researcher sees what he or she thinks he or she sees' (Kirk and Miller 1986, p. 21). Basically, three errors may occur: to see a relation, a principle etc. where they are not correct (type 1 error); to reject them where they are indeed correct (type 2 error); and finally to ask the wrong questions (type 3 error) (1986, pp. 29–30).

A basic problem in assessing the validity of qualitative research is how to specify the link between the relations that are studied and the version of them provided by the researcher. In other words: what would these relations look like, if they were not an issue of empirical research at that moment? And: is the researcher's version grounded in the versions in the field, in the interviewee's biography etc., and hence in the issue?

This implies less that the assumption be made of a reality existing independently of social constructions, i.e. perceptions, interpretations and presentations, than that the question should be asked as to how far the researcher's specific constructions are empirically grounded in those of the members. In this context, Hammersley (1992, pp. 50–2) outlines the position of a 'subtle realism'. This position starts from three premises. (1) The validity of knowledge cannot be assessed with certainty. Assumptions can only be judged for their plausibility and credibility. (2) Phenomena also exist independently of our claims concerning them. Our assumptions about them can only more or less approximate these phenomena. (3) Reality becomes accessible across the (different) perspectives on phenomena. Research aims at presenting reality not reproducing it.

If one starts from this position, the question of the validity of qualitative research turns into the question of how far the researcher's constructions are grounded in the constructions of those whom he or she studied (cf. Schütz 1962) and how far this grounding is transparent for others (see Chapter 3 on this). Thus the production of the data becomes one starting point for judging their validity (Gerhardt 1985) and the presentation of phenomena and of the inferences drawn from them becomes another one.

Analysing the interview situation

One approach for specifying the validity of interviews is to check formally if it was possible to guarantee the degree of authenticity which was aimed at during the interview. In the framework of biographical research, this is realized by answering the question of whether the respondent's presentation is a narrative or not. This is an attempt to answer the question of the validity of the statements received in this way by equating an unimpeded narrative (e.g. free of any interventions by the researcher) with a valid depiction. Various authors criticize this approach on the grounds that it only addresses a very limited part of the problem of validity (e.g. Bude 1985; Flick 1996; Gerhardt 1985).

More differentiated suggestions for judging the validity of interview data, and especially biographical self-presentations, are made by Legewie (1987, p. 141). According to this author, claims for validity made by a speaker in an interview have to be differentiated (and that means have to be judged separately in terms of the following considerations): '(a) that the contents of what is said is correct, (b) that what is said is socially appropriate in its relational aspect . . . and (c) that what is said is sincere in terms of the self-presentation' of the speaker. The point of departure for validating biographical statements is to analyse the interview situation for how far 'the conditions of non-strategic communication' were given and whether 'goals and particularities of the interview . . . are negotiated in the form of a more or less explicit . . . "working contract"' (1987, pp. 145–9). The main question here is whether the interviewee was given any cause to consciously or unconsciously construct a specific, i.e. biased, version of his or her experiences which does not or does not only correspond with his or her views in a limited way. The interview situation is analysed for any signs of such deformations. This should provide a basis for finding out which systematic deformations or deceptions in the text are a result of the interview situation and how far and how exactly they have to be taken into account in the interpretation. The reflections of the researcher can be further enhanced by involving the interviewee.

Communicative validation

Another version of specifying validity aims at involving the actors (subjects or groups) in the further research process. One way is to introduce communicative validation at a second meeting after the interview and its transcription (for concrete suggestions see Dann 1990; Scheele and Groeben 1988; Chapter 8 here).[1] The promise of further authenticity made here is twofold. On the one hand the interviewee's agreement with the contents of his or her statements is obtained after the interview. On the other hand, the interviewee him or herself does a structuration of his or her statements in terms of the complex relations the researcher is looking for (e.g. a subjective theory of trust as a form of everyday knowledge which is relevant for counselling: see Chapter 8 for an example).

For a more general application of such strategies, however, two questions remain to be satisfactorily answered. First, how can one design the methodological procedure of communicative validation in such a way that it really does justice to the issues under study and to the interviewees' views? Second, how can the question of grounding data and results further be answered beyond the subjects' agreement? One way of proceeding here is to attempt a general validation of the reconstructions in a more traditional way (see Flick 1987 for an overview).

Reformulations of the concept of validity

Mishler (1990) goes one step further in reformulating the concept of validity. He starts from the process of validating (instead of from the state of validity) and defines 'validation as the social construction of knowledge'

(1990, p. 417), by which we 'evaluate the "trustworthiness" of reported observations, interpretations, and generalizations' (1990, p. 419). Finally, 'Reformulating validation as the social discourse through which trustworthiness is established elides such familiar shibboleths as reliability, falsifiability, and objectivity' (1990, p. 420). As an empirical basis for this discourse and the construction of credibility, Mishler discusses the use of examples from narrative studies.

Lather (1993) picks up several postmodernist and poststructuralist theories. However, she does not reject the question of legitimation and thus the validation of scientific knowledge as a whole, but derives updated concepts of validity, which she sets in four frameworks:

- From Baudrillard she derives the idea of an 'ironic validity'. The background assumption is that more and more simulacra, as copies without originals, have replaced representations as copies of real objects (1993, p. 677), with the following consequence for the concept of validity: 'Contrary to dominant validity practices where the rhetorical nature of scientific claims is masked with methodological assurance, a strategy of ironic validity proliferates forms, recognizing that they are rhetorical and without foundation, post-epistemic, lacking in epistemological support.'

- From Lyotard (1984) she derives the idea of a 'paralogic/neo-pragmatic validity': scientific knowledge does not aim at corresponding with the reality but aims at discovering differences and at leaving contradictions in their tension. The validity of knowledge can be specified by answering the question of how far these goals have been reached.

- From Deleuze and Guattari (1976) and Derrida (1976), Lather takes the idea of 'rhizomatic validity'.

- She suggests, as a fourth framework, sensual validity or situated validity. Here the question of the genderedness of knowledge and in looking at scientific knowledge is asked.

How far these concepts contribute anything substantial to answering the question of whether qualitative data and results, or the research which produced them, manifest a minimum of credibility, remains an open matter.[2] Their main importance is that recent theoretical movements are taken up in order to outline ways to reformulate the concept of validity in the framework of a constructivist understanding of research.

Procedural validity

For the research process in ethnography, Wolcott suggests nine points which need to be realized in order to guarantee validity:

(1) The researcher should refrain from talking in the field but rather should listen as much as possible. He or she should (2) produce notes that are as exact as possible, (3) begin to write early, and in a way (4) which allows readers of his or her notes and reports to see for themselves. This means providing enough data for readers to make their own inferences and follow those of the researcher. The report should be as complete (5) and candid (6) as possible. The researcher should seek feedback on his or her findings and presentations in the field or from his or her colleagues (7). Presentations should be characterized by a balance (8) between the various aspects and (9) by accuracy in writing. (1990a, pp. 127–8)

These steps for guaranteeing validity in the research process can be summarized as an attempt to act sensitively in the field and above all as the transferral of the problem of validity in the research to the domain of writing about research (for this see the next chapter). Finally, Altheide and Johnson formulate the concept of 'validity as reflexive accounting', which creates a relation between researcher, issues and the process of making sense and locates validity in the process of research and the different relationships at work in it:

1 the relationship between what is observed (behaviours, rituals, meanings) and the larger cultural, historical, and organizational contexts within which the observations are made (the substance);
2 the relationship among the observer, the observed, and the setting (the observer);
3 the issue of perspective (or point of view), whether the observer's or the members', used to render an interpretation of the ethnographic data (the interpretation);
4 the role of the reader in the final product (the audience);
5 the issue of representational, rhetorical, or authorial style used by the author(s) to render the description and/or interpretation (the style). (1994, p. 489)

In the above suggestions validation is discussed within the framework of the total research process and the factors involved. These suggestions, however, remain at the programmatic level rather than at the level at which concrete criteria or starting points are formulated, in terms of which individual studies or parts of them may be assessed. All in all, attempts at using or reformulating validity and validation face several problems. Formal analyses of the way the data were produced, for example in the interview situation, do not tell us anything about the contents of these interviews and whether they have been appropriately treated in the further proceeding of the research. The concept of communicative validation (or member check) faces the problem that the subjects' consent becomes problematic as a criterion where the research systematically goes beyond the subject's viewpoint, for example in interpretations which want to permeate into social or psychological unconsciousness or which derive from the distinctiveness of various subjective viewpoints.[3] The reformulations of the concept of validity discussed here are marked by a certain fuzziness, which does not necessarily offer a solution for the problem of grounding qualitative research but rather provides problematizations and programmatics. As a general tendency, a shift from validity to validation and from assessing the individual step or part of the research towards increasing the transparency of the research process as a whole may be stated (see Chapter 20 for this).

Whether it makes sense or not to apply classical criteria to qualitative research is questioned, because 'the "notion of reality" in both streams of research is too heterogeneous' (Lüders and Reichertz 1986, p. 97). A similar reservation can already be found in Glaser and Strauss: they

> raise doubts as to the applicability of the canons of quantitative research as criteria for judging the credibility of substantive theory based on qualitative research. They suggest rather that criteria of judgement be based on generic elements of qualitative methods for collecting, analyzing and presenting data and for the way in which people read qualitative analyses. (1965b, p. 5)

From this scepticism, a series of attempts have been made over time to develop 'method-appropriate criteria' in order to replace criteria like validity and reliability. Approaches like triangulation and analytic induction, which have long been discussed, can be distinguished from more recent developments of new criteria.

TRIANGULATION

This key word is used to name the combination of different methods, study groups, local and temporal settings, and different theoretical perspectives in dealing with a phenomenon.

Denzin (1989b, pp. 237–41) distinguishes four types of triangulation. *Data triangulation* refers to the use of different data sources which should be distinguished from the use of different methods for producing data. As 'subtypes of data triangulation', Denzin makes a distinction between time, space and persons and suggests studying phenomena at different dates and places and from different persons. Thus he comes close to Glaser and Strauss's strategy of theoretical sampling. In both cases, the starting point is to purposively and systematically involve persons and study groups, local and temporal settings in the study.

As a second type of triangulation, Denzin names *investigator triangulation*. Different observers or interviewers are employed to detect or minimize biases resulting from the researcher as a person. This does not mean a simple division of labour or delegation of routine activities to assistants but rather a systematic comparison of different researchers' influences on the issue and the results of the research.

Theory triangulation is the third type in Denzin's systematology. The starting point is 'approaching data with multiple perspectives and hypotheses in mind . . . Various theoretical points of view could be placed side by side to assess their utility and power' (1989b, pp. 239–40). However, the purpose of the exercise is to extend the possibilities for producing knowledge.

As a fourth type, Denzin mentions *methodological triangulation*. Here again, two subtypes should be differentiated: within-method and between-method triangulation. An example for the first strategy is to use different subscales for measuring an item in a questionnaire, whereas an example for the second is to combine the questionnaire with a semi-structured interview.

Triangulation was first conceptualized as a strategy for validating results obtained with the individual methods. The focus, however, has shifted increasingly towards further enriching and completing knowledge and towards transgressing the (always limited) epistemological potentials of the individual method. Thus, Denzin now emphasizes that the 'triangulation of method, investigator, theory, and data remains the soundest strategy of theory construction' (1989b, p. 236).

An additional extension of this approach results from the systematic triangulation of the several theoretical perspectives (Flick 1992a) linked to the various qualitative methods – for example conducting interviews for reconstructing a subjective theory (e.g. about trust in counselling) and using conversation analysis to study how the subjective theory is mobilized and trust is invoked during counselling conversations. Thus, the orientation to the subject's point of view is linked to the perspective of producing social realities (see Chapter 2).

Triangulation may be used as an approach for further grounding the knowledge obtained with qualitative methods. Grounding here does not mean to assess results but to systematically extend and complete the possibilities of knowledge production. Triangulation is less a strategy for validating results and procedures than an alternative to validation (cf. Denzin and Lincoln 1994b; Flick 1992a) which increases scope, depth and consistency in methodological proceedings.

ANALYTIC INDUCTION

Analytic induction explicitly starts from a specific case. According to Bühler-Niederberger it can be characterized as follows:

> Analytic induction is a method of systematic interpretation of events, which includes the process of generating hypotheses as well as testing them. Its decisive instrument is to analyse the exception, the case which is deviant to the hypothesis. (1985, p. 476)

Box 18.1   Steps of analytic induction

1   A rough definition of the phenomenon to be explained is formulated.
2   A hypothetical explanation of the phenomenon is formulated.
3   A case is studied in the light of this hypothesis to find out whether the hypothesis corresponds to the facts in this case.
4   If the hypothesis is not correct, either the hypothesis is reformulated or the phenomenon to be explained is redefined in a way that excludes this case.
5   Practical certainty can be obtained after a small number of cases have been studied, but the discovery of each individual negative case by the researcher or another researcher refutes the explanation and calls for its reformulation.
6   Further cases are studied, the phenomenon is redefined and the hypotheses are reformulated until a universal relation is established; each negative case calls for redefinition or reformulation.

Source: adapted from Bühler-Niederberger 1985, p. 478

This procedure of looking for and analysing deviant cases is applied after a preliminary theory (hypothesis pattern or model etc.) has been developed. Analytic induction above all is oriented to examining theories and knowledge by analysing or integrating negative cases. The procedure of analytic induction includes the steps in Box 18.1.

As the 'analysis of negative cases', this concept is taken up by Lincoln and Guba (1985). There are links to questions of generalization of case studies (see below), but analytic induction has its own importance as a procedure for assessing analyses.

NEW CRITERIA

Since the middle of the 1980s, various attempts to develop new criteria for assessing qualitative research can be noted.

Trustworthiness, credibility, dependability

Lincoln and Guba (1985) propagate trustworthiness, credibility, dependability, transferability and confirmability as criteria for qualitative research.

The first of these criteria is considered to be the main one. They outline five strategies for increasing the credibility of qualitative research:

• activities for increasing the likelihood that credible results will be produced by a 'prolonged engagement' and 'persistent observation' in the field and the triangulation of different methods, researchers and data;

• 'peer debriefing': regular meetings with other people who are not involved in the research in order to disclose one's own blind spots and to discuss working hypotheses and results with them;

• the analysis of negative cases in the sense of analytic induction;

• appropriateness of the terms of reference of interpretations and their assessment;

• 'member checks' in the sense of communicative validation of data and interpretations with members of the fields under study.

Procedural dependability: auditing

Dependability is checked through a process of auditing, based on the procedure of audits in the domain of financing. Thus, an auditing trail is outlined in order to check procedural dependability in the following areas (see also Schwandt and Halpern 1988):

• the raw data, their collection and recording;

• data reduction and results of syntheses by summarizing, theoretical notes, memos etc., summaries, short descriptions of cases etc.;

• reconstructions of data and results of syntheses according to the structure of developed and used categories (themes, definitions, relationships), findings (interpretations and inferences) and the reports produced with their integration of concepts and links to the existing literature;

• process notes, i.e. methodological notes and decisions concerning the production of trustworthiness and credibility of findings;

• materials concerning intentions and dispositions like the concepts of research, personal notes and expectations of the participants;

• information about the development of the instruments including the pilot version and preliminary plans (see Lincoln and Guba 1985, pp. 320–7, 382–4).

This concept of auditing is discussed more generally in the framework of quality management (see Chapter 20 for this).

Thus, a series of starting points for producing and assessing the procedural rationality in the qualitative research process are outlined. In this way, proceedings and developments in the process of research can be revealed and assessed. In terms of the findings that have already been produced in a particular piece of research, the questions answered through the use of such an assessment procedure can more generally be summarized as follows, according to Huberman and Miles:

- Are findings grounded in the data? (Is sampling appropriate? Are data weighed correctly?)

- Are inferences logical? (Are analytic strategies applied correctly? Are alternative explanations accounted for?)

- Is the category structure appropriate?

- Can inquiry decisions and methodological shifts be justified? (Were sampling decisions linked to working hypotheses?)

- What is the degree of researcher bias (premature closure, unexplored data in the field notes, lack of search for negative cases, feelings of empathy)?

- What strategies were used for increasing credibility (second readers, feedback to informants, peer review, adequate time in the field)? (1994, p. 439)

Although the findings are the starting point for evaluating the research, an attempt is made to do this by combining a result-oriented view with a process-oriented procedure.

GENERALIZATION IN QUALITATIVE RESEARCH

Another aspect of grounding qualitative research is the generalization of concepts and relations that have been found in the sense of an analysis of the domains for which they may be applicable. At the same time, if the question is asked as to which considerations and steps have been applied in order to specify these domains, this is a starting point for the evaluation of such concepts. This is discussed as generalization. The central points to consider in such an evaluation are first the analyses themselves, and second the steps taken to arrive at more general statements. The problem of generalization in qualitative research is that its statements are often made for a certain context or specific cases and based on analyses of relations, conditions, processes etc. in them. This attachment to contexts often allows qualitative research a specific expressiveness. However, when attempts are made at generalizing the findings, this context link has to be given up in order to find out whether the findings are valid independently of and outside specific contexts. In highlighting this dilemma, Lincoln and Guba (1985) for example discuss this problem under the heading of 'the only generalization is: there is no generalization'. But, in terms of the 'transferability of findings from one context to another' and 'fittingness as to the degree of comparability of different contexts', they outline criteria and ways for judging the generalization of findings beyond a given context.

Correspondingly, various possibilities are discussed for mapping out the path from the case to the theory in a way which will allow the researcher to reach at least a certain generalization. A first step is to clarify which degree of generalization is sought and is possible to obtain with the concrete study, in order to derive appropriate claims for generalization. A second step is the cautious integration of different cases and contexts, in which the relations under study are empirically analysed. The generalizability of the results is often closely linked to the way the sampling is done. Theoretical sampling, for example, offers a way of designing the variation of the conditions under which a phenomenon is studied (Kleining 1982) as broadly as possible. The third step is the systematic comparison of the collected material. Here again, the procedures for developing grounded theories can be drawn on.

The Constant comparative method

In the process of developing theories, and additional to the method of 'theoretical sampling', Glaser (1969) suggests the 'constant comparative method' as a procedure for interpreting texts. It basically consists of four stages: '(1) comparing incidents applicable to each category, (2) integrating categories and their properties, (3) delimiting the theory, and (4) writing the theory' (1969, p. 220). For Glaser, the systematic circularity of this process is an essential feature: 'Although this method is a continuous growth process – each stage after a time transforms itself into the next – previous stages remain in operation throughout the analysis and provide continuous development to the following stage until the analysis is terminated' (1969, p. 220).

This procedure becomes a method of *constant* comparison when interpreters take care that they compare codings over and over again with codings and classifications that have already been made. Material which has already been coded is not finished with after its classification but is continually integrated into the further process of comparison.

Contrasting cases and ideal type analysis

The constant comparison is further developed and systematized in strategies of contrasting cases. The most consistent suggestions have been made by Gerhardt (1986b; 1988) based on the construction of ideal types which goes back to Max Weber (1904). This strategy includes the following steps: after reconstructing and contrasting the cases with one another, types are constructed; then 'pure' cases are tracked down; compared with these ideal types of processes, the understanding of the individual case can be made more systematic: after constructing further types, this process comes to an end by structure understanding, i.e. the understanding of relationships pointing beyond the individual case. The main instruments are the *minimal* comparison of cases which are as similar as possible, and the *maximal* comparison of cases which are as different as possible. They are compared for differences and correspondences. The comparisons become more and more concrete with respect to the range of issues included in the empirical material. The endpoints of this range receive special attention in the maximal comparison, whereas its centre is focused in the minimal comparison. In a similar way, Schütze (1983) suggests the minimal and maximal contrasting of individual cases for a comparative interpretation of narrative interviews. Haupert (1991) structures the cases according to 'reconstructive criteria' in order to develop a typology from such interviews. Biographies with maximal similarities are classified in groups which are labelled as empirical types in the further proceedings. For each type, specific everyday situations are distilled from the material and analysed across the individual cases.

Generalization in qualitative research is the gradual transfer of findings from case studies and their context to more general and abstract relations, for example a typology. The expressiveness of such patterns then can be specified for how far different theoretical and methodological perspectives on the issue – if possible by different researchers – have been triangulated and how negative cases were handled. The degree of generalization striven for in individual studies should also be taken into consideration. Then, the question of whether the intended level of generalization has been reached becomes a further criterion for evaluating results of qualitative research and of the process which led to them.

CRITERIA FOR EVALUATING THE BUILDING OF THEORIES

This connection of outcome and process-oriented considerations of the procedure of generalization in qualitative research is advanced one more step when the development of a grounded theory is the general aim of qualitative research. Corbin and Strauss (1990, p. 16) mention four points of departure for judging empirically grounded theories and the procedures that led to them. According to this suggestion, (1) the 'validity, reliability and credibility of the data', (2) the 'plausibility and the value of the theory itself', (3) the 'adequacy of the research process' which has 'generated, elaborated or tested the theory' and (4) the 'empirical grounding of the research findings' should be critically assessed. For evaluating the research process itself, they suggest seven criteria:

Criterion 1   How was the original sampling selected? On what grounds (selective sampling)?
Criterion 2   What major categories emerged?
Criterion 3   What were some of the events, incidents, actions, and so on that indicated some of these major categories?
Criterion 4   On the basis of what categories did theoretical sampling proceed? That is, how did theoretical formulations guide some of the data collection? After the theoretical sampling was carried out, how representative did these categories prove to be?
Criterion 5   What were some of the hypotheses pertaining to relations among categories? On what grounds were they formulated and tested?
Criterion 6   Were there instances when hypotheses did not hold up against what was actually seen? How were the discrepancies accounted for? How did they affect the hypotheses?
Criterion 7   How and why was the core category selected? Was the selection sudden or gradual, difficult or easy? On what grounds were the final analytic decisions made? How did extensive 'explanatory power' in relation to the phenomenon under study and 'relevance' . . . figure in decisions? (1990, p. 17).

Evaluating theory development ends up by answering the question of how far the concepts of the approach of Strauss – like theoretical sampling and the different forms of coding – were applied and whether this application corresponds with the methodological ideas of the authors. Thus efforts for evaluating proceedings and findings remain within the framework of their own system. A central role is given to the question of whether the findings and the theory are grounded in the empirical relations and data – if it is a grounded theory (building) or not. For an evaluation of the realization of this aim, Corbin and Strauss suggest criteria for answering the question of the empirical grounding of findings and theories:

Criterion 1   Are concepts generated? . . .
Criterion 2   Are the concepts systematically related? . . .
Criterion 3   Are there many conceptual linkages and are the categories well developed? Do the categories have conceptual density? . . .
Criterion 4   Is there much variation built into the theory? . . .
Criterion 5   Are broader conditions that affect the phenomenon under study built into its explanation? . . .
Criterion 6   Has 'process' been taken into account? . . .
Criterion 7   Do the theoretical findings seem significant and to what extent? (pp. 17–18)

The point of reference, here again, is the procedure formulated by the authors and whether it has been applied or not. Thus, the methodology of Strauss becomes more formalized. Its evaluation becomes more a formal one: were the concepts applied correctly? The authors themselves see this danger and therefore they included the seventh criterion of relevance in their list. They emphasize that a formal application of the procedures of grounded theory building does not necessarily make for 'good research'.

Box 18.2   Criteria for theory development in qualitative research

1   The degree to which generic/formal theory is produced.
2   The degree of development of the theory.
3   The novelty of the claims made.
4   The consistency of the claims with empirical observations, and the inclusion of representative examples of the latter in the report.
5   The credibility of the account to readers and/or those studied.
6   The extent to which findings are transferable to other settings.
7   The reflexivity of the account: the degree to which the effects on the findings of the researcher and of the research settings employed are assessed and/or the amount of information about the research process that is provided to readers.

Source: Hammersley 1992, p. 64

Points of reference like the originality of the results from the viewpoint of a potential reader, the relevance of the question and the relevance of the findings for the fields under study, or even for different fields, do not play any role here.[4]

Such aspects, however, are included in the criteria suggested by Hammersley (1992, p. 64) as a synopsis of various approaches for evaluating theories developed from empirical field studies (Box 18.2). These criteria are specific to the evaluation of qualitative research and its procedures, methods and results, and they start from theory building as one feature of qualitative research. The procedure which led to the theory, the degree of development of the theory which is the result of this process, and finally the transferability of the theory to other fields and back into the studied context, become central aspects of evaluating all research.

OLD OR NEW CRITERIA: NEW ANSWERS TO OLD QUESTIONS?

The approaches to grounding qualitative research discussed here provide a methodical approach to analysing understanding as an epistemological principle. Criteria are defined which serve to judge the appropriateness of the procedures which were applied. Central questions are how appropriately each case (whether a subject or a field) has been reconstructed, with how much openness it was approached, and what controls have been installed in the research process in order to assess this openness. One starting point is to problematize the construction of social realities in the field under study and in the research process. The decisive question, however, is whose constructions were addressed and were successful in the process of knowledge production and in the formulation of the results – those of the researcher, or those met in the studied field. Grounding qualitative research becomes a question of analysing the research as process. After discussing the alternatives mentioned, the impression remains that both strategies – the application of traditional criteria and the development of new, specific criteria – have featured in recent discussions and that neither has yet given a really satisfactory answer to the problem of grounding qualitative research.

The equation or connection of new and old criteria by Miles and Huberman (1994, p. 278) outlines an interesting perspective for structuring this field:

- objectivity/confirmability;

- reliability/dependability/auditability;

- internal validity/credibility/authenticity;

- external validity/transferability/fittingness;

- utilization/application/action orientation.

But at the same time this equation makes clear that attempts to reformulate criteria for qualitative research did not really lead to new solutions. Rather, the problems with traditional criteria derived from different backgrounds have to be discussed for the new criteria as well.

NOTES

1 For a while, communicative validation was also discussed for the interpretation of texts (e.g. by Heinze 1987). Not only due to the ethical problems which arise in the confrontation of interviewees with interpretations of their statements (see Köckeis-Stangl 1982), this notion of communicative validation has lost its importance.

2 One problem in approaches like Lather's is that questions and concepts of postmodernity are picked up with great enthusiasm. However, second-hand quotations predominate and the treatment of the concepts remains more or less oriented to the shells of the words. This impression is also given in several of the contibutions to Denzin and Lincoln (1994a) especially about the grounding of qualitative research. Thus more questions are raised than ways are mapped for treating problems linked to specifying validity.

3 Another aspect, which only can be mentioned here, is that research wants to produce knowledge which goes beyond what is immediately accessible for everyday reflection (for more details on this point see Flick 1987, p. 255).

4 This question is addressed less to Strauss's concept of research than to the attempts of evaluating it in Corbin and Strauss (1990).

FURTHER READING

Reliability

These texts give good overviews of the problematics of reliability in qualitative research.

Kirk, J.L., Miller, M. (1986), *Reliability and Validity in Qualitative Research*. Beverley Hills, CA: Sage.

Silverman, D. (1993), *Interpreting Qualitative Data: Methods for Analysing Talk, Text and Interaction*. London: Sage.

Validity

These texts give good overviews of the problematics of validity in qualitative research.

Hammersley, M. (1990), *Reading Ethnographic Research: A Critical Guide*. London: Longman.

Hammersley, M. (1992), *What's Wrong with Ethnography?* London: Routledge.

Kvale, S. (ed.) (1989), *Issues of Validity in Qualitative Research*. Lund: Studentlitteratur.

Triangulation

These texts discuss the strategy of triangulation in qualitative research.

Denzin, N.K. (1989b), *The Research Act* (3rd edn). Englewood Cliffs, NJ: Prentice-Hall.

Flick, U. (1992a), Triangulation Revisited: Strategy of or Alternative to Validation of Qualitative Data. *Journal for the Theory of Social Behavior*, 22, pp. 175–97.

New criteria

In this text, the authors most consistently try to develop new criteria for qualitative research.

Lincoln, Y.S., Guba, E.G. (1985), *Naturalistic Inquiry*. London: Sage.

Generalization

This is still the classic text on generalization in qualitative research.

Glaser, B.G. (1969), The Constant Comparative Method of Qualitative Analysis. In: McCall, G.J., Simmons, J.L. (eds), *Issues in Participant Observation*. Reading, MA: Addison-Wesley.

Theory evaluation

These two references give a good overview of how to evaluate theories grounded in and resulting from qualitative research.

Corbin, J., Strauss, A. (1990), Grounded Theory Research: Procedures, Canons and Evaluative Criteria. *Qualitative Sociology*, 13, pp. 3–21.

Hammersley, M. (1992), *What's Wrong with Ethnography?* London: Routledge.

WRITING QUALITATIVE RESEARCH

The question of how to display research findings and proceedings has come to the fore in qualitative research – especially in ethnography – since the middle of the 1980s. In the social sciences, text is not only an instrument for documenting data and a basis for interpretation and thus an epistemological instrument, but also and above all an instrument of mediating and communicating findings and knowledge. Sometimes, writing is even seen as the core of social science:

> To do social science means mainly to produce texts . . . Research experiences have to be transformed into texts and to be understood on the basis of texts. A research process has findings only when and as far as these can be found in a report, no matter whether and which experiences were made by those who were involved in the research. The observability and practical objectivity of social science phenomena is constituted in texts and nowhere else. (Wolff 1987, p. 333)

In this context, writing becomes relevant in qualitative research in three respects: for presenting the findings of a project; as a starting point for evaluating the proceedings which led to them and thus the results themselves; and finally as a point of departure for reflexive considerations about the overall status of research altogether.

PRAGMATIC FUNCTION OF WRITING: PRESENTATION
OF RESULTS

The various alternatives for presenting findings can be located between two poles. At one end, there is the aim of developing a theory from the data and interpretations according to the model of Strauss (1987). At the other end are the 'tales from the field' (van Maanen 1988), which are intended to illustrate the relations the researcher met.

Theories as a form of presentation

In the previous chapter, criteria for judging theories in the sense of Strauss (1987) were discussed. The presentation of such a theory requires, according to Strauss and Corbin:

> (1) A clear analytic story. (2) Writing on a conceptual level, with description kept secondary. (3) The clear specification of relationships among categories, with levels of conceptualization also kept clear. (4) The specification of variations and their relevant conditions, consequences, and so forth, including the broader ones. (1990, p. 229)

In order to attain these goals, the authors suggest as a first step that the researcher outlines a logical draft of the theory. In this draft the analytic logic of the story is developed and the contours of the theory are noted. A clear summary of the central draft of the theory should be the first part of this draft. As a third step, the authors suggest that a visual presentation of the 'architecture' of the central draft is made (1990, pp. 230–1). They thus lay the main stress in the presentation on clarifying the central concepts and lines of the developed theory. A visualization for example in the form of concept networks, trajectories etc. is a way of presenting the theory in a concise form. In order to avoid falling into the trap of wanting to write the perfect manuscript (which is never finished), Strauss and Corbin suggest letting things go at the right moment and accepting a certain degree of imperfection in the theory and presentation (1990, pp. 235–6). Finally, they suggest taking the potential readership of the manuscript into account and formulating the text for the target readership. The suggestions of Lofland (1974) for presenting findings in the form of theories head in a similar direction. He mentions as criteria for writing the same criteria for evaluating such reports, namely ensuring that:

> (1) The report was organized by means of a *generic* conceptual framework; (2) the generic framework employed was *novel*; (3) the framework was *elaborated* or developed in and through the report; (4) the framework was *eventful* in the sense of being abundantly documented with qualitative data; (5) the framework was interpenetrated with the empirical materials. (1974, p. 102)

Tales from the field

Van Maanen (1988) distinguishes three basic forms of presenting research findings and processes in ethnographic studies, which can be transferred to other forms of qualitative research.

Realist tales are characterized by four conventions. First, the author is absent from the text: observations are reported as facts or documented by using quotations from statements or interviews. Interpretations are not formulated as subjective formulations. Second, emphasis in the presentation is laid on the typical forms of what is studied. Therefore, many details are analysed and presented. Third, the viewpoints of the members of a field or of interviewees are emphasized in the presentation: how did they experience their own life in its course? What is health for the interviewees? Finally, presentations may seek to give the impression of 'interpretive omnipotence' (1988, p. 51). The interpretation does not stop at subjective viewpoints but goes beyond them by various and far-reaching interpretations. The author demonstrates that he or she is able to provide a grounded interpretation. The subject's statements for example are transferred theoretically to a more general level, maybe by using 'experience-distant concepts' (Geertz) taken from social science literature for expressing relations. One example of this form of interpretive omnipotence is the presentation of findings after applying objective hermeneutics (see Chapter 16), in which the real causes for activities are sought in the elaborated structures far beyond the acting subject (see Reichertz 1988 on this as well).

Confessional tales, on the other hand, are characterized by a personalized authorship and authority. Here, the author expresses the role that he or she played in what was observed, in his or her interpretations and also in the formulations that are used. The author's viewpoints are treated as an issue in the presentation as well as problems, breakdowns, mistakes etc. (van Maanen 1988, p. 79) in the field. Nevertheless, it is attempted to present one's own findings as grounded in the issue that was studied. Naturalness in the presentation is one means of creating the impression of 'a fieldworker and a culture finding each other and, despite some initial spats and misunderstandings, in the end making a match' (1988, p. 79). The result is a mixture of descriptions of the studied object and the experiences made in studying it. An example of this form of presentation is the description of entering the field as a learning process given by Lau and Wolff (1983) or descriptions of failing to successfully enter the field (Kroner and Wolff 1986).

Impressionist tales are written in the form of dramatic recall:

> Events are recounted roughly in the order in which they are said to have occurred and carry with them all the odds and ends that are associated with the remembered events. The idea is to draw an audience into an unfamiliar story world and to allow it, as far as possible, to see, hear, and feel as the fieldworker saw, heard, and felt. Such tales seek to imaginatively place the audience in the fieldwork situation. (van Maanen 1988, p. 103)

The knowledge in the report is presented step by step in a fragmentary way. Narratives are often chosen as a form of presentation. The aim is to maintain the tension for the readers and to convey consistency and credibility. But impressionist reports are never completely finished. Their meaning is further elaborated in the contact with the reader (1988, p. 120). A good example is the presentation of the Balinese cockfight of Geertz (1973).

Other forms are the *critical story*, which seeks to bring social issues to the reader's attention, and *formal stories*, which aim rather at the presentation of theoretical relationships.

In these forms of reports, different emphases are placed on findings and processes. Sometimes, these forms of reports complement each other, e.g. initially a realistic tale is given and only in a second publication is provided a version of the field contact which is designed more as a confession. On the other hand, conventions of writing ethnographic reports have changed, as van Maanen documents for his own styles of writing: today in general fewer realist and more impressionist or confessional tales are published. This change has occurred in two respects: more works are not only written in these styles, but also accepted for publication. There is a shift from realist tales to confessions and also an increasing awareness that there exists neither the perfect theory nor the perfect report about it. Thus, the dimension of partial failure and the limits of one's own knowledge should be taken into account as elements of the findings which are worthy of presentation.[1]

The ability to write and how to learn it

With regard to the presentation of findings – whether as theory or as story – attention will (have to) increasingly turn to the question of writing and writing competencies in the context of qualitative research. Where findings cannot be briefly reduced to numbers, to a statistical distribution or to tables, considerations like Becker's (1986b) about writing as an (in-)competence of social scientists become particularly relevant. The background of Becker's considerations is his own experience with seminars on writing aimed especially for social scientists. Becker notes a certain fear in social scientists of taking one's own position which for him is one reason for the limited persuasiveness of texts in social sciences: 'We write that way because we fear that others will catch us in obvious error if we do anything else, and laugh at us. Better to say something innocuous but safe than something bold you might not be able defend against criticism' (1986b, pp. 8–9).

Considerations about grounding social science findings by systematically integrating negative cases and by contrasting extremely different cases (see the previous chapter) are particularly helpful here. They inspire a more positive handling of findings and results, which encourages the researcher to write and to present them more unambiguously and concretely: 'Bullshit qualifications, making your statements fuzzy, ignore the philosophical and methodological tradition which holds that making generalizations in a strong universal form identifies negative evidence which can be used to improve them' (1986b, p. 10).

According to Becker, the fact that the mode of presentation attracts more attention in every form of scientific knowledge production should lead to considering the potential reader as a central focus in the design of the text in which the research is presented. Findings and results never exist in pure form and are never communicable in this form, but are at least co-determined by their potential readership. To actively use this as a resource in shaping social science texts is another suggestion Becker makes (not only for the participants in his writing seminars):

> Making your work clearer involves considerations of audience. Who is it supposed to be clearer to? Who will read what you write? What do they have to know so that they will not misread or find what you say obscure or unintelligible? You will write one way for the people you work with closely on a joint project, another way for professional colleagues in other specialities and disciplines, and differently yet for the 'intelligent layman'. (1986b, p. 18)

Questions of how to present findings and processes will increasingly influence methodological discussions in qualitative research, if the trend towards a textual science continues. Texts (including those in social sciences) seek to and indeed do design a certain version of the world (according to Goodman 1978) and seek to persuade with this version other scientists in particular and (potential) readers more generally. This persuasion will indeed be achieved not only by the 'how' of the presentation but also by the 'what' in that presented. However, the function and effect of social science texts depend on taking the following experience into account: 'We talked about scientific writing as a form of rhetoric, meant to persuade, and which forms of persuasion the scientific community considered okay and which illegitimate' (Becker 1986b, p. 15). Correspondingly, it is not only the technique of writing which has attracted more attention recently. Both the constructive and interpretive processes in producing and empirically reworking texts, and the questions of grounding which have to be directed to text and construction, version and interpretation, findings and results, have come to the fore.[2]

LEGITIMIZING FUNCTION OF WRITING

That the communication of social science knowledge is essentially dependent on the forms in which it is presented has been neglected for a long time. Recently, however, this issue has been brought to the fore in methodological discussions within different areas of the social sciences, as Bude makes clear:

> One is made aware that scientific knowledge is always presented scientific knowledge. And the consequence is that a 'logic of presentation' has to be considered as well as a 'logic of research'. How researchers' constitution of experiences is linked to the way those experiences are saved in presentations has only begun to become an issue for reflection and research. (1989, p. 527).

As mentioned above, the background to these considerations is the methodological discussions in different areas of the social sciences: considerations in historical sciences (Ginzburg 1990; Koselleck 1990) and the thoughts of Clifford Geertz (1988) about the role of the 'anthropologist as author'. The latter provides less an image of the studied culture *per se* than a specific presentation of this culture, which is clearly marked by his or her style of writing. Thus Geertz deals with four classic researchers in anthropology (Malinowski, Evans-Pritchard, Lévi-Strauss, Benedict) as four classic authors of anthropological texts and regards their texts from a literary viewpoint. In his considerations, the discussion that takes place in modern anthropology about the 'crisis of ethnographic representation' plays a central role.[3] In this discussion, the problems with traditional understandings of representation, which were mentioned in Chapter 3, are taken up and focused on the problem of the representation of the other (i.e. here, the other culture): 'The turn towards the text discloses a dimension in the scientific process of knowledge, which remained underexposed up to now. Where knowledge is thematized as the production of text, as the transcription of discourse and practice, the conditions of possibility for discussing ethnographic practices of representation are created' (Fuchs and Berg 1993, p. 64). In the ethnography of foreign and faraway cultures and the attempt to make them understandable to readers who do not have direct experience of them, the problem of presentation may be evident. However, in researchers' attempts to make a certain everyday life, a biography, an institutional milieu from their own cultural context comprehensible to readers, the problem of presentation, though less obvious, is equally relevant: 'Ethnography always has to struggle with the misrelation of limited personal experience, on which the process of knowledge is based, and the claim for an authoritative knowledge about a whole culture, which it makes with its product, i.e. the texts' (1993, p. 73).

As soon as social science adopts this critical re-examination of the conditions of the production of scientific texts and of their significance for what is described, explained or narrated in these texts,[4] the discussion about the appropriate form of displaying its findings is entered into. Writing then is not only a part of the research process[5] but also a method of research (Richardson 1994) which, like other methods, is subject to the changes in historical and scientific contexts. Postmodernity has especially influenced scientific writing in the field of qualitative research in a lasting way and has questioned it in its self-evidence. Special importance is

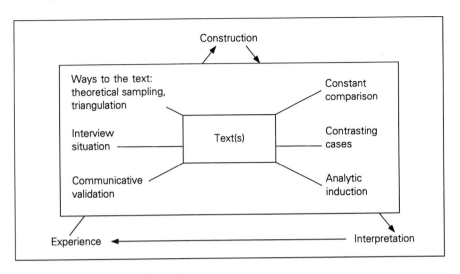

FIGURE 19.1 *Grounding the text*

attributed to writing in the research process, because the 'new criteria' for assessing qualitative research as a whole, discussed in the previous chapter, begin from the ways in which processes and results are displayed. Where trustworthiness and credibility replace reliability and validity of data and findings as the central criteria (e.g. in Lincoln and Guba 1985), the problem of grounding is transferred to the level of the writing and reporting:

> The research report with its presentation of and reflection on the methodo-
> logical proceedings, with all its narratives about access to and the activities in
> the field, with its documentations of various materials, with its transcribed
> observations and conversations, interpretations and theoretical inferences is
> the only basis for answering the question of the quality of the investigation.
> (Lüders 1995, p. 325)

Thus, if the findings and procedures of scientific research are mainly judged according to their presentation and to the stylistic and other qualities of the report or article, the border between science and (fine) literature becomes blurred. In each case, the text is brought to the fore of the discussion about the grounding of qualitative research. In addition to the discussions in Chapter 3 (see Figure 3.2), the text becomes the central element for judging the translation of experiences into constructions and interpretations. The credibility of the presentation can be specified in the suggestions for realizing the criteria for grounding qualitative research, which were treated in the previous chapter: from communicative validation across the analysis of the interview situation, from a consequent application of theoretical sampling and of triangulation of methods and perspectives to the methodological starting points for generalization of findings by the constant comparison and contrasting of cases, to the analysis of negative cases (see Figure 19.1).

Reichertz (1992) goes one step beyond a text-centred treatment of credibility. He makes it clear that this form of persuasion concerning credibility is produced not only in the text but also in the interaction of author, text and reader:

> The decisive point, however, is the attitude which is expressed in the text, with which the ethnographer turns toward his own interpretations and those of his colleagues in order to relate them to each other according to the needs of the individual case. It is not the way of accounting claimed for in the writing, which is relevant for the reader, but the attitude of accounting, which is shown in the text, which of course always has to use semiotic means, and these are means which are sensitive to cheating. (1992, p. 346)

REFLEXIVE FUNCTION OF WRITING

Research, then, includes not only the interaction between the researcher and the issue, but also the interaction between the researcher and his or her potential readers, for whom he or she finally writes his or her presentation. This relationship – as well as the text produced for this purpose and the writing linked to it – is determined in multiple ways: 'contextually . . . rhetorically . . . institutionally . . . generically . . . politically . . . historically' (Clifford 1986, p. 6).

More generally, such considerations push the relationship between author, text and readers and the conditions of producing scientific texts to the fore and in front of the relationship between researcher and issue, which is only documented in the text in summary form. A similar reflection can be noted for the production of research in (natural) science (see Knorr-Cetina 1981). In this case, social science (as it always did) is dealing with the 'other' – that is, concretely the (natural) scientists and their laboratories and the practices involved in the manufacturing of knowledge. The discussion about writing in ethnography and more generally in qualitative research, however, has led to self-reflection in social science research. Here, the role and the self-awareness of the qualitative researcher is increasingly questioned: 'The qualitative researcher is not an objective, authoritative, politically neutral observer standing outside and above the text' (Bruner 1993, quoted in Lincoln and Denzin 1994, p. 576).

This leads to the question of what validity can be claimed for what is presented, given that the form of presentation used by the author essentially determines what is presented and how. This question is discussed under the heading of the authority of the text:

> By the *authority of the text* we reference the claim any text makes to being accurate, true, and complete. Is a text, that is, faithful to the context and the individuals it is supposed to represent? Does the text have the right to assert

that it is a report to the larger world that addresses not only the researcher's interests, but also the interests of those studied? (1994, p. 578)

Here, questions about the claims of qualitative research arise – claims for an appropriate analysis and presentation of the contexts and persons that were studied and their legitimacy. The questioning of the authority of the text leads to a questioning of the authority and legitimacy of the research altogether. But, in such discussions, the original motive for the research – to produce knowledge about contexts of living and subjective points of view and their contexts – is in danger of getting lost in an endless discourse of self-referentiality.[6]

DISSOLUTION OF SCIENCE INTO STYLES OF WRITING?

It is ironic that just as qualitative research has – with difficulties but successfully – achieved its place amongst the sciences, it now faces the danger of getting lost in endless debates about the role and problems of writing. Perhaps it does make sense to consider the writing styles of established ethnographers as authors (Geertz 1988 on Lévi-Strauss and others; Wolff 1992 again on Geertz), in order to differentiate the style of writing in ethnography from that in other genres. Nevertheless, the claim made by qualitative research – for doing science, for specifying the borders with other genres of presentation, but also for marking the borders of a good, successful study from another, less successful or even failed study – should not be given up. In favouring the discussion about writing in the research, one must neither give up the discussion about quality in research – and not only that of a good and credible text – nor reduce the emphasis on research practice.

NOTES

1 How far Bude's (1989) suggestion of using 'the essay as a form of presenting social science knowledge' may map a path in this context awaits further clarification. The same is the case for the profit and speciality of sociological narratives discussed by the same author in a different context (Bude 1993).
2 This impression results not only from the publications about ethnography, but more generally in reading the handbook edited by Denzin and Lincoln (1994a) which is very strongly marked by the ongoing discussions about writing ethnographies and culture in times of postmodernity.
3 This discussion is documented in great detail in Berg and Fuchs (1993) and Clifford and Marcus (1986).

4 That it should do this has been stated more generally by René König: 'The ideas of the "foreign" or of the "foreign distance", which are fundamental for the ethnographer's work, are relevant for the sociologist as well who studies his or her own reality; because the idea that he or she as a member of the given social reality has a substantial "foreknowledge" at hand, which can be elaborated by the corresponding presentation as scientific knowledge, is nowadays everything other than the case' (1984, p. 23).

5 For this aspect, beyond Becker (1986b), see also Wolcott (1990b) and Richardson (1990).

6 Lincoln and Denzin see a similar danger: 'Endless self-referential criticisms by poststructuralists can produce mountains of texts with few referents to concrete human experience' (1994, p. 577).

FURTHER READING

These texts go further into the details of the problems mentioned here concerning the different functions of writing in qualitative research.

Becker, H.S. (1986b), *Writing for Social Scientists*. Chicago: University of Chicago Press.

Clifford, J., Marcus, G.E. (eds) (1986), *Writing Culture: The Poetics and Politics of Ethnography*. Berkeley, CA: University of California Press.

Geertz, C. (1988), *The Anthropologist as Author*. Stanford, CA: Stanford University Press.

Van Maanen, J. (1988), *Tales of the Field: On Writing Ethnography*. Chicago: University of Chicago Press.

$$\boxed{20}$$

PERSPECTIVES

In this final chapter, some perspectives and trends will be outlined which, it can be reasonably expected, will provide the impetus for qualitative research in forthcoming years. These are trends whose realization has already begun (the computer entering qualitative research), which have been prevalent for a long time but have not been realized in a satisfactory way (the combination with quantitative research), which will make possible new forms of assessing the quality of research (process evaluation and quality management), or which call to mind traditional fields of tension in qualitative research (between methods and attitude) and their relevance for ways of teaching the subject.

COMPUTERS IN QUALITATIVE RESEARCH

That qualitative research is undergoing a technological change and that this is influencing the essential character of qualitative research has already become clear in the discussion about new technologies of recording and the new forms of data they have made possible for the first time (see Chapter 14). In the last ten years, a potentially far-reaching technological change has begun in the analysis of data, which is linked to the introduction of computers in qualitative research. Here, the general changes in working patterns in the social sciences brought about by the personal computer and word processing may be noted (see Flick 1996 on this), but it is also important to note the specific developments in and for qualitative research. If these developments become more established than they have up to now, considerable changes in qualitative research practice will probably result. In the meantime, initial overviews of the permanently developing market have been published. Some of them have been written from the program developer's point of view (Richards and Richards 1994) and some from that of the user (Weitzman and Miles 1995).

Ways of using computers in qualitative research

Generally speaking, the following ways of using computers and software in the context of qualitative research can be noted:

1 Making notes in the field.
2 Writing up or transcribing field notes.
3 Editing: correcting, extending or revising field notes.
4 Coding: attaching key words or tags to segments of text to permit later retrieval.
5 Storage: keeping text in an organized database.
6 Search and retrieval: locating relevant segments of text and making them available for inspection.
7 Data 'linking': connecting relevant data segments with each other, forming categories, clusters or networks of information.
8 Memoing: writing reflective commentaries on some aspect of the data, as a basis for deeper analysis.
9 Content analysis: counting frequencies, sequence or locations of words and phrases.
10 Data display: placing selected or reduced data in a condensed, organized format, such as a matrix or network, for inspection.
11 Conclusion drawing and verification: aiding the analyst to interpret displayed data and to test or confirm findings.
12 Theory building: developing systematic, conceptually coherent explanations of findings; testing hypotheses.
13 Graphic mapping: creating diagrams that depict findings or theories.
14 Preparing interim and final reports. (Miles and Huberman 1994, p. 44)

Some other aspects could be added to this list, most notably the transcription of interviews, the writing of a research diary, communication with other researchers on computer networks, e-mail, the Internet and so on, and writing articles about one's own research or its methods. Most of these activities can be more or less comfortably carried out with the usual word processors (1, 2, 3, 8, 14, and with the skilful use of costly and powerful programs also 4, 6, 9: cf. Weitzman and Miles 1995, p. 5). Thus the first way of using computers has been outlined: the simple and straightforward use of word processors and/or the creative use of their programs to perform specific functions. If their options are not sufficient, however, the researcher may turn to existing software for specific ends or even develop his or her own program. Many of the programs available today have been created in this way – starting from specific necessities in a concrete research project. Some programs have had their range of options extended in a way which allows them to be used for research questions and data sorts other than those originally intended.

Special programs for analysing qualitative data

As a result of these developments around 25 programs are now available which have been developed especially for analysing qualitative data. However, accompanying this there has been a lack of clarity as to the exact nature of the supply and range of products available on the market. Additionally, all these programs are subject to specific limitations resulting from their original developmental context and purpose and the emphases of the program.

Leading questions for analysing programs

For an initial stocktaking (Flick 1991a) of the programs available at that time, the leading questions in Box 20.1 were used for assessing computer programs for qualitative research (Flick 1991c, p. 800). Although in the meantime more developed programs have become available, these questions should still be asked before using them. A more recent orientation review has been provided by Weitzman and Miles (1995), who give some hints for the decision for or against the use of computers for the assistance of qualitative analyses and for specific programs and also provide a criteria based test and comparison of 24 programs.

Key questions before deciding on a program

Weitzman and Miles (1995, pp. 7–9) start from a series of key questions which should be asked before deciding on a program or on using computers generally:

- What kind of computer user is given? Here, they give criteria for four levels (from the beginner to the hacker). Furthermore, the question arises as to which kind of computer is to be used or is already used (PC or Apple?). Finally, they raise the question of the researcher's own experience with qualitative research: beginners in qualitative research as well as beginners in using computers are usually over-challenged by

Box 20.1   Leading questions for assessing computer programs in qualitative research

- *Data-related questions* For which kind of data was the program conceived? For which data can it be used beyond these original data? For which data should it not be used?
- *Activity-related questions* Which activities can be carried out with this program, and which should not be carried out with it?
- *Process-related questions* How did the program influence the handling of data and the part played by the researcher or interpreter according to the experiences had up to now? Which new options did it open? What has become more difficult or laborious in the process of interpretation owing to the program?
- *Technical questions* What are the necessary conditions in the hardware (type of computer, RAM, hard disk, graphics card, screen etc.) or in the software (systems software, other programs needed?) or in networking options to other programs (SPSS, word processors, databases)?
- *Competence-related questions* Which specific and above all technical skills does the program require from the user (programming skills, perhaps in specific programming languages etc.)?

Source: Flick 1991c, p. 800

the more demanding programs and the options they offer and by the decision about which program to use.

- Is the decision to use a program made for a concrete research project or for general research use over the coming years? Two questions are linked to this point. First, what is the balance of the costs in training with the program and maybe with the computer and the preparation of the data for the computer against the benefits of the time that will be saved and the new options provided by the use of the computer, especially if only a very limited amount of data is to be analysed with the computer? Second, how far is the program selected according to the current conditions (the kind of data, the research question etc.) and how far with respect to later, perhaps more complex studies?

- What kind of data and project are given: one or more data sources; case or comparative study; structured or open data; uniform or various inputs of data; size of the databases?

- What kind of analysis is planned: exploratory or confirming; pre-defined coding scheme or one to be developed; multiple or simple coding; one passage through the data or multi-step analysis; delicacy of the analyses; interest in the context of the data; how the data are to be presented; only qualitative or also numeric analyses?

- How important is the proximity of the data in the process of analysing them? Should the text which is interpreted always be accessible (on the screen) or only the categories etc.?

- Limits of costs: is it affordable to buy the program and the computers needed to use it?

Another question should be added: whether the effort needed to become familiar with computers and the program can be afforded in general and at that moment. A researcher helplessly facing mountains of data shortly before the funding of a project ends, and furthermore who is not very experienced in using computers, will not be saved by a computer program for analysing data – at least not in the short run.

Types of programs

The programs available at the moment can be summarized into various types (Richards and Richards 1994; Weitzman and Miles 1995):

- Word processors, which allow one not only to write but also to edit texts, and to search for words or word sequences at least in a limited way.

- Text retrieval programs, which specifically allow one to search, summarize, list etc. certain word sequences.

- Text administration programs for administering, searching, sorting and ordering text passages.

- Code-and-retrieve programs for splitting the text into segments to which codes are assigned, and for retrieving or listing all segments of the text which were marked with each code. Marking, ordering, sorting and linking texts and codes is supported and both text and code are presented and administered together.

- Code based theory building: additionally, these programs support theory building by supporting steps and operations at the level of the text (attachment of one or more passages to a code) but also at the conceptual level (relations between codes, super- and subcategories, networks of categories), always going back to the attached text passages. In some programs, more or less powerful graphic editors are included and it is possible to integrate video data.

- Conceptual networking is possible in the last group, which offer extensive options for developing and presenting conceptual networks and networks of categories, and various ways to visualize relations among the various parts of the network.

For all these options offered by the different programs, it should be considered that it is of course not the programs which develop the theory – just as it is not the word processor that writes an article. Both support these activities by simplifying, facilitating, and accelerating certain steps and making new ways of presentation possible.

An example: ATLAS/ti

This program was developed by Muhr (1991; 1994) in a research project at the Technical University of Berlin (Böhm et al. 1994). It is based on the approach of grounded theory and theoretical coding according to Strauss (1987; see Chapter 15). Weitzman and Miles file this program[1] in their highest category, but above all in the group of the 'code based theory builders'. It supports operations on the textual and the conceptual level (see above). A 'hermeneutic unit' is formed on the screen that unifies the primary text (e.g. the interview to interpret) and the interpretations or codings related to it. The program shows the primary text with all codes attached to it and comments in different windows on the screen. It offers some functions, which are present on the screen in the form of symbols (retrieval, copy, cut, coding, networking etc.).

Apart from the retrieval of sequences of words in the text and the attachment of codes, the presentation of codes and categories in conceptual networks is helpful. The relation to the passage to which the categories and supercategories are linked is maintained and can be presented immediately on the screen. Codings can be listed on the screen or printed. Interfaces to SPSS and other programs are integrated. Furthermore it is possible for different authors to work on the same text on different computers. The evaluation of the program by Weitzmann and Miles (1995, p. 228) is extremely positive.

Questions and problems in using computers in qualitative research

Up to now, the utilization of programs which were developed specially for analysing qualitative data is still rather limited, whereas word processors have become indispensable in the research process. One reason that analytic programs have not become more established is that they are relatively new. Some programs have recently passed from the phase of development into a phase of being more or less manageable, reliable and user-friendly in their application. Alternatively, as with the pioneering programs for computer-aided content analysis on big machines in computer centres, they are already hopelessly outdated. However, potential users are still tied to computers, even though all the modern programs run on PCs, other desktop computers or laptops. This leads to problems of access (not every qualitative researcher can be animated by computers) and of accessibility (as well as the program, the system and the machine itself has to be learnt, managed and used). Accessibility should be understood in a local and temporal sense as well: you have to conduct analyses on the computer at the places and times it is available (see Flick 1994b).

Another question is the usefulness of computer programs for the different approaches of interpretation. For sequential analyses, the options in the different programs are much less relevant than in coding and categorizing approaches. If computers increasingly enter the domain of text interpretation, and if in the long run it becomes more and more normal to use them, the question has to be asked whether this has an impact on those procedures in the interpretation of data which are less or not at all compatible with computer programs. In the worst case, the spread of computers in this domain might have the consequence that certain alternatives in the methodological range disappear owing to their incompatibility with the computer (program). Note how today tape recordings are widely used for documenting qualitative data, and sometimes they are regarded as a precondition for qualitative research in general. Those phenomena and procedures that escape this kind of recording (e.g. during participant observation) may then be regarded as secondary (e.g. in the textbook of Bohnsack 1991). Similarly, Richards and Richards, developers of one of the leading programs (NUD•IST), state: 'The computer method can have dramatic implications for the research process and outcomes, from unacceptable restrictions on analysis to unexpected opening out of possibilities' (1994, p. 445).

Computers will become established in qualitative research like anywhere else. One will have to wait to see how this changes research. Perhaps the use of computers will lead to new ways of documenting procedures and to a higher transparency in the research process. Thus it may contribute to increasing the grounding of qualitative interpretations.

QUALITATIVE AND QUANTITATIVE RESEARCH

In the beginning, qualitative methods were often developed in the context of a critique of quantitative methods and research strategies (see Kohli 1978 for the example of interviewing, and more generally Cicourel 1964). The debates about the 'right' understanding of science are not settled yet (see Becker 1996), but in both domains a broad research practice has developed which speaks for itself, independent of the fact that there is good and bad research on both sides. On the other hand the combination of both strategies has crystallized as a perspective, which is discussed and practised in various forms.

Appropriateness of the methods as a point of reference

The debate about qualitative and quantitative research which was originally oriented to epistemological and philosophical standpoints (for overviews see Becker 1996; Bryman 1988) has increasingly moved towards questions of research practice such as the appropriateness of each approach. Wilson states for the relation of both methodological traditions: 'qualitative and quantitative approaches are complementary rather than competitive methods . . . [and the] use of a particular method . . . must rather be based on the nature of the actual research problem at hand' (1982, p. 58). Authors like McKinlay (1993; 1995) and Baum (1995) argue in a similar direction in the field of public health research. The suggestion is that rather than fundamental considerations determining the decision for or against qualitative or quantitative methods, this decision should be determined by the appropriateness of the method to the issue under study and the research questions.

Combination of qualitative and quantitative methods

This also applies to the decision about using both methods. Here however we find different positions in the discussion.

Dominance of quantitative research over qualitative research

This dominance can still be found very often, for example where an exploratory, preliminary study with open interviews precedes the actual collection of data with questionnaires. Arguments such as the representativeness of the sample are often used for substantiating the claim that only the quantitative data lead to results in the actual sense of the word, whereas qualitative data play a more illustrative part. Statements in the open interviews are then tested and 'explained' by their confirmation and frequency in the questionnaire data.

Dominance of qualitative research over quantitative research

This position is held more seldom but more radically. For Oevermann et al. (1979, p. 16) for example, quantitative methods in any case are merely 'research economic short cuts of the process of generating data', whereas qualitative methods, particularly the objective hermeneutics he has developed (see Chapter 16), are able to provide the actual scientific explanations of facts. Kleining (1982) underlines that qualitative methods can live very well without the later use of quantitative methods, whereas quantitative methods need qualitative methods for explaining the relations they find. Cicourel (1981) sees qualitative methods as being especially appropriate to answering micro sociological questions and quantitative methods to answering macro sociological questions. McKinlay (1995), on the other hand, makes it clear that in public health qualitative methods rather lead to relevant results at the level of socio-political topics and relations owing to their complexity. Thus, reasons for the dominance of qualitative research can be found at the level of research programmatic and at the level of the appropriateness to the issue under study.

Defining fields of application

Another position in this discussion aims at seeing the research strategies separately but side by side, again depending on the issue and the research question. The researcher who wants to know something about the subjective experience of a chronic mental illness should conduct biographic interviews with some patients and analyse them in great detail. The researcher who wants to find out something about the frequency and distribution of such diseases in the population should run an epidemiological study on this topic. For the first question, qualitative methods are appropriate, and for the second, quantitative methods are suitable; each method refrains from entering the territory of the other.

Triangulation of qualitative and quantitative research

Triangulation (see Chapter 18) can mean combining several qualitative methods (see Flick 1992a), but it can also mean combining qualitative and quantitative methods (see Jick 1983). Here, the different methodological perspectives complement each other in the study of an issue and this is conceived as the complementary compensation of the weaknesses and blind spots of each single method. The slowly establishing insight 'that qualitative and quantitative methods should be viewed as complementary rather than as rival camps' (Jick 1983, p. 135) is the background of such a conception. But, the different methods remain autonomous, operating side by side, their meeting point being the issue under study.

Transformation of qualitative data into quantitative data

Another form of combination is to transform the data from one strategy into the other. Repeatedly, there have been attempts to quantify statements of open or narrative interviews (e.g. Mühlefeld et al. 1981). Observations can also be analysed in terms of their frequency. The frequencies in each category can be specified and compared. Engel and Wuggenig (1991) present a series of statistical methods for calculating such data.

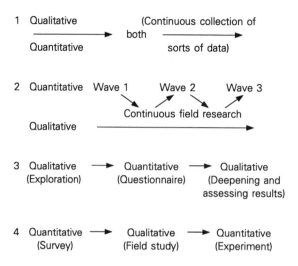

FIGURE 20.1 *Research designs for the integration of qualitative and quantitative research*
Source: adapted from Miles and Huberman 1994, p. 41

Transformation of quantitative data into qualitative data

The inverse transformation is normally even more difficult. Questionnaire data hardly allow the disclosure of the context of each answer, which can only be achieved by the explicit use of additional methods such as complementary interviews for a part of the sample. Whereas analysing the frequency of certain answers in interviews may provide additional insights for those interviews, the additional explanation for why certain patterns of answering can be found in large numbers in questionnaires requires the collection and involvement of new sorts of data (interviews, field observations).

Integration of qualitative and quantitative research

A more demanding strategy is to integrate both traditions of research in one design. Miles and Huberman (1994, p. 41) outline four types of designs for realizing this form of combinations, as in Figure 20.1. In the first design, both strategies are pursued in parallel. Continuous observation of the field provides a basis to which the several waves in a survey are related or from which these waves are derived and shaped in the second design. The third combination begins with a qualitative method (e.g. a semi-structured interview) which is followed by a questionnaire study as an intermediate step, before finally the results from both steps are deepened and assessed in a second qualitative phase. In the fourth design, a complementary field study adds more depth to the results of a survey in the first step, and is followed by an experimental intervention in the field for testing the results of the first two steps (see Patton 1990 for similar suggestions of mixed designs).

The problems in combining qualitative and quantitative research have not yet been solved satisfactorily. Attempts to integrate both approaches often end up in forms of one after the other (with different preferences), side by side (with various degrees of independence of both strategies) or dominance (also with different preferences). The integration is often restricted to the level of the research design – a combinatory use of various methods with different degrees of interrelation. On the other hand, the differences in the two streams of research concerning appropriate designs (see Chapter 4) and appropriate forms of assessing the procedures, data and results continue to exist. The question of how to take these differences into account in the combination of both strategies remains to be further discussed.

QUALITY IN QUALITATIVE RESEARCH: PROCESS EVALUATION AND QUALITY MANAGEMENT

The question of grounding qualitative research has not yet been answered in a definite way (see Chapter 18). Starting from this observation, the need to try new ways of evaluation and to specify quality in qualitative research results. One starting point comes from the processual character of qualitative research (see Chapter 4) as well as from procedural specifications of reliability and of the evaluation of theory building (see Chapter 18): to specify and even more to produce the grounding of qualitative research in relation to the research process.

Process evaluation

Qualitative research is embedded in a process in a special way. It does not make sense to ask and answer questions of sampling or concerning special methods in an isolated way. Whether a sampling is appropriate can only be answered with regard to the research question, to the results, to the generalizations that are aimed at and to the methods used. Abstract measures like the representativity of a sample, which can be judged generally, do not have any benefit here. A central starting point for answering such questions is the sounding of the research process, which means whether the sampling that was applied harmonizes with the concrete research question and with the concrete process. Activities for optimizing qualitative research in the concrete case have to start from the stages of the qualitative research process (see Flick 1991b). Correspondingly a shift in the accent in evaluating qualitative methods and their use, from a mere evaluation of the application to a process evaluation, can be noted (Flick 1995b).

This kind of process evaluation has been realized in the Berlin research association 'Public Health', in which 23 research projects worked with qualitative and/or quantitative methods on various health-related questions. For example, questions of networking among social services and programmes, ways of how to design an everyday life outside hospital, citizens' participation in health-relevant urban planning and administration, and the organization of preventive interventions were studied. The different projects use narrative and semi-structured interviews, participant observations, conversation analysis or theoretical coding, among other methods. A cross-sectional project 'Qualitative Methods in Health Sciences' (Flick 1992b) served as a methodological support and process evaluation. Starting from a processual understanding of qualitative research, a continuous programme of project consultations, colloquia and workshops was established. In this programme, the different projects in this association were consulted and evaluated according to the stages of the qualitative research process (formulation and circumscription of the research question, sampling, collection and interpretation of data, grounding and generalization of results). This programme serves to define a framework for a discussion of methodological questions of operationalization of the research question and the application of methods across projects. The leitmotiv of this shift in emphasis – from an evaluation which views methods and their application isolatedly to a process evaluation which takes the specific character of the research process and issue into account – is that the application of qualitative methods above all should be judged with regard to its embedding in the process of research and to the issue of the study, and less for its own sake.

Thus, the aspect of grounding is shifted to the level of the research process. The aim of this shift is also to underscore a different understanding of quality in qualitative research and to relate it to a concrete project.

Quality management

Impulses for further developments can be provided by the general discussion about quality management (Kamiske and Brauer 1995), which takes place mainly in the area of industrial production but also in public services (Murphy 1994). This discussion certainly cannot be transferred to qualitative research with no restrictions. But some of the concepts and strategies used in this discussion may be adopted to promote a discussion about quality in research which is appropriate to the issues and research concepts. The concept of auditing is discussed in both areas (see Chapter 18; Lincoln and Guba 1985), and provides first intersections: 'An audit is understood as a systematic, independent examination of an activity and its results, by which the existence and appropriate application of specified demands are evaluated and documented' (Kamiske and Brauer 1995, p. 5).

In particular, the 'procedural audit' is interesting for qualitative research. It should guarantee that 'the pre-defined demands are fulfilled and are useful for the respective application ... Priority is always given to an enduring remedy of causes of mistakes, not just the simple detection of mistakes' (1995, p. 8). Such specifications of quality are not conducted abstractly, e.g. for certain methods *per se*, but with regard to the client orientation (pp. 95–6) and the co-workers' orientation (pp. 110–1).

For the first point, the question arises as to who the clients of qualitative research actually are. Quality management differentiates between internal and external clients. Whereas the latter are the consumers of the product, the former are those who are involved in its production in a broader sense (e.g. employees in other departments). For qualitative research, this distinction may be translated as follows. External clients are those outside the project for whom its results are produced (overseers, reviewers etc. as external clients). Internal clients then are those for and with whom one attempts to obtain the result (interviewees, institutions under study etc.). Concepts like 'member checks' or communicative validation (see Chapter 18) explicitly take this orientation into account. Designing the research process, and proceeding in a way which gives enough room to those who are studied, realizes this orientation implicitly. For an evaluation, both aspects may be analysed explicitly: how far did the study succeed in answering its research question (orientation on external clients), and did it give enough room to the perspectives of those who were involved as interviewees for example (orientation on internal clients)?

The co-worker orientation seeks to take into account that 'quality arises from applying suitable techniques but on the basis of a corresponding mentality' (p. 110). Transferred to qualitative research, this underlines that not only does the application of methods essentially determine its quality, but also the attitude with which the research is conducted. Another point of departure here is 'to give responsibility (for quality) to the co-workers by introducing self-assessments instead of outside control' (p. 111). Quality in the qualitative research process can be realized – as elsewhere – if it is produced and assessed together with the researchers involved. First, they define together what should be and is understood as quality in this context. Quality management then includes 'activities ... defining the quality policy, the goals and the responsibilities and realizing these by means of quality planning, quality steering, quality assessment/quality management and quality improvement' (ISO 9004, quoted in Kamiske and Brauer 1995, p. 149).

These guiding principles of quality management are summarized in Box 20.2. They can be realized by defining the goals, documenting process and problems, and regularly reflecting jointly about process and problems. Joint processual evaluation in connection with consultation, training and retraining, as outlined above, can be an instrument for realizing quality management in qualitative research. Other strategies will follow and advance the discussion about the appropriate realization and evaluation of qualitative research. A definition of quality in research, and how to realize and

---

Box 20.2   Principles of quality management in the qualitative research process

- A definition of the goals to be reached and the standards of the project to be kept, which should be as clear as possible; all researchers and co-workers have to be integrated in this definition.
- A definition of how these goals and standards, and more generally the quality to be obtained, can be reached; and therefore a consensus about the way to apply certain methods, perhaps through joint interview training and its analysis; are preconditions for quality in the research process.
- A clear definition of the responsibilities for obtaining quality in the research process.
- The transparency of the judgement and the assessment of quality in the process.

---

guarantee it in the process which is appropriate to the issue, and the experience that quality can only be produced through a combination of methods and a corresponding attitude, are links to the discussion about quality management.

DIDACTIC QUESTIONS

Overviews of methods in qualitative research face two basic problems. First, the field of alternatives summarized under the label of qualitative research is still very heterogeneous. Therefore such overviews run the risk of giving a unified presentation to an issue which is and will remain rather ambiguous. The canonization and codification which are sometimes demanded or attempted may miss the point of creating a unity which really can be realized, and it remains to be asked how desirable such a creation of unity really is. It seems more instructive to clarify the different theoretical, methodological and general aims of the various alternatives.

On the other hand, these overviews face the problem that a stress on methods runs the risk of obscuring rather than illuminating the idea that qualitative research is not merely an application of methods in the sense of technologies. It is not only the tension of technique and art in the methods, but also that qualitative research includes a specific research attitude. This attitude is linked to the primacy of the issue over the methods, to the orientation of the process of research and to the attitude with which the researcher should meet his or her 'object'. In addition to curiosity, openness and flexibility in handling the methods, a special degree of reflection about the issue, about the appropriateness of the research question and methods, and also about his or her own perceptions and blind spots, is part of this attitude. Two consequences result from this.

In a didactic of qualitative methods, the need arises to find a way between conveying techniques (how to formulate a generative narrative question in the narrative interview, what is an axial code) and the necessary attitude. Curiosity and flexibility cannot be taught in lectures about the history and methods of qualitative research. The appropriate use of qualitative methods often results from experience, from problems, from failing and continuing in the field. The pure methodological level has to be separated from the level of application – as in every research. The concrete field with its obstructions and necessities often makes difficult an optimal application of a certain interview technique. But the problems in qualitative methods are intensified because the scope of application and the need for flexibility are so great in most of the methods that a lot of decisions can only be made in the situation of applying them. In the successful case, this flexibility opens a way to the subjective viewpoint of the interviewee; in a failed case, it makes an orientation in the application more difficult, and the bureaucracy of the interview guide results, as Hopf (1978) warns. If it is applied consequently and successfully, the narrative interview gives the interviewee the chance to unfold his or her life history without being disturbed. Then it gives the interviewer the chance to receive and file narratives and presentations in their temporal and sequential context. In failure the situation becomes a caricature which is described by Kreissl and Wolfersdorff-Ehlert as a 'paradoxical request . . . I don't want anything from you, just tell me your story' (1985, p. 103). With success, procedures like theoretical coding or objective hermeneutics allow one to find a way into the structure of the text or of the case; in failure, they leave the researcher in the situation described by Südmersen (1983) as 'help, I am stifled by texts'.

An understanding of qualitative research can hardly be mediated only theoretically. Beyond that, the instruction should include practical experience in applying methods and in the contact with concrete research subjects. Projects combining teaching and research, which allow one to work continuously for a longer period on a research question with one or more methods, may give a framework for gaining the practical experience which is necessary to make an understanding of the options and limits of qualitative methods possible. Procedures of interviewing and interpreting data can only be taught and learned in combination with their practical application and in a joint analysis of experiences and problems.

Beyond the fundamental certitude that qualitative research cannot function at all, which is still formulated by sceptics and opponents of these approaches, the failure of qualitative research is discussed much too seldom. Given the various overviews and handbooks which are available now, the impression arises sometimes that qualitative methods are based on a validated knowledge which only has to be applied correctly. But the analysis of failures in qualitative research strategies (see for example

Borman et al. 1986; or more concretely about entrance into the research field and failures in this process see Kroner and Wolff 1986; Lau and Wolff 1983) can provide insights into how they function in contact with concrete fields, institutions or human beings.

QUALITATIVE RESEARCH: ART OR METHOD?

The other side of the coin is the overemphasis on the part played by art in qualitative research. For several methods, it is explicitly claimed that they are art and to be taught as art (e.g. for objective hermeneutics). For other methods, sometimes the impression is given that their applications by those who have developed them is the best measure for assessing their potential. Other theoretical and methodological presentations and applications clearly fall behind the creator's claims for the insights they can give into process and procedures. Furthermore, the handbook of Denzin and Lincoln (1994a) gives the impression of qualitative research as art in many passages. Several chapters have titles like: 'Interview: The Art of Science' (Fontana and Frey 1994) and then provide relatively little concrete advice on (in this case) how to design and conduct an interview. The description of the state of the art in qualitative research, which Denzin and Lincoln (1994b) provide as an introduction, gives the impression that questions of methods and how to apply them are strongly pushed to the back or filed as being outdated and in the 'modernist phase' of earlier times, in favour of the crises of representation and legitimation which are discussed. This may be linked to the strong orientation to ethnography which characterizes the presentation of qualitative research in this handbook. According to Hammersley and Atkinson (1983) or Lüders (1995) it is characteristic for ethnography that single methods are integrated in a pragmatic-pluralistic attitude or vanish behind such an attitude. The great attention which has been attracted by the question of writing qualitative research, and the crises and problems linked to it in this context, will definitely neither accelerate the development of methods nor promote the application of the developed methods and will not necessarily lead to more and better research. Perhaps qualitative research should be understood as art *and* method. Progress should rather be expected from the combination of methodological developments and their successful and reflected application in as many fields and research questions as possible. That the need for this kind of research is increasing has been underlined by Clifford Geertz in his recent considerations about the 'world in pieces':

> The same dissolution of established groupings and familiar subdivisions, which made the political world so unwieldy and unfathomable, has also made interpretation more complicated: how people see things and react to them, how they imagine things, judge and handle them, is increasingly beyond our

knowledge. Analysing culture today is a much more difficult enterprise than it was in those days, when we knew, or better believed we knew, what matched what and what did not . . . We need new ways of thinking that are able to handle peculiarities, individualities, strangeness, discontinuities, contrasts and singularities and to respond to something Charles Taylor has recently called 'deep diversity' – a plurality of belongings and ways of being. We nevertheless lack approaches able to provide a feeling of interconnectedness, which is neither comprehensive nor uniform, neither original nor immutable, and nevertheless is real in its plurality . . . What other choice do we have except to plunge into the depths of concrete cases at the expense of losing general validity, security and intellectual balances? (1996, pp. 23–4)

NOTE

1   Technical preconditions are: IBM-compatible DOS computer (386DX, 40 MHz) with 8 MB RAM, VGA graphics card, DOS 3.0 and higher, mouse, hard disk. A Windows 95 version is now available. For more information about the program and contact with other users, see also the author's homepage on the Internet: http://www.atlasti.de.

FURTHER READING

Computers

These texts give concrete suggestions for using computers in qualitative research and also address problems associated with their use.

Richards, T.J., Richards, L. (1994), Using Computers in Qualitative Research. In: Denzin, N., Lincoln, Y.S. (eds), *Handbook of Qualitative Research*, pp. 445–62. London: Sage.

Weitzman, E., Miles, M.B. (1995), *Computer Programs for Qualitative Data Analysis: A Software Source Book*. London: Sage.

Qualitative and quantitative research

A very pragmatic and very thoughtful text about methods and problems in linking both kinds of research.

Miles, M.B., Huberman, A.M. (1994), *Qualitative Data Analysis: A Sourcebook of New Methods* (2nd edn). Newbury Park, CA: Sage.

REFERENCES

Adler, P.A., Adler, P. (1987), *Membership Roles in Field Research*. Beverly Hills, CA: Sage.

Adler, P.A., Adler, P. (1994), Observational Techniques. In: Denzin, N., Lincoln, Y.S. (eds), *Handbook of Qualitative Research*, pp. 377–93. London: Sage.

Agar, M.H. (1980), *The Professional Stranger*. New York: Academic Press.

Agger, B. (1991), Critical Theory, Poststructuralism, Postmodernism: Their Sociological Relevance. *American Review of Sociology*, 17, pp. 105–31.

Altheide, D.L., Johnson, J.M. (1994), Criteria for Assessing Interpretive Validity in Qualitative Research. In: Denzin, N., Lincoln, Y.S. (eds), *Handbook of Qualitative Research*, pp. 485–99. London: Sage.

Amann, K., Knorr-Cetina, K. (1991), Qualitative Wissenschaftssoziologie. In: Flick, U., Kardorff, E.v., Keupp, H., Rosenstiel, L.v., Wolff, S. (eds), *Handbuch Qualitative Sozialforschung*, pp. 419–25. Munich: Psychologie Verlags Union.

Arbeitsgruppe Bielefelder Soziologen (1973), *Alltagswissen, Interaktion und gesellschaftliche Wirklichkeit*, Vols 1–2. Reinbek: Rowohlt.

Aster, R., Merkens, H., Repp, M. (eds) (1989), *Teilnehmende Beobachtung. Werkstattberichte und methodologische Reflexionen*. Frankfurt: Campus.

Atkinson, P., Hammersley, M. (1994) Ethnography and Participant Observation. In: Denzin, N., Lincoln, Y.S. (eds), *Handbook of Qualitative Research*, pp. 236–47. London: Sage.

Barthes, R. (1996), *Camera Lucida: Reflections on Photography*. New York: Hill and Wang.

Bateson, G., Mead, M. (1942), *Balinese Character: A Photographic Analysis*, Vol. 2. New York: New York Academy of Sciences.

Baum, F. (1995), Researching Public Health: Behind the Qualitative–Quantitative Methodological Debate. *Social Science and Medicine*, 40, pp. 459–68.

Beck, U. (1986), *Risikogesellschaft: Auf dem Weg in eine andere Moderne*. Frankfurt: Suhrkamp (translation: *Risk Society*, London: Sage, 1992).

Beck, U., Bonß, W. (eds) (1989), *Weder Sozialtechnologie noch Aufklärung? Analysen zur Verwendung sozialwissenschaftlichen Wissens*. Frankfurt: Suhrkamp.

Becker, H.S. (1986a), *Doing Things Together: Selected Papers*. Evanston, IL: Northwestern University Press.

Becker, H.S. (1986b), *Writing for Social Scientists*. Chicago: University of Chicago Press.

Becker, H.S. (1996), The Epistemology of Qualitative Research. In: Jessor, R., Colby, A., Shweder, R.A. (eds), *Ethnography and Human Development*, pp. 53–72. Chicago: University of Chicago Press.

Becker, H.S., Geer, B. (1960), Participant Observation: Analysis of Qualitative Data.

In: Adams, R.N., Preiss, J.J. (eds), *Human Organization Research*, pp. 267–89. Homewood, IL: Dorsey.

Becker, H.S., Geer, B., Hughes, E.C., Strauss, A.L. (1961), *Boys in White: Student Culture in Medical School*. Chicago: University of Chicago Press.

Berg, E., Fuchs, M. (eds) (1993), *Kultur, soziale Praxis, Text: Die Krise der ethnographischen Repräsentation*. Frankfurt: Suhrkamp.

Bergmann, J.R. (1980), Interaktion und Exploration: Eine konversationsanalytische Studie zur sozialen Organisation der Eröffnungsphase von psychiatrischen Aufnahmegesprächen. Konstanz, dissertation.

Bergmann, J.R. (1981), Ethnomethodologische Konversationsanalyse. In: Schröder, P., Steger, H. (eds), *Dialogforschung: Jahrbuch 1980 des Institut für deutsche Sprache*, pp. 9–51. Düsseldorf: Schwann.

Bergmann, J.R. (1985), Flüchtigkeit und methodische Fixierung sozialer Wirklichkeit: Aufzeichnungen als Daten der interpretativen Soziologie. In: Bonß, W., Hartmann, H. (eds), *Entzauberte Wissenschaft: Zur Realität und Geltung soziologischer Forschung*, pp. 299–320. Göttingen: Schwartz.

Bergmann, J.R. (1991a), Studies of Work/Ethnomethodologie. In: Flick, U., Kardorff, E.v., Keupp, H., Rosenstiel, L.v., Wolff, S. (eds), *Handbuch Qualitative Sozialforschung*, pp. 269–72. Munich: Psychologie Verlags Union.

Bergmann, J.R. (1991b), Konversationsanalyse. In: Flick, U., Kardorff, E.v., Keupp, H., Rosenstiel, L.v., Wolff, S. (eds), *Handbuch Qualitative Sozialforschung*, pp. 213–18. Munich: Psychologie Verlags Union.

Bergold, J.B., Flick, U. (eds) (1987), *Ein-Sichten: Zugänge zur Sicht des Subjekts mittels qualitativer Forschung*. Tübingen: DGVT.

Bertaux, D. (ed.) (1981), *Biograpy and History: The Life History Approach in Social Sciences*. Beverly Hills, CA: Sage.

Billig, M. (1987), *Arguing and Thinking: A Rhetorical Approach to Social Psychology*. Cambridge: Cambridge University Press.

Billman-Mahecha, E. (1990), *Egozentrismus und Perspektivenwechsel*. Göttingen: Hogrefe.

Blumer, H. (1938), Social Psychology. In: Schmidt, E. (ed.), *Man and Society*, pp. 144–98. New York: Prentice-Hall.

Blumer, H. (1969), *Symbolic Interactionism: Perspective and Method*. Berkeley and Los Angeles: University of California Press.

Böhm, A., Legewie, H., Muhr, T. (1992), Kursus Textinterpretation: Grounded Theory. Berlin: Technische Universität, Bericht aus dem IfP Atlas 92-3, MS.

Böhm, A., Muhr, T., Mengel, A. (eds) (1994), *Texte verstehen: Konzepte, Methoden, Werkzeuge*. Konstanz: Universitätsverlag (Schriften zur Informationswissenschaft).

Bohnsack, R. (1991), *Rekonstruktive Sozialforschung: Einführung in Methodologie und Praxis qualitativer Forschung*. Opladen: Leske and Budrich.

Bonß, W. (1982), *Die Einübung des Tatsachenblicks: Zur Struktur und Veränderung empirischer Sozialforschung*. Frankfurt: Suhrkamp.

Bonß, W. (1991), Soziologie. In: Flick, U., Kardorff, E.v., Keupp, H., Rosenstiel, L.v., Wolff, S. (eds), *Handbuch Qualitative Sozialforschung*, pp. 36–39. Munich: Psychologie Verlags Union.

Bonß, W., Hartmann, H. (1985), Konstruierte Gesellschaft, rationale Deutung: Zum Wirklichkeitscharakter soziologischer Diskurse. In: Bonß, W., Hartmann, H. (eds), *Entzauberte Wissenschaft: Zur Realität und Geltung soziologischer Forschung*, pp. 9-48. Göttingen: Schwartz.

Borman, K.M., LeCompte, M., Goetz, J.P. (1986), Ethnographic Research and

Qualitative Research Design and Why It Doesn't Work. *American Behavioral Scientist*, 30, pp. 42–57.

Bortz, J. (1984), *Lehrbuch der empirischen Forschung*. Heidelberg: Springer.

Bruce, G. (1992), Comments. In: Svartnik, J. (ed.), *Directions in Corpus Linguistics: Proceedings of Nobel Symposium 82, Stockholm*. Berlin: De Gruyter.

Bruner, E.M. (1993), Introduction: The Ethnographic Self and the Personal Self. In: Benson, P. (ed.), *Anthropology and Literature*. pp. 1–26. Urbana: University of Illinois Press.

Bruner, J. (1987), Life as Narrative. *Social Research*, 54, pp. 11–32.

Bruner, J. (1990), *Acts of Meaning*. Cambridge, MA: Harvard University Press.

Bruner, J. (1991), The Narrative Construction of Reality. *Critical Inquiry*, 18, pp. 1–21.

Bruner, J., Feldman, C. (1996), Group Narrative as a Cultural Context of Autobiography. In: Rubin, D. (ed.), *Remembering our Past: Studies in Autobiographical Memory*, pp. 291–317. Cambridge: Cambridge University Press.

Bryman, A. (1988), *Quantity and Quality in Social Research*. London: Unwin Hyman.

Bude, H. (1984), Rekonstruktion von Lebenskonstruktionen: Eine Antwort auf die Frage, was die Biographieforschung bringt. In: Kohli, M., Robert, G. (eds), *Biographie und soziale Wirklichkeit: Neuere Beiträge und Forschungsperspektiven*, pp. 7–28. Stuttgart: Metzler.

Bude, H. (1985), Der Sozialforscher als Narrationsanimateur: Kritische Anmerkungen zu einer erzähltheoretischen Fundierung der interpretativen Sozialforschung. *Kölner Zeitschrift für Soziologie und Sozialpsychologie*, 37, pp. 327–36.

Bude, H. (1989), Der Essay als Form der Darstellung sozialwissenschaftlicher Erkenntnisse. *Kölner Zeitschrift für Soziologie und Sozialpsychologie*, 41, pp. 526–39.

Bude, H. (1991), Die Rekonstruktion kultureller Sinnsysteme. In: Flick, U., Kardorff, E.v., Keupp, H., Rosenstiel, L.v., Wolff, S. (eds), *Handbuch Qualitative Sozialforschung*, pp. 101–13. Munich: Psychologie Verlags Union.

Bude, H. (1993), Die soziologische Erzählung. In: Jung, T., Müller-Doohm, S. (eds), *'Wirklichkeit' im Deutungsprozeß: Verstehen und Methoden in den Kultur- und Sozialwissenschaften*, pp. 409–29. Frankfurt: Suhrkamp.

Bude, H. (1994), Das Latente und das Manifeste. Aporien einer 'Hermeneutik des Verdachts'. In: Garz, D. (ed.), *Die Welt als Text*, pp. 114–24. Frankfurt: Suhrkamp.

Bude, H. (1995), Verallgemeinerung und Darstellung. Workshop des Projektes Q1b im Berliner Forschungsverbund Public Health (mimeo).

Bühl, W. (ed.) (1972), *Verstehende Soziologie*. Munich: Nymphenburger Verlagsanstalt.

Bühler-Niederberger, D. (1985), Analytische Induktion als Verfahren qualitativer Methodologie. *Zeitschrift für Soziologie*, 14, pp. 475–85.

Charmaz, K. (1995), Grounded Theory. In: Smith, J.A., Harré, R., Langenhove, L.v. (eds), *Rethinking Methods in Psychology*, pp. 27–49. London: Sage.

Cicourel, A.V. (1964), *Method and Measurement in Sociology*. New York: Free Press.

Cicourel, A.V. (1981), Notes on the Integration of Micro- and Macrolevels of Analysis. In: Knorr-Cetina, K., Cicourel, A.V. (eds), *Advances in Social Theory and Methodology: Towards an Integration of Micro- and Macro-Sociologies*, pp. 51–80. London: Routledge and Kegan Paul.

Clifford, J. (1986), Introduction: Partial Truths. In: Clifford, J., Marcus, G.E. (eds), *Writing Culture: The Poetics and Politics of Ethnography*, pp. 1–26. Berkeley, CA: University of California Press.

Clifford, J., Marcus, G.E. (eds) (1986), *Writing Culture: The Poetics and Politics of Ethnography*. Berkeley, CA: University of California Press.

Collier, J. (1957), Photography in Anthropology: A Report on Two Experiments. *American Anthropologist*, 59, pp. 843–59.

Corbin, J., Strauss, A. (1990), Grounded Theory Research: Procedures, Canons and Evaluative Criteria. *Qualitative Sociology*, 13, pp. 3–21.

Coulter, J. (1983), *Rethinking Cognitive Theory*. London: Macmillan.

D'Andrade, R.G. (1987), A Folk Model of the Mind. In: Holland, D., Quinn, N., (eds), *Cultural Models in Language and Thought*, pp. 112–49. Cambridge: Cambridge University Press.

Dabbs, J.M. (1982), Making Things Visible. In: Van Maanen, J., Dabbs, J.M., Faulkner, R. (eds), *Varieties of Qualitative Research*, pp. 31–64. London: Sage.

Dann, H.D. (1990), Subjective Theories: A New Approach to Psychological Research and Educational Practice. In: Semin, G. R., Gergen, K.J. (eds), *Everyday Understanding: Social and Scientific Implications*, pp. 204–26. London: Sage.

Decker, F. (1979), Forschung und Erfahrung: Wandlungen eines Projekts. In: Horn, K. (ed.), *Aktionsforschung*, pp. 111–63. Frankfurt: Syndikat.

Deleuze, G., Guattari, F. (1976), *Rhizome: Introduction*. Paris: Minuit.

Denzin, N.K. (1978), *The Research Act* (2nd edn). Chicago: Aldine.

Denzin, N.K. (1988), *Interpretive Biography*. London: Sage.

Denzin, N.K. (1989a), *Interpretative Interactionism*. London: Sage.

Denzin, N.K. (1989b), *The Research Act* (3rd edn). Englewood Cliffs, NJ: Prentice-Hall.

Denzin, N.K. (1989c), Reading *Tender Mercies*: Two Interpretations. *Sociological Quarterly*, 30, pp. 1–190.

Denzin, N.K. (ed.) (1993), *Studies in Symbolic Interactionism*, Vol. 15. Greenwich, CT: JAI.

Denzin, N.K. (1994), The Art and Politics of Interpretation. In: Denzin, N., Lincoln, Y.S. (eds), *Handbook of Qualitative Research*, pp. 500–15. London: Sage.

Denzin, N., Lincoln, Y.S. (eds) (1994a), *Handbook of Qualitative Research*. London: Sage.

Denzin, N., Lincoln, Y.S. (1994b), Introduction: Entering the Field of Qualitative Research. In: Denzin, N., Lincoln, Y.S. (eds), *Handbook of Qualitative Research*, pp. 1–18. London: Sage.

Derrida, J. (1976), *Die Schrift und die Differenz*. Frankfurt: Suhrkamp (original: *L'Ecriture et la différence*, Paris: Editions du Seuil, 1967).

Devereux, G. (1967), *From Anxiety to Methods in the Behavioral Sciences*. The Hague: Mouton.

Dixon, R.A., Gould, O.N. (1996), Adults Telling and Retelling Stories Collaboratively. In: Baltes, P.B., Staudinger, U. (eds), *Interactive Minds: Lifespan Perspectives on the Social Foundation of Cognition*, pp. 221–41. Cambridge: Cambridge University Press.

Dörner, D. (1983), Empirische Psychologie und Alltagsrelevanz. In: Jüttemann, G. (ed.), *Psychologie in der Veränderung*, pp. 13–29. Weinheim: Beltz.

Douglas, J.D. (1976), *Investigative Social Research*. Beverly Hills, CA: Sage.

Dreher, M., Dreher, E. (1982), Gruppendiskussion. In: Huber, G.L., Mandl, H. (eds), *Verbale Daten*, pp. 141–64. Weinheim: Beltz.

Drew, P. (1995), Conversation Analysis. In: Smith, J.A., Harré, R., Langenhove, L.v. (eds), *Rethinking Methods in Psychology*, pp. 64–79. London: Sage.

Edwards, D., Potter, J. (1992), *Discursive Psychology*. London: Sage.

Ehlich, K., Switalla, B. (1976), Transkriptionssysteme: Eine exemplarische Übersicht. *Studium Linguistik*, 2, pp. 78–105.

Engel, U., Wuggenig, U. (1991), Statistische Auswertungsverfahren nominalskalierter Daten. In: Flick, U., Kardorff, E.v., Keupp, H., Rosenstiel, L.v., Wolff, S. (eds), *Handbuch Qualitative Sozialforschung*, pp. 237–42. Munich: Psychologie Verlags Union.

Englisch, F. (1991), Bildanalyse in struktural-hermeneutischer Einstellung: Methodische Überlegungen und Analysebeispiele. In: Garz, D., Kraimer, K. (eds), *Qualitativ-empirische Sozialforschung*, pp. 133–76. Opladen: Westdeutscher Verlag.

Erdheim, M. (1984), *Die gesellschaftliche Produktion von Unbewußtheit*. Frankfurt: Suhrkamp.

Faltermaier, T. (1994), *Gesundheitsbewußtsein und Gesundheitshandeln: Über den Umgang mit Gesundheit im Alltag*. Weinheim: Beltz PsychologieVerlags Union.

Fielding, N.G., Fielding, J.L. (1986), *Linking Data*. Beverly Hills, CA: Sage.

Fielding, N.G., Lee, R.M. (eds) (1991), *Using Computers in Qualitative Research*. London: Sage.

Fleck, L. (1935), *Entstehung und Entwicklung einer wissenschaftlichen Tatsache*. Frankfurt: Suhrkamp (translation: *Genesis and Development of a Scientific Fact*, eds Trenn, T.J., Merton, R.K., 1979). Chicago: University of Chicago Press.

Flick, U. (1987), Methodenangemessene Gütekriterien in der qualitativ-interpretativen Forschung. In: Bergold, J.B., Flick, U. (eds), *Ein-Sichten: Zugänge zur Sicht des Subjekts mittels qualitativer Forschung*, pp. 246–63. Tübingen: DGVT-Verlag.

Flick, U. (1989), *Vertrauen, Verwalten, Einweisen: Subjektive Vertrauenstheorien in sozialpsychiatrischer Beratung*. Opladen: Deutscher Universitätsverlag.

Flick, U. (1991a), Ad-hoc Gruppe 'Verwendung von Computern in der Qualitativen Forschung'. In: Glatzer, W. (ed.), *Modernisierung moderner Gesellschaften: 25. Dt. Soziologentag, Beiträge der Sektions- und Ad-hoc-Gruppen*, pp. 800–20. Opladen: Westdeutscher Verlag.

Flick, U. (1991b), Stationen des qualitativen Forschungsprozesses. In: Flick, U., Kardorff, E.v., Keupp, H., Rosenstiel, L.v., Wolff, S. (eds), *Handbuch Qualitative Sozialforschung*, pp. 148–75. Munich: Psychologie Verlags Union.

Flick, U. (1991c), Vom Ersticken in Texten zum Absturz ins Programm? Verwendung von Computern in der Qualitativen Forschung. In: Glatzer, W. (ed.), *Modernisierung moderner Gesellschaften: 25. Dt. Soziologentag, Beiträge der Sektions- und Ad-hoc-Gruppen*, pp. 800–3. Opladen: Westdeutscher Verlag.

Flick, U. (1992a), Triangulation Revisited: Strategy of or Alternative to Validation of Qualitative Data. *Journal for the Theory of Social Behavior*, 22, pp. 175–97.

Flick, U. (1992b), Querschnittsprojekt 'Q1a: Qualitative Methoden in den Gesundheitswissenschaften'. Berlin: Projektantrag im Rahmen des Berliner Forschungsverbundes Public Health, MS.

Flick, U. (ed.) (1993), *La perception quotidienne de la Santé et la Maladie. Théories subjectives et Représentations sociales*. Paris: L'Harmattan.

Flick, U. (1994a), Social Representations and the Social Construction of Everyday Knowledge: Theoretical and Methodological Queries. *Social Science Information*, 33, pp. 179–97.

Flick, U. (1994b), Hermeneuten-Zirkel am PC: Erfahrungen mit ATLAS/ti aus einem Lehr-Forschungsprojekt. In: Böhm, A., Muhr, T., Mengel A. (eds), *Texte verstehen: Konzepte, Methoden, Werkzeuge*, pp. 198–209. Konstanz: Universitätsverlag.

Flick, U. (1995a), Social Representations. In: Harré, R., Smith, J., Langenhove, L.v. (eds), *Rethinking Psychology*, pp. 70–96. London: Sage.

Flick, U. (1995b), Qualitative Forschung in der Sozialpsychiatrie: Methoden und Anwendung. *Psychiatrische Praxis*, 3, pp. 91–6.

Flick, U. (1996), *Psychologie des technisierten Alltags*. Opladen: Westdeutscher Verlag.

Flick, U. (ed.) (1998), *Psychology of the Social*. Cambridge: Cambridge University Press.

Flick, U., Niewiarra, S. (1994), Alltag, Lebensweisen und Gesundheit. Berlin: Technische Universität, Bericht 94-5 aus dem Institut für Psychologie, MS.

Flick, U., Kardorff, E.v., Keupp, H., Rosenstiel, L.v., Wolff, S. (eds) (1991), *Handbuch Qualitative Sozialforschung* (2nd edn 1995). Munich: Psychologie Verlags Union.

Fontana, A., Frey, J.H. (1994), Interviewing: The Art of Science. In: Denzin, N., Lincoln, Y.S. (eds), *Handbook of Qualitative Research*, pp. 361–76. London: Sage.

Freud, S. (1958), Recommendations to Physicians Practising Psycho-Analysis (1912). In: *The Standard Edition of the Complete Psychological Works of Sigmund Freud* (trans. J. Strachey), Vol. XII, pp. 109–20. London: Hogarth.

Friedrichs, J. (1973), *Methoden empirischer Sozialforschung*. Reinbek: Rowohlt.

Friedrichs, J., Lüdtke, H. (1973), *Teilnehmende Beobachtung*. Weinheim: Beltz.

Fuchs, M., Berg, E. (1993), Phänomenologie der Differenz: Reflexionsstufen ethnographischer Repräsentation. In: Berg, E., Fuchs, M. (eds), *Kultur, soziale Praxis, Text. Die Krise der ethnographischen Repräsentation*, pp. 11–108. Frankfurt: Suhrkamp.

Fuchs, W. (1984), *Biographische Forschung: Eine Einführung in Praxis und Methoden*. Opladen: Westdeutscher Verlag.

Garfinkel, H. (1967), *Studies in Ethnomethodology*. Englewood Cliffs, NJ: Prentice-Hall.

Garfinkel, H. (1986), *Ethnomethodological Studies of Work*. London: Routledge and Kegan Paul.

Garfinkel, H., Sacks, H. (1970), On Formal Structures of Practical Actions. In: McKinney, J., Tiryyakian, E. (eds), *Theoretical Sociology*. New York: Appleton.

Garz, D. (ed.) (1994), *Die Welt als Text*. Frankfurt: Suhrkamp.

Garz, D., Kraimer, K. (1994), Die Welt als Text. Zum Projekt einer hermeneutisch-rekonstruktiven Sozialwissenschaft. In: Garz, D. (ed.), *Die Welt als Text*, pp. 7–21. Frankfurt: Suhrkamp.

Gebauer, G., Wulf, C. (1995), *Mimesis: Culture, Art, Society*. Berkeley, CA: University of California Press.

Geertz, C. (1973), *The Interpretation of Cultures: Selected Essays*. New York: Basic Books.

Geertz, C. (1983), *Local Knowledge: Further Essays in Interpretatitve Anthropology*. New York: Basic Books.

Geertz, C. (1988), *The Anthropologist as Author*. Stanford, CA: Stanford University Press.

Geertz, C. (1996), *Welt in Stücken: Kultur und Politik am Ende des 20. Jahrhunderts*. Wien: Passagen.

Gerdes, K. (ed.) (1979), *Explorative Sozialforschung: Einführende Beiträge aus 'Natural Sociology' und Feldforschung in den USA*. Stuttgart: Enke.

Gergen, K.J. (1985), The Social Constructionist Movement in Modern Psychology. *American Psychologist*, 40, pp. 266–75.

Gerhardt, U. (1985), Erzähldaten und Hypothesenkonstruktion: Überlegungen zum Gültigkeitsproblem in der biographischen Sozialforschung. *Kölner Zeitschrift für Soziologie und Sozialpsychologie*, 37, pp. 230–56.

Gerhardt, U. (1986a), *Patientenkarrieren: Eine medizinsoziologische Studie*. Frankfurt: Suhrkamp.

Gerhardt, U. (1986b), Verstehende Strukturanalyse: Die Konstruktion von Idealtypen bei der Auswertung qualitativer Forschungsmaterialien. In: Soeffner, H.G. (ed.), *Sozialstruktur und soziale Typik*, pp. 31–83. Frankfurt: Campus.

Gerhardt, U. (1988) Qualitative Sociology in the Federal Republic of Germany. *Qualitative Sociology*, 11, pp. 29–43.

Ginzburg, C. (1990), Veranschaulichung und Zitat: Wahrheit in der Geschichte. In: Braudel, F., Natalie, Z.D., Febvre, L., Ginzburg, C., LeGoff, J., Koselleck, R., Monigiliano, A. (eds), *Der Historiker als Menschenfresser: Über den Beruf des Geschichtsschreibers*. Berlin: Wagenbach.

Girtler, R. (1984), *Methoden der qualitativen Sozialforschung*. Wien: Böhlau.

Girtler, R. (1991), Forschung in Subkulturen. In: Flick, U., Kardorff, E.v., Keupp, H., Rosenstiel, L.v., Wolff, S. (eds), *Handbuch Qualitative Sozialforschung*, pp. 385–90. Munich: Psychologie Verlags Union.

Glaser, B.G. (1969), The Constant Comparative Method of Qualitative Analysis. In: McCall, G.J., Simmons, J.L. (eds), *Issues in Participant Observation*. Reading, MA: Addison-Wesley.

Glaser, B.G. (1978), *Theoretical Sensitivity*. Mill Valley, CA: University of California Press.

Glaser, B.G., Strauss, A.L. (1965a), *Awareness of Dying*. Chicago: Aldine.

Glaser, B.G., Strauss, A.L. (1965b), Discovery of Substantive Theory: A Basic Strategy underlying Qualitative Research. *The American Behavioral Scientist*, 8, pp. 5–12.

Glaser, B.G., Strauss, A.L. (1967), *The Discovery of Grounded Theory: Strategies for Qualitative Research*. New York: Aldine.

Goffman, E. (1961), *Asylums: Essays on the Social Situation of Mental Patients and Other Inmates*. New York: Anchor Doubleday.

Gold, R.L. (1958), Roles in Sociological Field Observations. *Social Forces*, 36, pp. 217–23.

Goodman, N. (1978), *Ways of Worldmaking*. Indianapolis: Hackett.

Grathoff, R. (1978), Alltag und Lebenswelt als Gegenstand der phänomenologischen Sozialtheorie. In: Hammerich, K., Klein, M. (eds), *Kölner Zeitschrift für Soziologie und Sozialpsychologie*, Sonderheft 20: *Materialien zur Soziologie des Alltags*, pp. 67–85.

Groeben, N. (1990), Subjective Theories and the Explanation of Human Action. In: Semin, G.R., Gergen, K.J. (eds), *Everyday Understanding: Social and Scientific Implications*, pp. 19–44. London: Sage.

Gross, P. (1981), Ist die Sozialwissenschaft eine Textwissenschaft? In: Winkler, P. (ed.), *Methoden der Analyse von Face-to-Face-Situationen*, pp. 143–68. Stuttgart: Metzler.

Guba, E.G. (ed.) (1990), *The Paradigm Dialog*. Newbury Park, CA: Sage.

Guba, E.G., Lincoln, Y.S. (1994), Competing Paradigms in Qualitative Research. In: Denzin, N., Lincoln, Y.S. (eds), *Handbook of Qualitative Research*, pp. 105–17. London: Sage.

Habermas, J. (1967), *Zur Logik der Sozialwissenschaften*. Tübingen: Mohr.

Habermas, J. (1985), *Die neue Unübersichtlichkeit*. Frankfurt: Suhrkamp (translation in: *The Habermas Reader*. Cambrdige: Polity, 1996).

Hall, E.T. (1986), Foreword. In: Collier, J., Collier, M. (eds), *Visual Anthropology: Photography as a Research Method*, pp. xii–xvii. Albuquerque, NM: University of New Mexico Press.

Hammersley, M. (1990), *Reading Ethnographic Research: A Critical Guide*. London: Longman.

Hammersley, M. (1992), *What's Wrong with Ethnography?* London: Routledge.

Hammersley, M., Atkinson, P. (1983), *Ethnography: Principles in Practice*. London: Tavistock.

Harper, D. (1994), On the Authority of the Image: Visual Methods at the Crossroads. In: Denzin, N., Lincoln, Y.S. (eds), *Handbook of Qualitative Research*, pp. 403–12. London: Sage.

Harré, R. (1998), The Epistemology of Social Representations. In: Flick, U. (ed.), *Psychology of the Social*, pp. 129–37. Cambridge: Cambridge University Press

Harré, R., Stearns, P. (eds) (1995), *Discursive Psychology in Practice*. London: Sage.

Haupert, B. (1991), Vom narrativen Interview zur biographischen Typenbildung. In: Garz, D., Kraimer, K. (eds), *Qualitativ-empirische Sozialforschung*, pp. 213–54. Opladen: Westdeutscher Verlag.

Haupert, B. (1994), Objektiv-hermeneutische Fotoanalyse am Beispiel von Soldatenfotos aus dem zweiten Weltkrieg. In: Garz, D. (ed.), *Die Welt als Text*, pp. 281–314. Frankfurt: Suhrkamp.

Heinze, T. (1987), *Qualitative Sozialforschung*. Opladen: Westdeutscher Verlag.

Heritage, J. (1985), Recent Developments in Conversation Analysis. *Sociolinguistics*, 15, pp. 1–17.

Herkommer, S. (1979), *Gesellschaftsbewußtsein und Gewerkschaften*. Hamburg: VSA.

Hermanns, H. (1984), Ingenieurleben: Der Berufsverlauf von Ingenieuren in biographischer Perspektive. In: Kohli, M., Robert, G. (eds), *Biographie und soziale Wirklichkeit: Neuere Beiträge und Forschungsperspektiven*, pp. 164–91. Stuttgart: Metzler.

Hermanns, H. (1991), Narratives Interview. In: Flick, U., Kardorff, E.v., Keupp, H., Rosenstiel, L.v., Wolff, S. (eds), *Handbuch Qualitative Sozialforschung*, pp. 182–5. Munich: Psychologie Verlags Union.

Herzlich, C. (1973), *Health and Illness: A Social Psychological Analysis*. London: Academic Press.

Hildenbrand, B. (1983), *Alltag und Krankheit: Ethnographie einer Familie*. Stuttgart: Klett-Cotta.

Hildenbrand, B. (1987), Wer soll bemerken, daß Bernhard krank wird? Familiale Wirklichkeitskonstruktionsprozesse bei der Erstmanifestation einer schizophrenen Psychose. In: Bergold, J.B., Flick, U. (eds), *Ein-Sichten: Zugänge zur Sicht des Subjekts mittels qualitativer Forschung*, pp. 151–62. Tübingen: DGVT.

Hildenbrand, B. (1991), Fallrekonstruktive Forschung. In: Flick, U., Kardorff, E.v., Keupp, H., Rosenstiel, L.v., Wolff, S. (eds), *Handbuch Qualitative Sozialforschung*, pp. 256–60. Munich: Psychologie Verlags Union.

Hildenbrand, B., Jahn, W. (1988), 'Gemeinsames Erzählen' und Prozesse der Wirklichkeitskonstruktion in familiengeschichtlichen Gesprächen. *Zeitschrift für Soziologie*, 17, pp. 203–17.

Hirst, W., Manier, D. (1996), Remembering as Communication: A Family Recounts its Past. In: Rubin, D. (ed.), *Remembering our Past: Studies in Autobiographical Memory*, pp. 271–90. Cambridge: Cambridge University Press.

Hitzler, R. (1988), *Sinnwelten: Ein Beitrag zum Verstehen von Kultur*. Opladen: Westdeutscher Verlag.

Hitzler, R., Honer, A. (1991), Qualitative Verfahren zur Lebensweltanalyse. In: Flick, U., Kardorff, E.v., Keupp, H., Rosenstiel, L.v., Wolff, S. (eds), *Handbuch Qualitative Sozialforschung*, pp. 382–4. Munich: Psychologie Verlags Union.

Hoffmann-Riem, C. (1980), Die Sozialforschung einer interpretativen Soziologie: Der Datengewinn. *Kölner Zeitschrift für Soziologie und Sozialpsychologie*, 32, pp. 339–72.

Hollingshead, A.B., Redlich, F. (1958), *Social Class and Mental Illness*. New York: Wiley.

Holzkamp, K. (1986), Die Verkennung von Handlungsbegründungen als empirische Zusammenhangsannahmen in sozialpsychologischen Theorien: Methodologische

Fehlorientierungen infolge von Begriffsverwirrung. *Zeitschrift für Sozialpsychologie*, 17, pp. 216–39.

Hopf, C. (1978), Die Pseudo-Exploration: Überlegungen zur Technik qualitativer Interviews in der Sozialforschung. *Zeitschrift für Soziologie*, 7, pp. 97–115.

Hopf, C. (1985), Nichtstandardisierte Erhebungsverfahren in der Sozialforschung: Überlegungen zum Forschungsstand. In: Kaase, M., Küchler, M. (eds), *Herausforderungen der empirischen Sozialforschung*, pp. 86–108. Mannheim: ZUMA.

Hopf, C. (1991), Qualitative Interviews in der Sozialforschung. In: Flick, U., Kardorff, E.v., Keupp, H., Rosenstiel, L.v., Wolff, S. (eds), *Handbuch Qualitative Sozialforschung*, pp. 177–81. Munich: Psychologie Verlags Union.

Hopf, C., Weingarten, E. (eds) (1979), *Qualitative Sozialforschung*. Stuttgart: Klett-Cotta.

Hradil, S. (ed.) (1992), *Zwischen Bewußtsein und Sein*. Opladen: Leske and Budrich.

Huber, G.L. (1991), Computerunterstützte Auswertung Qualitativer Daten. In: Flick, U., Kardorff, E.v., Keupp, H., Rosenstiel, L.v., Wolff, S. (eds), *Handbuch Qualitative Sozialforschung*, pp. 243–8. Munich: Psychologie Verlags Union.

Huberman, A.M., Miles, M.B. (1994), Data Management and Analysis Methods. In: Denzin, N., Lincoln, Y.S. (eds), *Handbook of Qualitative Research*, pp. 428–44. London: Sage.

Humphreys, L. (1973), Toilettengeschäfte. In: Friedrichs, J. (ed.), *Teilnehmende Beobachtung abweichenden Verhaltens*, pp. 254–87. Stuttgart: Enke.

Humphreys, L. (1975), *Tearoom Trade: Impersonal Sex in Public Places* (enlarged edn). New York: Aldine.

Iser, W. (1991), *Das Fiktive und das Imaginäre*. Frankfurt: Suhrkamp.

Jacob, E. (1987), Qualitative Research Traditions: A Review. *Review of Educational Research*, 57, pp. 1–50.

Jessor, R., Colby, A., Shweder, R.A. (eds) (1996), *Ethnography and Human Development*. Chicago: Chicago University Press.

Jick, T. (1983), Mixing Qualitative and Quantitative Methods: Triangulation in Action: In: Maanen, v. (ed.), *Qualitative Methodology*, pp. 135–48. London: Sage.

Joas, H. (1987), Symbolic Interactionism. In: Giddens, A., Turner, J.H. (eds), *Social Theory Today*, pp. 82–115. Cambridge: Polity.

Jodelet, D. (1991), *Madness and Social Representations*. Hemel Hempstead: Harvester Wheatsheaf.

Jorgensen, D.L. (1989), *Participant Observation: A Methodology for Human Studies*. London: Sage.

Jüttemann, G. (ed.) (1985), *Qualitative Forschung in der Psychologie*. Weinheim: Beltz.

Kamiske, G.F., Brauer, J.P. (1995), *Qualitätsmanagement von A bis Z: Erläuterungen moderner Begriffe des Qualitätsmanagements* (2nd edn). Munich: Hanser.

Keupp, H. (1982), Sozialepidemiologie. In: Keupp, H., Rerrich, D. (eds), *Psychosoziale Praxis: Ein Handbuch in Schlüsselbegriffen*, pp. 23–32. Munich: Urban and Schwarzenberg.

Kirk, J.L., Miller, M. (1986), *Reliability and Validity in Qualitative Research*. Beverley Hills, CA: Sage.

Kleining, G. (1982), Umriss zu einer Methodologie qualitativer Sozialforschung. *Kölner Zeitschrift für Soziologie und Sozialpsychologie*, 34, pp. 224–53.

Knorr-Cetina, K. (1981), *The Manufacture of Knowledge: An Essay on the Constructivist and Contextual Nature of Science*. Oxford: Pergamon Press.

Knorr-Cetina, K. (1989), Spielarten des Konstruktivismus. *Soziale Welt*, 20, pp. 69–79.

Knorr-Cetina, K., Mulkay, M. (eds) (1983), *Science Observed: Perspectives on the Social Studies of Science*. London: Sage.

Köckeis-Stangl, E. (1982), Methoden der Sozialisationsforschung. In: Hurrelmann, K., Ulich, D. (eds), *Handbuch der Sozialisationsforschung*, pp. 321–70. Weinheim: Beltz.

Koepping, K.P. (1987) Authentizität als Selbstfindung durch den anderen: Ethnologie zwischen Engagement und Reflexion, zwischen Leben und Wissenschaft. In: Duerr, H.P. (ed.), *Authentizität und Betrug in der Ethnologie*, pp. 7–37. Frankfurt: Suhrkamp.

Kohli, M. (1978), 'Offenes' und 'geschlossenes' Interview: Neue Argumente zu einer alten Kontroverse. *Soziale Welt*, 9, pp. 1–25.

Kohli, M., Robert, G. (eds) (1984), *Biographie und soziale Wirklichkeit: Neuere Beiträge und Forschungsperspektiven*. Stuttgart: Metzler.

König, R. (1984), Soziologie und Ethnologie. *Kölner Zeitschrift für Soziologie und Sozialpsychologie*, Sonderheft 26: *Ethnologie als Sozialwissenschaft*, pp. 17–35.

Koselleck, R. (1990), Darstellung, Ereignis und Struktur. In: Braudel, F., Natalie, Z.D., Febvre, L., Ginzburg, C., LeGoff, J., Koselleck, R., Monigiliano, A. (eds), *Der Historiker als Menschenfresser: Über den Beruf des Geschichtsschreibers*. Berlin: Wagenbach.

Kraimer, K. (ed.) (1998), *Die Fallanalyse*. Frankfurt: Suhrkamp.

Kreissl, R., Wolfersdorff-Ehlert, C. (1985), Selbstbetroffenheit mit summa cum laude? Mythos und Alltag qualitativer Methoden in der Sozialforschung. In: Bonß, W., Hartmann, H. (eds), *Entzauberte Wissenschaft: Zur Realität und Geltung soziologischer Forschung*, pp. 91–110. Göttingen: Schwartz.

Kroner, W., Wolff, S. (1986), Der praktische Umgang mit Wissenschaft: Reflexionen zu einem mißglückten Einstieg in das Forschungsfeld. In: Lüdtke, H. (ed.), *Freizeitforschung*, pp. 127–54. Opladen: Leske and Budrich.

Krüger, H. (1983), Gruppendiskussionen: Überlegungen zur Rekonstruktion sozialer Wirklichkeit aus der Sicht der Betroffenen. *Soziale Welt*, 34, pp. 90–109.

Krüger, H., Marotzki, W. (eds) (1994), *Erziehungswissenschaftliche Biographieforschung*. Opladen: Leske and Budrich.

Küchler, M. (1980), Qualitative Sozialforschung: Modetrend oder Neuanfang? *Kölner Zeitschrift für Soziologie und Sozialpsychologie*, 32, pp. 373–86.

Kunstforum (1991), *Imitation und Mimesis*, 114, July/August.

Kvale, S. (ed.) (1989), *Issues of Validity in Qualitative Research*. Lund: Studentlitteratur.

Kvale, S. (1991), Validierung: Von der Beobachtung zu Kommunikation und Handeln. In: Flick, U., Kardorff, E.v., Keupp, H., Rosenstiel, L.v., Wolff, S. (eds), *Handbuch Qualitative Sozialforschung*, pp. 427–432. Munich: Psychologie Verlags Union.

Kvale, S. (1996), *InterViews: An Introduction to Qualitative Research Interviewing*. London: Sage.

Lamnek, S. (1988), *Qualitative Sozialforschung. Vol. 1: Methodologie*. Munich: Psychologie Verlags Union.

Lamnek, S. (1989), *Qualitative Sozialforschung. Vol. 2: Methoden und Techniken*. Munich: Psychologie Verlags Union.

Lather, P. (1993), Fertile Obsession: Validity after Post-Structuralism. *Sociological Quarterly*, 35, pp. 673–93.

Lau, T., Wolff, S. (1983), Der Einstieg in das Untersuchungsfeld als soziologischer Lernprozeß. *Kölner Zeitschrift für Soziologie und Sozialpsychologie*, 35, pp. 417–37.

Legewie, H. (1987), Interpretation und Validierung biographischer Interviews. In: Jüttemann, G., Thomae, H. (eds), *Biographie und Psychologie*, pp. 138–50. Berlin: Springer.

Legewie, H. (1994), Globalauswertung. In: Böhm, A., Muhr, T., Mengel, A. (eds),

Texte verstehen: Konzepte, Methoden, Werkzeuge, pp. 100–14. Konstanz: Universitätsverlag.

Lincoln, Y.S., Denzin, N.K. (1994), The Fifth Moment. In: Denzin, N., Lincoln, Y.S. (eds), *Handbook of Qualitative Research*, pp. 575–87. London: Sage.

Lincoln, Y.S., Guba, E.G. (1985), *Naturalistic Inquiry*. London: Sage.

Livingston, E. (1986), *The Ethnomethodological Foundations of Mathematics*. London: Routledge and Kegan Paul.

Lofland, J.H. (1974), Styles of Reporting Qualitative Field Research. *American Sociologist*, 9, pp. 101–11.

Lofland, J., Lofland, L.H. (1984), *Analyzing Social Situations* (2nd edn). Belmont, CA: Wadsworth.

Lüders, C. (1991), Deutungsmusteranalyse: Annäherungen an ein risikoreiches Konzept. In: Garz, D., Kraimer, K. (eds), *Qualitativ-empirische Sozialforschung*, pp. 377–408. Opladen: Westdeutscher Verlag.

Lüders, C. (1995), Von der Teilnehmenden Beobachtung zur ethnographischen Beschreibung: Ein Literaturbericht. In: König, E., Zedler P. (eds), *Bilanz qualitativer Forschung*, Vol. I, pp. 311–42. Weinheim: Deutscher Studienverlag.

Lüders, C., Reichertz, J. (1986), Wissenschaftliche Praxis ist, wenn alles funktioniert und keiner weiß warum: Bemerkungen zur Entwicklung qualitativer Sozialforschung. *Sozialwissenschaftliche Literaturrundschau*, 12, pp. 90–102.

Lunt, P., Livingstone, S. (1996), Rethinking the Focus Group in Media and Communications Research. *Journal of Communication*, 46, pp. 79–98.

Lyotard, J.F. (1984), *The Postmodern Condition: A Report on Knowledge*. Manchester: Manchester University Press.

Malinowski, B. (1916), *Magic, Science and Religion and Other Essays*. New York: Natural History Press, 1948.

Mangold, W. (1973), Gruppendiskussionen. In: König, R. (ed.), *Handbuch der empirischen Sozialforschung*, pp. 228–59. Stuttgart: Enke.

Matthes, J. (1984), Über die Arbeit mit lebensgeschichtlichen Erzählungen in einer nicht-westlichen Kultur. In: Kohli, M., Robert, G. (eds), *Biographie und soziale Wirklichkeit: Neuere Beiträge und Forschungsperspektiven*, pp. 284–95. Stuttgart: Metzler.

Matthes, J. (1985), Die Soziologen und ihre Wirklichkeit: Anmerkungen zum Wirklichkeitsverhältnis der Soziologie. In: Bonß, W., Hartmann, H. (eds), *Entzauberte Wissenschaft: Zur Realität und Geltung soziologischer Forschung*, pp. 49–64. Göttingen: Schwartz.

Mayring, P. (1983), *Qualitative Inhaltsanalyse: Grundlagen und Techniken* (2nd edn 1988). Weinheim: Deutscher Studien Verlag.

McKinlay, J.B. (1993), The Promotion of Health through Planned Sociopolitical Change: Challenges for Research and Policy. *Social Science and Medicine*, 38, pp. 109–17.

McKinlay, J.B. (1995), Towards Appropriate Levels, Research Methods and Healthy Public Policies. In: Guggenmoos-Holzmann, I., Bloomfield, K., Brenner, H., Flick, U. (eds), *Quality of Life and Health: Concepts, Methods, and Applications*, pp. 161–82. Berlin: Blackwell Science.

Mead, M. (1963), Anthropology and the Camera. In: Morgan, W.D. (ed.), *The Encyclopedia of Photography*, Vol. I, pp. 163–84. New York.

Merkens, H. (1989), Einleitung. In: Aster, R., Merkens, H., Repp, M. (eds), *Teilnehmende Beobachtung: Werkstattberichte und methodologische Reflexionen*, pp. 9–18. Frankfurt: Campus.

Merton, R.K. (1987), The Focused Interview and Focus Groups: Continuities and Discontinuities. *Public Opinion Quarterly*, 51, pp. 550–6.

Merton, R.K., Kendall, P.L. (1946), The Focused Interview. *American Journal of Sociology*, 51, pp. 541–57.

Merton, R.K., Fiske, M., Kendall, P.L. (1956), *The Focused Interview*. Glencoe, IL: Free Press.

Meuser, M., Nagel, U. (1991), ExpertInneninterviews: Vielfach erprobt, wenig bedacht: Ein Beitrag zur qualitativen Methodendiskussion. In: Garz, D., Kraimer, K. (eds), *Qualitativ-empirische Sozialforschung*, pp. 441–68. Opladen: Westdeutscher Verlag.

Middleton, D., Edwards, D. (eds) (1990), *Collective Remembering*. London: Sage.

Miles, M.B., Huberman, A.M. (1994), *Qualitative Data Analysis: A Sourcebook of New Methods* (2nd edn). Newbury Park, CA: Sage.

Mishler, E.G. (1986), The Analysis of Interview Narratives. In: Sarbin, T.R. (ed.), *Narrative Psychology*, pp. 233–55. New York: Praeger.

Mishler, E.G. (1990), Validation in Inquiry-Guided Research: The Role of Exemplars in Narrative Studies. *Harvard Educational Review*, 60, pp. 415–42.

Morgan, D.L. (1988), *Focus Groups as Qualitative Research*. Newbury Park, CA: Sage.

Morris, C. (1975), *Zeichen, Wert, Ästhetik*. Frankfurt: Suhrkamp.

Morse, J.M. (1994), Design in Funded Qualitative Research. In: Denzin, N., Lincoln, Y.S. (eds), *Handbook of Qualitative Research*, pp. 220–35. London: Sage.

Moscovici, S. (1973), Foreword. In: Herzlich, C. (ed.), *Health and Illness: A Social Psychological Analysis*. London: Academic Press.

Mühlefeld, C., Windolf, R., Lampert, N., Krüger, K. (1981), Auswertungsprobleme offener Interviews. *Soziale Welt*, 32, pp. 325–52.

Muhr, T. (1991), ATLAS/ti: A Prototype for the Support of Text Interpretation. *Qualitative Sociology*, 14, pp. 349–71.

Muhr, T. (1994), ATLAS/ti: Ein Werkzeug für die Textinterpretation. In: Böhm, A., Muhr, T., Mengel, A. (eds), *Texte verstehen: Konzepte, Methoden, Werkzeuge*, pp. 317–24. Konstanz: Universitätsverlag.

Müller-Doohm, S. (1993), Visuelles Verstehen: Konzepte kultursoziologischer Bildhermeneutik. In: Jung, T., Müller-Doohm, S. (eds), *'Wirklichkeit' im Deutungsprozeß*, pp. 438–56. Frankfurt: Suhrkamp.

Murphy, J.A. (1994), *Dienstleistungsqualität in der Praxis*. Munich: Hanser.

Niemann, M. (1989), Felduntersuchungen an Freizeitorten Berliner Jugendlicher. In: Aster, R., Merkens, H., Repp, M. (eds), *Teilnehmende Beobachtung: Werkstattberichte und methodologische Reflexionen*, pp. 71–83. Frankfurt: Campus.

Nießen, M. (1977), *Gruppendiskussion: Interpretative Methodologie, Methodenbegründung, Anwendung*. Munich: Fink.

Nothdurft, W. (1987), Gesprächsanalyse subjektiver Konfliktorganisationen: Ein natürliches Design zur Rekonstruktion individuellen Konfliktverständnisses. In: Bergold, J.B., Flick, U. (eds), *Ein-Sichten: Zugänge zur Sicht des Subjekts mittels qualitativer Forschung*, pp. 98–114. Tübingen: DGVT.

O'Connell, D., Kowall, S. (1995), Basic Principles of Transcription. In: Smith, J.A., Harré, R., Langenhove, L.v. (eds), *Rethinking Methods in Psychology*, pp. 93–104. London: Sage.

Oerter, R. (1995), Persons' Conception of Human Nature: A Cross-Cultural Comparison. In: Valsiner, J. (ed.), *Comparative Cultural and Constructivist Perspectives. Vol. III: Child Development within Culturally Structured Environments*, pp. 210–42. Norwood, NJ: Ablex.

Oerter, R., Oerter, R., Agostiani, H., Kim, H.-O., Wibowo, S. (1996). The Concept of

Human Nature in East Asia: Etic and Emic Characteristics. *Culture & Psychology*, 2, pp. 9–51.

Oevermann, U. (1983), Zur Sache: Die Bedeutung von Adornos methodologischem Selbstverständnis für die Begründung einer materialen soziologischen Struktur-analyse. In: Friedeburg, L.v., Habermas, J. (eds), *Adorno-Konferenz 1983*, pp. 234–92. Frankfurt: Suhrkamp.

Oevermann, U., Allert, T., Konau, E., Krambeck, J. (1979), Die Methodologie einer 'objektiven Hermeneutik' und ihre allgemeine forschungslogische Bedeutung in den Sozialwissenschaften. In: Soeffner, H.G. (ed.), *Interpretative Verfahren in den Sozial- und Textwissenschaften*, pp. 352–433. Stuttgart: Metzler.

Patton, M.Q. (1990), *Qualitative Evaluation and Research Methods* (2nd edn). London: Sage.

Petermann, W. (1991), Fotografie- und Filmanalyse. In: Flick, U., Kardorff, E.v., Keupp, H., Rosenstiel, L.v., Wolff, S. (eds), *Handbuch Qualitative Sozialforschung*, pp. 228–31. Munich: Psychologie Verlags Union.

Pollock, F. (1955), *Gruppenexperiment: Ein Studienbericht*. Frankfurt: Europäische Verlagsanstalt.

Potter, J., Wetherell, M. (1995), Discourse Analysis. In: Smith, J.A., Harré, R., Langenhove, L.v. (eds), *Rethinking Methods in Psychology*, pp. 80–92. New Delhi: Sage

Potter, J., Wetherell, M. (1998), Social Representations, Discourse Analysis and Racism. In: Flick, U. (ed.), *Psychology of the Social*, pp. 138–55. Cambridge: Cambridge University Press.

Ragin, C.C., Becker, H.S. (eds) (1992), *What is a Case? Exploring the Foundations of Social Inquiry*. Cambridge: Cambridge University Press.

Reichertz, J. (1988), Verstehende Soziologie ohne Subjekt. *Kölner Zeitschrift für Soziologie und Sozialpsychologie*, 40, pp. 207–21.

Reichertz, J. (1989), Hermeneutische Auslegung von Feldprotokollen? Verdrießliches über ein beliebtes Forschungsmittel. In: Aster, R., Merkens, H., Repp, M. (eds), *Teilnehmende Beobachtung: Werkstattberichte und methodologische Reflexionen*, pp. 84–102. Frankfurt: Campus.

Reichertz, J. (1991), Objektive Hermeneutik. In: Flick, U., Kardorff, E.v., Keupp, H., Rosenstiel, L.v., Wolff, S. (eds), *Handbuch Qualitative Sozialforschung*, pp. 223–7. Munich: Psychologie Verlags Union.

Reichertz, J. (1992), Beschreiben oder Zeigen: Über das Verfassen ethnographischer Berichte. *Soziale Welt*, 43, pp. 331–50.

Richards, T.J., Richards, L. (1994), Using Computers in Qualitative Research. In: Denzin, N., Lincoln, Y.S. (eds), *Handbook of Qualitative Research*, pp. 445–62. London: Sage.

Richardson, L. (1990), *Writing Strategies: Reaching Diverse Audiences*. London: Sage.

Richardson, L. (1994), Writing: A Method of Inquiry. In: Denzin, N., Lincoln, Y.S. (eds) *Handbook of Qualitative Research*, pp. 516–29. London: Sage.

Ricoeur, P. (1981), *Mimesis and Representation. Annals of Scholarship*, 2, pp. 15–32.

Ricoeur, P. (1984), *Time and Narrative*, Vol. 1. Chicago: University of Chicago Press.

Riemann, G. (1987), *Das Fremdwerden der eigenen Biographie: Narrative Interviews mit psychiatrischen Patienten*. Munich: Fink.

Riemann, G., Schütze, F. (1987), Trajectory as a Basic Theoretical Concept for Analyzing Suffering and Disorderly Social Processes. In: Maines, D. (ed.), *Social Organization and Social Process: Essays in Honor of Anselm Strauss*, pp. 333–57. New York: Aldine de Gruyter.

Rogers, C.R. (1944), The Nondirective Method as a Technique for Social Research. *American Journal of Sociology*, 50, pp. 279–93.

Ruff, F.M. (1990), *Ökologische Krise und Umweltbewußtsein: zur psychischen Verarbeitung von Umweltbelastungen*. Wiesbaden: Deutscher Universitätsverlag.

Ruff, F.M. (1991), Gesundheitsgefährdungen durch Umweltbelastungen: Ein neues Deutungsmuster. In: Flick, U. (ed.), *Alltagswissen über Gesundheit und Krankheit: Subjektive Theorien und soziale Repräsentationen*, pp. 101–16. Heidelberg: Asanger.

Ruff, F.M. (1993), Les Nuisances environnementales portent atteinte à la santé: Un nouveau schème explicatif. In: Flick, U. (ed.), *La Perception quotidienne de la santé et de la maladie*, pp. 123–42. Paris: L'Harmattan.

Sacks, H. (1992), *Lectures on Conversation*, Vols 1, 2 (ed. G. Jefferson). Oxford: Blackwell.

Sacks, H., Schegloff, E., Jefferson, G. (1974), A Simplest Systematics for the Organization of Turntaking for Conversation. *Language*, 4, pp. 696–735.

Sahle, R. (1987), *Gabe, Almosen, Hilfe*. Opladen: Westdeutscher Verlag.

Saldern, M.v. (ed.) (1986), *Mehrebenenanalyse: Beiträge zur Erfassung hierarchisch strukturierter Realität*. Munich: Psychologie Verlags Union.

Sanjek, R. (ed.) (1990), *Fieldnotes: The Making of Anthropology*. Albany, NY: State University of New York Press.

Sarbin, T.R. (ed.) (1986), *Narrative Psychology: The Storied Nature of Human Conduct*. New York: Praeger.

Schatzman, L., Strauss, A.L. (1973), *Field Research*. Englewood Cliffs, NJ: Prentice-Hall.

Scheele, B., Groeben, N. (1988), *Dialog-Konsens-Methoden zur Rekonstruktion Subjektiver Theorien*. Tübingen: Francke.

Schegloff, E., Sacks, H. (1974), Opening Up Closings. In: Turner, R. (ed.), *Ethnomethodology*, pp. 233–64. Harmondsworth: Penguin.

Schneider, G. (1985), Strukturkonzept und Interpretationspraxis der objektiven Hermeneutik. In: Jüttemann, G. (ed.), *Qualitative Forschung in der Psychologie*, pp. 71–91. Weinheim: Beltz.

Schneider, G. (1988), Hermeneutische Strukturanalyse von qualitativen Interviews. *Kölner Zeitschrift für Soziologie und Sozialpsychologie*, 40, pp. 223–44.

Schneider, G. (1994), Sozialwissenschaftliche Hermeneutik und 'strukturale' Systemtheorie: Zu den Grenzen und Entwicklungsmöglichkeiten der 'objektiven Hermeneutik'. In: Garz, D. (ed.), *Die Welt als Text*, pp. 153–94. Frankfurt: Suhrkamp.

Schütz, A. (1962), *Collected Papers*, Vol. 1. Den Haag: Nijhoff.

Schütze, F. (1976), Zur Hervorlockung und Analyse von Erzählungen thematisch relevanter Geschichten im Rahmen soziologischer Feldforschung. In: Arbeitsgruppe Bielefelder Soziologen (eds), *Kommunikative Sozialforschung*, pp. 159–260. Munich: Fink.

Schütze, F. (1977), Die Technik des narrativen Interviews in Interaktionsfeldstudien, dargestellt an einem Projekt zur Erforschung von kommunalen Machtstrukturen. Manuskript der Universität Bielefeld, Fakultät für Soziologie.

Schütze, F. (1983), Biographieforschung und narratives Interview. *Neue Praxis*, 3, pp. 283–93.

Schwandt, T.A., Halpern, E.S. (1988), *Linking Auditing and Meta-Evaluation: Enhancing Quality in Applied Research*. London: Sage.

Shweder, R.A. (1996), True Ethnography: The Lore, the Law, and the Lure. In: Jessor, R., Colby, A., Shweder, R.A. (1996) (eds), *Ethnography and Human Development*, pp. 15–32. Chicago: University of Chicago Press.

Silverman, D. (1985), *Qualitative Methodology and Sociology*. Aldershot: Gower.

Silverman, D. (1993), *Interpreting Qualitative Data: Methods for Analysing Talk, Text and Interaction*. London: Sage.

Smith, J.A. (1995) Semi-Structured Interview and Qualitative Analysis. In: Smith, J.A., Harré, R., Langenhove, L.v. (eds), *Rethinking Methods in Psychology*, pp. 9–26. London: Sage.

Spöhring, W. (1989), *Qualitative Sozialforschung*. Stuttgart: Teubner.

Spradley, J.P. (1979), *The Ethnographic Interview*. New York: Holt, Rinehart and Winston.

Spradley, J.P. (1980), *Participant Observation*. New York: Holt, Rinehart and Winston.

Sprenger, A. (1989), Teilnehmende Beobachtung in prekären Handlungssituationen: Das Beispiel Intensivstation. In: Aster, R., Merkens, H., Repp, M. (eds), *Teilnehmende Beobachtung: Werkstattberichte und methodologische Reflexionen*, pp. 35–56. Frankfurt: Campus.

Stegmüller, W. (1973), *Probleme und Resultate der Wissenschaftstheorie und Analytischen Philosophie. Vol. 2.2.: Theoriestrukturen und Theoriedynamik*. Berlin: Springer.

Steinert, H. (ed.) (1973), *Symbolische Interaktion: Arbeiten zu einer reflexiven Soziologie*. Stuttgart: Klett.

Stewart, D.M., Shamdasani, P.N. (1990), *Focus Groups: Theory and Practice*. Newbury Park, CA: Sage.

Strauss, A.L. (1987), *Qualitative Analysis for Social Scientists*. Cambridge: Cambridge University Press.

Strauss, A.L. (1995), Im Gespräch (mit Heiner Legewie und Barbara Schervier-Legewie). *Journal für Psychologie*, 3, pp. 64–75.

Strauss, A.L., Corbin, J. (1990), *Basics of Qualitative Research*. London: Sage.

Strauss, A.L., Schatzmann, L., Bucher, R., Ehrlich, D., Sabshin, M. (1964), *Psychiatric Ideologies and Institutions*. New York: Free Press.

Streeck, J. (1991), Sprachanalyse als empirische Geisteswissenschaft: Von der 'Philosophy of Mind' zur 'kognitiven Linguistik'. In: Flick, U., Kardorff, E.v., Keupp, H., Rosenstiel, L.v., Wolff, S. (eds), *Handbuch Qualitative Sozialforschung*, pp. 90–100. Munich: Psychologie Verlags Union.

Stryker, S. (1976), Die Theorie des Symbolischen Interaktionismus. In: Auwärter, M., Kirsch, E., Schröter, K. (eds), *Seminar: Kommunikation, Interaktion, Identität*, pp. 257–74. Frankfurt: Suhrkamp.

Südmersen, I. (1983), Hilfe, ich ersticke in Texten! Eine Anleitung zur Aufarbeitung narrativer Interviews. *Neue Praxis*, 13, pp. 294–306.

Thomas, W.I., Znaniecki, F. (1918–20), *The Polish Peasant in Europe and America*, Vols 1, 2. New York: Knopf.

Toulmin, S. (1990), *Cosmopolis: The Hidden Agenda of Modernity*. New York: Free Press.

Van Maanen, J. (1988), *Tales of the Field: On Writing Ethnography*. Chicago: University of Chicago Press.

Wahl, K., Gravenhorst, L., Honig, S.M. (1982), *Wissenschaftlichkeit und Interessen: Zur Herstellung subjektivitätsorientierter Sozialforschung*. Frankfurt: Suhrkamp.

Weber, M. (1904), Die 'Objektivität' sozialwissenschaftlicher und sozialpolitischer Erkenntnis. In: Winkelmann, J. (ed.), *Max Weber: Gesammelte Aufsätze zur Wissenschaftslehre*, pp. 146–214. Tübingen: Mohr.

Weber, M. (1919), Wissenschaft als Beruf. In: Winkelmann, J. (ed.), *Max Weber: Gesammelte Aufsätze zur Wissenschaftslehre*, pp. 582–613. Tübingen: Mohr.

Weingarten, E., Sack, F., Schenkein, J. (eds) (1976), *Ethnomethodologie: Beiträge zu einer Soziologie des Alltagshandelns*. Frankfurt: Suhrkamp.

Weitzman, E., Miles, M.B. (1995), *Computer Programs for Qualitative Data Analysis: A Software Sourcebook.* London: Sage.

Wiedemann, P.M. (1986), *Erzählte Wirklichkeit: Zur Theorie und Auswertung Narrativer Interviews.* Munich: Psychologie Verlags Union.

Wiedemann, P.M. (1991), Gegenstandsnahe Theoriebildung. In: Flick, U., Kardorff, E.v., Keupp, H., Rosenstiel, L.v., Wolff, S. (eds), *Handbuch Qualitative Sozialforschung,* pp. 440–5. Munich: Psychologie Verlags Union.

Wilson, T.P. (1982), Quantitative 'oder' qualitative Methoden in der Sozialforschung. *Kölner Zeitschrift für Soziologie und Sozialpsychologie,* 34, pp. 469–86.

Winograd, T., Flores, F. (1986), *Understanding Computers and Cognition.* Reading, MA: Addison-Wesley.

Witzel, A. (1982), *Verfahren der qualitativen Sozialforschung–Überlick und Alternativen.* Frankfurt: Campus.

Witzel, A. (1985), Das problemzentrierte Interview. In: Jüttemann, G. (ed.), *Qualitative Forschung in der Psychologie,* pp. 227–55. Weinheim: Beltz.

Wolcott, H.F. (1990a), On Seeking – and Rejecting – Validity in Qualitative Research. In: Eisner, W., Peshkin, A. (eds), *Qualitative Inquiry in Education: The Continuing Debate,* pp. 121–52. New York: Teachers College Press.

Wolcott, H.F. (1990b), *Writing up Qualitative Research.* London: Sage.

Wolff, S. (1986), Das Gespräch als Handlungsinstrument: Konversationsanalytische Aspekte sozialer Arbeit. *Kölner Zeitschrift für Soziologie und Sozialpsychologie,* 38, pp. 55–84.

Wolff, S. (1987), Rapport und Report: Über einige Probleme bei der Erstellung plausibler ethnographischer Texte. In: Ohe, W.v.d. (ed.), *Kulturanthropologie: Beiträge zum Neubeginn einer Disziplin,* pp. 333–64. Berlin: Reimer.

Wolff, S. (1991), Gregory Bateson, Margaret Mead, *Balinese Character* (1942): Qualitative Forschung als disziplinierte Subjektivität. In: Flick, U., Kardorff, E.v., Keupp, H., Rosenstiel, L.v., Wolff, S. (eds), *Handbuch Qualitative Sozialforschung,* pp. 135–41. Munich: Psychologie Verlags Union.

Wolff, S. (1992), Die Anatomie der Dichten Beschreibung: Clifford Geertz als Autor. In: Matthes, J. (ed.), *Zwischen den Kulturen? Sozialwissenschaftlen vor dem Problem des Kulturvergleichs,* pp. 339-361. Soziale Welt Sonderband 8. Göttingen: Schwartz.

Wolff, S. (1993), Der Einstieg in das Untersuchungsfeld. Workshop des Projektes Q1b im Berliner Forschungsverbund Public Health, Mimeo.

Wolff, S., Knauth, B., Leichtl, G. (1988), Kontaktbereich Beratung: Eine konversationsanalytische Untersuchung zur Verwendungsforschung. Hildesheim: Projektbericht, MS.

Wuggenig, U. (1990), Die Photobefragung als projektives Verfahren. *Angewandte Sozialforschung,* 16, pp. 109–31.

Wundt, W. (1900–20), *Völkerpsychologie.* Leipzig: Engelmann.

Znaniecki, F. (1934), *The Method of Sociology.* New York: Farrar and Rinehart.

NAME INDEX

SUBJECT INDEX